COMPUTERS, SCIENCE and MANAGEMENT DYNAMICS

A research study
prepared for

**FINANCIAL EXECUTIVES
RESEARCH FOUNDATION**

by

Robert J. Fahey
Douglas A. Love
Paul F. Ross
    Arthur D. Little, Inc.

Financial Executives Research Foundation
50 West 44th Street, New York, N. Y. 10036

Library of Congress Catalog Card Number: 72-102175
Printed in the United States of America

First Printing

Foreword

THE RESEARCH ARM of Financial Executives Institute has followed closely the growing use, and importance, of the computer. In 1955 it published an annotated bibliography of the literature then available on the computer. This was so well received that three additional volumes were published—two in 1956 and the final one in 1958. In addition, the Research Foundation published "Appraising the Economics of Electronic Computers" in 1956, and "Business Experience with Electronic Computers" in 1959.

Today, the literature on computers is so extensive as to almost defy classification and analysis. Yet, the current computer revaluation has so many implications for the future that all management executives, no matter what their individual responsibility, must be alert to the constant change or time will have passed them by.

Several years ago the Trustees of Financial Executives Research Foundation saw the need for a forward-looking study dealing with the impact of computers on management technology. While the study originally was to have concentrated on management technology and the computer, it soon became evident that a much wider focus was needed, as the current title suggests. The Trustees were fortunate in securing the services of Arthur D. Little, Inc., to undertake the necessary research. Research of this type, however, cannot be done in a vacuum and many people gave generously of their time, ideas and imagination. The Trustees are particularly grateful for the contributions of the Project Advisory Committee listed on page vii.

Donald P. Jones, President
FERF

iii

iv

Contents

PROJECT ADVISORY COMMITTEE

ALEXANDER L. STOTT
Vice President & Comptroller
American Telephone & Telegraph Co.

MARSHALL K. EVANS
Vice President—Operations
Westinghouse Electric Corporation

WILLIAM H. FEATHERS
Vice President
Union Carbide Corporation

JAMES D. GALLAGHER
McCall Information Services Co.

DOUGLAS HAMILTON
Vice President—Finance
Sylvania Electric Products, Inc.

WILLIAM F. HOLMES
Exec. Development Director
Lever Brothers

DONALD P. JONES
Vice President
Sun Oil Co.

NORMAN J. REAM
Principal
S. D. Leidesdorf and Co.

STEVENS L. SHEA
Vice President—Organization Planning
Fireman's Fund American Insurance Co.

BEN MAKELA
Research Director
Financial Executives Research Foundation

CHAPTER 1

Coping with the Computer Revolution: Executive Development Versus Obsolescence

*Significance of the Computer to the Organization / The
Manager's Responsibility / The Myth of the Computer*

THE COMPUTER PRESENTS the individual corporate executive
with a powerful force for change. The changes in corporate operations
effected by the computer, significant as they have already been, are
scarcely yet perceived. Nevertheless, certain patterns of computer use
and effect are already clear enough to suggest their probable extension. The purpose of this book is to provide a guide for the executive
who seeks an understanding of the computer and its implications—
both opportunities and problems—for his company and himself.

By changing procedures, organization structure, the corporate possession of knowledge, and the means of its communication, computer
use ultimately affects practically every element of corporate life.
Among these elements are both individual positions at the middle-
management level and skill and knowledge requirements at top-management levels. In the early 1970's, the computer will be in too common use for the middle-level manager, interested in performing his
responsibilities better and qualifying for their enlargement, to depend
solely on subordinates' or peers' judgments about computers and their
application to his area of responsibility. By the late 1970's or early
1980's, some large companies, at least, will be led by men whose
knowledge of computers is thorough enough to permit their personal
use of computers in strategic thinking and policy planning. The present manager must develop and extend his practical understanding of
the computer's capabilities, limitations, potentialities, and costs. If he
does not, he risks obsolescence as a manager.

Any thinking manager recognizes that few jobs in healthy, growing companies go unchanged for longer than a few years, that companies must continually adapt to internal and external change, and that the organization and its jobs change as a result. He also recognizes that he must adapt to a changing environment just as his company does—by growth, by the acquisition of new knowledge and skills. For today's manager, that growth must be in his understanding of computer technology.

The central significance of the computer for the manager is its relationship to his own duties and to the organization for which he works. How the computer is perceived by others in the company—his subordinates, peers, and superiors—will influence heavily on how well he, and they, can function as managers or workers in the computer environment. It is ironic that the computer, a machine of logic, has become the occasion of considerable anxiety, much of it founded on myths about the computer itself. Thus, a manager seeking understanding for himself and for others of the computer and its meaning to his organization must devote some portion of his time to coping with "computer mythology." He must confront and deal with false as well as accurate beliefs because both condition the attitudes of his co-workers, and to that degree are therefore equally important. He must be able to recognize, on the basis of personal knowledge, what the computer is—a powerful management tool, not hardware alone, but a combination of skilled people, procedures and machine. He must accept an underlying reality which the computer enforces—that mathematics is a powerful means for approaching management problems.

A. *Significance of the Computer to the Organization*

Basically, a corporation is a common purpose in which a number of human beings share and to which they contribute their personal services or their capital, expecting some return. Organization theorists have come to a more complex view of the corporation, in which it is seen as a combination of "systems"—an authority/responsibility system, a reward/penalty system, a communication system, a social system, and others. These systems obviously are interrelated. A corporation must determine how the computer can facilitate the operation of its other "systems" in the overall corporate purpose. Its management must therefore continuously distinguish between what is potential in the computer and what is actual with respect to its capacity to forward the corporation's overall purposes. Thus the concepts of costs, manageable rates of change, and other constraints are part of its management, just as much as identifying its benefits.

The advent of the computer has focussed managerial attention upon the information system of the corporation. (The information system itself will be discussed in the next chapter.) It is here that the computer has had its most direct and greatest impact upon corporate organization. Even the concept of an information system was not far developed before the advent of the computer, but as the computer is applied within a company it is necessary that its application follow some rationale, and so the idea of the information system becomes useful. Other forces have worked to bring the information-system concept into wider use.

As management as a profession has developed, increasing weight has been placed on its intellectual aspects—economic theory, the behavioral sciences, and the natural sciences. Increasing value has been attached to information per se as an ingredient of the management process, and particularly of the decision-making process. Because the computer is a machine for systematically handling large amounts of information, it is a powerful tool for management to employ. However, the computer should not be viewed simply as an instrument for providing the same information more cheaply and quickly than conventional clerical systems, and in the same format and fashion. To view the computer merely as an accounting device which mechanizes information systems is to dismiss a primary potential of the machine—its potential for providing otherwise unavailable information, and hence as a tool for exploratory and creative activities. In short, computers are useful for management's own research, i.e., answering its own questions on the basis of new factual knowledge.

As a research device, the computer can provide the manager new insights into and better understanding of the economic nature of his company, how it works, and what is good and what is bad for its operations under assumed or forecast conditions. Inventory control, capital allocation, construction design optimization, all are tasks that can be opened to a wider range of possible solutions for a given problem by the new computing power available to the manager. Greater effectiveness and economy can result. The managerial knowledge of economics can be brought into fuller play and practice in the enterprise. The commodity of cheaper calculating power, harnessed and directed by programmers and mathematicians, has made more immediate practical application of economic theory at the corporate level.

As a socializing force, the computer can help managers to think and act with a better understanding of the framework of the corporate organization, not just their own department. The department syndrome, the consideration and promotion of limited departmental objectives which may vary from corporate interests, is a serious problem in corporate performance today because of overall corporate size and complexity. Educational and value differences and conflicts among specialists within departments aggravate this problem. For example, the scientist or engineer engaged in product development often has difficulty communicating with sales or marketing personnel and seeing their needs. The fundamental need for each to understand the other and for both to understand the broader corporation is so great that it is almost always constructive to increase their understanding of the economic and technical realities facing both departments. The computer can aid such mutual understanding. Mutual confrontation of the whole cycle of product development according to revenue, cost and time "models" reflecting the state and direction of the corporation's broader activities can provide a basis for more meaningful communication among managers of complementary departments engaged in the same corporate process, be it production or new product development and introduction. Computer models can help to refine corporate goals and strategies, and, in turn, corporate objectives, divisional and departmental tasks and standards, placing them in a context which is entirely practical for day-to-day decision making.

B. The Manager's Responsibility

Because the corporation must master the computer, the manager must master the computer. To make aggressive use of the computer, the manager must understand its capabilities and limitations. His task is not that of the technical personnel who work in conjunction with the machine, it is that of the decision maker. He must lay down policy, interpret policy, and decide continuously how his department can use the computer to the advantage of the entire corporation.

The computer is so variable a tool that a manager's first responsibility is to define the problems and the priorities of problems in which he seeks its assistance and the role he wants the computer to play. Basically he can use the computer in five ways and must consider potential uses of the computer in each of these modes within his department:

    (1) *As an information storage device,* for storing data for possible retrieval by decision makers;

(2) As an *operating machine,* for systematizing major tasks of the operating departments, such as payroll accounting;

(3) As a *management control device,* for measuring organizational performance and cost and providing control information;

(4) As a *learning and research device,* for exploring new ways of understanding and doing his job; and

(5) As a *planning device,* for analyzing alternative assumptions and/or management choices about future company and departmental environment or operations to determine their effects on company or department performance.

Because the experienced manager knows what problems face his department better than anyone else, he is in the best position to evaluate the kind of help the computer can provide. His position as manager is not endangered by the new "computer scientists" unless his failure to familiarize himself with computer technology has placed the responsibility for the computer application decision in their hands.

C. *The Myth of the Computer*

The computer is subject to easy myth making. Such myth making has often resulted in overestimating the computer's potential and underestimating its costs. It has also given rise to a widely-held belief that computers will replace individuals in their jobs. Let the manager take note that although computers have probably created more jobs than they have eliminated, the newly created jobs require new skills and too frequently new people. Because the computer is a force for change, and people tend to fear and resist change, its way must be prepared. Only an understanding of people as well as the computer, and the development of sound people policies can prevent the growth of the myth that the computer is to be resisted because it must put people out of work. Thus, the corporate manager's success with the computer is likely to depend on his attitude toward change, his understanding of the people over which he has supervisory authority, his understanding of computer technology, and his own resourcefulness in introducing behavioral change in his organization.

The manager's attitude toward the computer should be devoid of misconceptions. Any manager who finds himself intimately involved with computers must take care to separate what is real from what is almost real, both with respect to benefits and costs. The computer can help make decisions, for example, but to say that the computer can make decisions is a deception. It is true, for example, that the computer can be arranged so that it will compare two different values, choose the greater of these values, and then indicate its choice to some other machine so that the other machine will take some action, such as turning off a valve or starting a fire. But, the decision was not made by the machine; it was made by the engineer who designed the system to work in the sequence followed by the computer. The machine acts in a pattern established not by itself, but by a decision maker or decision makers. Even in the more advanced programs under which computers "learn," their learning is artificial and is guided by human design.

The manager should recognize that the computer is not only an accounting device but a magnificent tool for managerial discovery. A manager, by understanding the application of the computer to the department, can understand his department better. He can develop new insights into his business if he is in touch with the computer's applications to his operation; he begins to see new relationships between variables that he wants to control and variables that he can control; he begins to perceive changes in the environment of his operations that he otherwise would not perceive as early. He has, in short, an improved means for viewing himself, his subordinates, and the work they are performing or trying to perform.

The manager who fails to take advantage of the opportunity that computers provide, who refuses to adapt to what is changing in the management environment, is missing the chance to improve both his competitive position among the managers within his company and the position of his company within his industry. The manager who fails to take advantage of the new managerial tools faces obsolescence, for other managers who can deal effectively with the problems of change will exploit the opportunity computers offer and will be better managers as a result.

A. Theoretical Framework

CHAPTER 2

Management Information Systems

Introduction / Definition of Terms / General Concept of an Enterprise / Desirable Characteristics of Management Information Systems / The Development of MIS's

A. Introduction

COMPUTER SYSTEMS use computers, programs, and data to accomplish management tasks. A management information system (MIS) combines computer systems and management organization and communication.

The term *management information system* has been used for about ten years, but it often has been too narrowly construed. The usual image generated by this term is that of a configuration of procedures and equipment, which furnishes a manager with reports (usually summaries of operating data) he can use in support of his decision making. However, the total management information system within an organizational environment is richer and more complex than that reflected in paperwork or computer data flow. It includes a large and very important amount of interpersonal information exchange—during discussions and meetings, telephone conversations, and even golf games. Indeed, some extremely successful organizations of small to medium size—such as abound in the garment industry—base decisions almost exclusively on information communicated orally; the telephone is sometimes the main technology on which they depend. These organizations demonstrate remarkable ability to respond quickly to changes in their environment—the rapidly changing world of fashion.

Experience with MIS has revealed that the patterns of information flow within an organization determine the structure of that organization. This insight was formally developed in the physical sciences as the study of cybernetics (adaptive control systems); a fundamental precept of cybernetics is that information and organization are inseparable. Regarding the formal paperwork-and-mechanical information system as separable from the informal human system leads to serious difficulties. As a matter of fact, this misconception may be cited as one of the main reasons that many of the extensive computer systems set up within the last few years, presumably to aid management, have actually been fairly useless. In too many cases, such systems handle routine data very well, but produce management reports and summaries which are not useful to the real managers and decision makers.

We approach the important job of defining MIS's from several angles: (1) by defining each of the three words describing the concept, (2) by advancing a general concept of an enterprise, (3) by discussing desirable MIS characteristics, and (4) by tracing the development of MIS's.

B. Definition of Terms

1. MANAGEMENT

By management—not the function but the people—we mean all those having the authority to make decisions committing the firm or its resources. According to this definition, a production foreman and a material-control clerk are included in management—the former because he has the authority to make decisions affecting the allocation of a firm's principal resources, production workers; the latter because he frequently makes decisions affecting the timing and quantity of purchases. A production worker, on the other hand, is excluded by the definition; he may have resources—material, tools, etc.—to commit, but he does not have the authority to make decisions that effect such commitments. Thus, the management function may be exercised by an employee irrespective of his place on an organization chart, irrespective of the number of people reporting to him.

By management—the function—we mean both planning and decision making. The distinction between the two, although it may be considered academic, is useful; failure to recognize this distinction is the source of much organizational malaise. A decision represents a commitment of resources to a course of action; a plan is a preliminary or conditional decision. A plan becomes an actual decision if no better approach develops between the time the plan is drawn up and the time it is implemented.

2. INFORMATION

Information is simply that which informs, that which is descriptive of elements relevant to the performance of managerial functions. Thus, a single fact arising out of a business transaction is information if it is presented to a person to whom it is relevant. The criterion of relevance we use is that the information be of assistance in making management plans or decisions, that it reduce uncertainty.

The raw material of information is data. Raw data itself is generally not information; it usually must be evaluated before it becomes useful management information. Management information is classified according to its uses as follows:

- Operating information: working documents—movie tickets, checks, invoices, etc.—which make possible the routine functioning of the business.
- Decision-making information: analyses that permit the evaluation and comparison of the results of alternative courses of action.
- Performance evaluation information: measures by which the progress of an activity can be determined.

3. SYSTEMS

A system is a collection of elements—such as procedures, equipment, and persons—with a set of relations among them which are dictated by a common goal or goals. A management information system, then, is a collection of procedure descriptions, equipment, and persons brought together to provide those who make decisions committing the firm or its resources with descriptions of the elements relevant to the performance of their function. In short, an MIS provides information needed by managers in conducting the business.

C. General Concept of an Enterprise

Our discussion of the term *management information system* emphasizes the decision-making aspect of business enterprises. This view is in accord with the predominant trend in the literature about management, generated by economists, statistical theorists, and mathematicians. The literature on management by psychologists, sociologists, and many of its practitioners, however, tends to emphasize such aspects of business and organization as leadership, creativity, multiple goals and suboptimization, and social responsibility. We shall incorporate this latter category of literature into the decision-making framework by characterizing its contributions as adding to the body of knowledge on how to make better management decisions. This literature presents divergent views as to what constitutes the essence of an organization; we prefer a general concept of an enterprise which manifests the central role of information.

The concept of an information-oriented enterprise can be most clearly articulated in the form of a series of propositions, each of which provides a definition which aids in the understanding of the others, both separately and together

- Any *enterprise*—business, social, or political—may be characterized as a (changing) collection of problems to be solved.
- *Managing* is the process of assigning and solving problems.
- *Organization* is the result of assigning problems to those most qualified to solve them economically.
- *Data* are unevaluated messages (problem elements) for specific uses.
- *Data Processing* is the collection, storage, retrieval, and manipulation of data.
- *Information* is evaluated data, including knowledge, relevant to the elements of a problem and in the possession of the appropriate decision maker.
- *Knowledge* is the stock of what there is to be known about the best decision to be made; it includes precedent and experience, habit, "rules of thumb" and formal problem-solving techniques.
- A *management information system* is a method for bringing together problems and the relevant information.

Within this concept, all the elements constituting the purpose, structure, and meaning of organization and information are related in a manner which emphasizes the importance of information retrieval and transfer in an enterprise. The computer is central to this operation.

D. Desirable Characteristics of Management Information Systems

A well-conceived MIS has several distinguishing characteristics. These pertain to either or both of the two main elements of such systems: (1) the mechanism (how and by what means the system operates) and (2) the content (the kinds of information developed and communicated by the system and the decisions they support). These systems should basically of course provide information in the right *form* to the right *person* at the right *time*. To elaborate:

An MIS is open-ended. Both mechanism and content are flexible; they can be expanded to take advantage of new opportunities (new data, new techniques, or new hardware) or to assist in making new kinds of decisions.

An MIS is discriminating. One of the goals of an MIS is to restrict the output of the system. Information disposal (efficient storage or division) is as important as information retrieval. The unfortunate result of many MIS installations is the inundation of executives with too many reports and figures. This "information overload" stems from the lack of system discrimination regarding information priority and appropriate levels of aggregation. In this respect, a well-designed MIS manifests itself in four ways

- Each level and position of management can receive all the information that can be used in the conduct of each manager's job; but
- Each level and position of management actually receives on a regular basis only the information it can and must act on. (This characteristic represents a reversal of the trend in business to make reports universal; moreover, it negates the value of equipment manufacturers' making more and more printout available.)
- Information is presented to the manager when action is possible and appropriate.
- Information presented to the manager is current, or timely.

An MIS is logically complete. Good MIS's are developed only after a systematic examination has been made of (1) the nature of the various management functions; (2) the results the manager of each function is expected to achieve; (3) the control actions (controllable elements of performance) the manager can take to achieve these results; (4) the influence these actions have on the actual results; (5) the ways in which information can be developed to determine and understand the relation between cause and effect; (6) the ways in which the flow of information can be directed to achieve desired action; and (7) the economic rewards and penalties for developing various types of information.

An MIS should benefit the company first, and then its subordinate parts. Students of organizational behavior are impressed by the existence, significance, and impact of the divergent (as distinct from the common) goals of organizations. One of the principal problems of introducing an MIS is the resistance to it because of the constraints it imposes on individuals, departments, or divisions, on attaining subgoals at the expense of the firm as a whole.

An MIS should be randomly accessible. In addition to assembling and interrelating information and turning out smoothly, effectively, and accurately all three kinds of management information—operating, decision-making, and performance evaluation information—an MIS must be able to interrogate itself in unanticipated or unusual ways at random intervals.

E. _The Development of MIS's_

The development of MIS's can be described in terms of progress in several dimensions: their support of higher-order decisions, their support of a real-time environment, their application to more kinds of problems, and their use of new problem-solving techniques.

1. SUPPORT OF HIGHER-ORDER DECISION-MAKING

Industry's initial acceptance of computers has been based on the possibility of obtaining lower-cost solutions to highly structured problems. Contributing significantly to the salability of the computer was its ability to reduce the cost of clerical operations, particularly accounting functions such as payroll and billing. The mathematical techniques employed in such applications are primarily addition and subtraction, although percentages or ratios are sometimes calculated. One of the more important functions conducted is the preparation, for reporting purposes, of several data summaries (aggregates) and cross tabulations.

The second level of computer use is as an optimizing device. Mathematical models of business problems or manufacturing processes are constructed and programmed into the computer. The computer is then given the data required in the problem statement and instructed to solve the model for an optimum solution. The solution is then either given to a decision maker as "information" or relayed directly to a control device, which takes the action required to keep a process within control. Typical applications using this approach are production scheduling, inventory control, and process control.

Optimizing models require complete information about the particular problem at hand, the structure—the mathematical equations required to accurately specify the problem—and the data must be available. Also, there must be only one goal (e.g., maximum profits or minimum cost) and that must be measurable. Finally, optimization models generally presuppose quantitative knowledge of each of the system parameters (or, at least, given probability distributions for each parameter). Because of these constraints, optimizing models often are employed in the solution of subproblems. These solutions, in turn, provide information for the solution by people of complex problems that cannot be so clearly formulated.

The third level of computer use involves simulation techniques. The distinction between optimization models and simulation models is amount of information required. Simulation techniques generally are employed when not enough is known about a problem to construct an optimization model. The functions involved may be too complex to yield to known mathematical optimizing techniques; there may be too many parameters in the problem in which uncertainty must be explicitly dealt with; there may be more than one goal to be optimized simultaneously; or it may not be possible to measure quantitatively progress toward a goal. In such cases, a model is constructed which represents the behavior of the system, including probability distributions for those system elements about which there is uncertainty. Subsequent to programming the computer with this model, simulations are run on the computer. These runs are much like controlled experiments, one condition at a time being varied.

The performance of the simulated system is monitored, and its response to changing conditions is recorded. In this way, the real-life system counterpart of the computer model can be improved, and the conditions under which it operates can be controlled according to a multiple set of goals or qualitative measures of success.

In the fourth and highest level of use, the computer is employed as a "heuristic" problem solver.[1] In a heuristic program, a solution method is not explicitly and sequentially predetermined, but some of the characteristics of human problem solving are incorporated. Chief among these characteristics is the use of "rule of thumb" procedures, the ability to measure progress toward a solution, and the ability to learn from past mistakes and success. To date, such programs have been successful only in relatively synthetic games; however, it is hoped that this "artificial intelligence" approach will yield techniques suitable for use in the solution of real-life business problems.

2. SUPPORT OF A REAL-TIME ENVIRONMENT

The ability of any system to sustain optimum control over a rapidly changing process is affected severely by the cycle time between when the control system senses and measures a change in the process, and when the corrective action has the desired effect. Business management is analogous to this situation. The problem facing management is not what actions should be taken to cope with present conditions, for these actions should have been taken some time ago; rather, the problem is what action must be taken now to meet future conditions. The appropriateness of the selected actions will depend on the timeliness of the information provided to management. A real-time environment for decision making contributes to the success of the control actions.

Recognition of this need for a real-time environment was evidenced during World War II, when persons in positions of authority tended to gravitate toward communications centers rather than formally assigned locations in times of crises. This tendency has since been formally incorporated in the design of military command and control centers, of which SAGE is probably the first. The industrial counterpart of SAGE is the DuPont Co.'s chart room, which was in existence before the advent of modern computer science. The executives of the DuPont Co. gather at frequent intervals to be briefed on the status of operations and plans. They have the opportunity to question the custodians of the chart room system at random.

An important trend in modern management is the adoption and

---

[1] The word "heuristic" characterizes those problem-solving proceedings which, for lack of a formal solution, rely on unprovable solutions to small pieces of a larger problem and the trial-and-error accumulation of results which lead to a satisfactory rather than optimum solution of the larger problem.

automation of this concept through the use of computers and automated displays. Many of the questions asked at such briefings can be answered in a reasonable time only by a computer. In addition, with a computer, it is possible to try out several solutions to problems prior to real-life implementation. The basic characteristics of a real-time command and control center are that it can be queried at random intervals, not just at weekly meetings, and that the information is up to the minute. These characteristics are difficult to achieve, particularly for an enterprise as a whole; nonetheless, the trend is to achieve these aims for larger and larger segments of businesses.

3. APPLICATION TO NEW KINDS OF PROBLEMS

The extension of computer use has been horizontal, involving more aspects of a business, as well as vertical, dealing with more complex problem structures. The traditional use of computers in business is in the accounting function. The first extension of the use of the computer was into inventory control. Programs were written to assist managers in making decisions concerning the product operations of businesses and to deal with problems in production scheduling. There followed more universal programs, linking optimal production scheduling to optimal inventory control. Soon these techniques were broadened to include purchasing policy and, finally, distribution. Attention now is being focused on the use of computers in marketing and marketing research. Developments in this area will be joined with prior developments, and a universal program for the optimum strategy for purchasing, production scheduling, inventory control, distribution, and marketing eventually will evolve.

In addition to controlling the flow of product (including manufacturing process control and scheduling), computer systems have been used to improve control of the flow of cash and personnel. Large sums of corporate cash must be managed, and much attention has been given to their full employment to earn returns while in liquid form, and to provide the liquidity necessary to cope with nonsynchronous inflows and outflows and chance shortages. Personnel requirements, search, and screening also have been computerized.

The above-mentioned computer applications include primarily the use of the computer in the day-to-day operation of a business. More far reaching in its impact on the corporation is the computer's potential as an aid to planning. In this application, the computer is used to explore different ways to organize and conduct a business. Professional management consultants and scientists are aware that the process of defining an operation well enough to allow a computer to be of help leads to improved knowledge of the process itself and, in turn, to improvements in its design and functioning. A manager working with a computer model of the process for which he is responsible invariably discovers a better way to organize and conduct the process itself. This benefit of computer use is frequently neglected, even though it often outweighs the cost-reduction benefits originally intended.

Another extension of the use of computers is data storage and communication. Information retrieval, a large and growing discipline, is based on the capability of modern computer memory designs to store vast quantities of randomly accessible data. Computer memories can accept and transmit data internally at very rapid speeds as long as intermediate printouts do not have to be made (to communicate with the outside world). This capability affords the rapid low-cost transmission of data between computers by way of computer-to-computer "talk."

4. USE OF NEW PROBLEM-SOLVING TECHNIQUES

The use of the computer as a decision-making aid has depended on the development of new and/or more powerful problem-solving techniques. These techniques can be characterized in four ways.

First, as noted above, computer-oriented problem-solving techniques have been extended to cope with progressively less well-structured problems. Solution techniques have progressed from clerical manipulations to optimizing techniques, simulation, and heuristic problem solving.

Second, solution techniques developed for one class of problems have been applied to other kinds of problems. For example, "linear programming" was developed primarily to determine the least-cost combinations of constituents in products such as feeds and petroleum and chemical products. These techniques are now applied in such diverse fields as warehouse location and investment portfolio balancing.

Third, ways have been found to extend the generality and power of previously existing solution methods. For example, "linear programming" has been extended to "quadratic" and "dynamic" programming.

Fourth, new analytical techniques are applied in business applications. Frequently, mathematical games or puzzles which initially had no apparent real-life applications have become the sole means of solving whole classes of business problems.

CHAPTER 3

Computer Support of Decision-Making

*Introduction / Modern Decision Theory / The
Computer as a Decision-Making Aid / The Accuracy
of Decisions*

A. *Introduction*

THE DEVELOPMENT of scientific, statistical, modern, or formal
decision-making, as it has been variously referred to, has taken place
at the crossroads of several disciplines. The large and growing volume
of literature on decision-making reflects several of its characteristics:

(1) It is a complex process, not easily described in linear (or
sequential) terms;
(2) There are several kinds of decisions, each being measured
by the level within an organization at which it is made;
(3) The appropriate criteria for making a decision depend on
the psychological makeup of the decision maker(s) and
the kind and magnitude of the decision to be made; and
(4) The large and growing number of mathematical-statistical
problem-solving techniques that can be combined in an
almost infinite number of ways.

To relate information management to business organization and
management in a decision-making context, we will first describe modern decision theory. Second, we will consider the computer as a decision-making aid within the context of the general theory of decision-
making set forth. At each juncture of the decision-making process, the
computer's ability to perform a useful economic role will be evaluated.
Third, we will discuss the measurement of the accuracy of decisions—
formal or informal, computer-based or not computer-based.

21

B. *Modern Decision Theory*

Modern decision theory is a method and a framework, large and flexible enough to encompass all kinds of decisions and decision-making methods. Figure 1 is a block diagram of such a decision system. We use the block diagram in our analysis of this formal decision system because it provides a means of viewing the system as a whole and one component of the system within the context of the whole. Each component of the system is described below in terms of its inputs, functions, and outputs.

1. DATA, INFORMATION, AND KNOWLEDGE

The raw materials for decision-making are data, information, knowledge, and a decision problem. Knowledge of the decision problem is used to process data and obtain information of value in making a decision. The bank of data includes the results of prior decisions, which may be classified as either (1) conditioning or actually giving rise to the need for the existing decision or (2) experience gained from past decisions which were similar to the present one.

2. PREDICTION, VALUATION, CRITERIA SELECTION

The principal components of the decision-making system are prediction, valuation, and criteria selection. The operation and output of these components within a particular system depends on the analytical framework being used—the "classical" model of decision-making or the "modern" (or "statistical") decision theory.[1]

Prediction: Decisions are concerned with possible future events or conditions. Thus, every decision involves some kind of forecasting effort. The scope of the forecasting effort is determined by economic considerations; forecasting costs must be balanced against expected gains on the value of more accurate information about the future.

The classical approach to predicting outcomes does not cope explicitly with uncertainty. Mutually exclusive outcomes are assigned probabilities of zero or one—either events will occur or they will not. The statistical approach, on the other hand, tries to cope explicitly

---

[1] A comprehensive discussion of both analytical frameworks is included in Appendix A.

Figure 1
MODERN DECISION SYSTEM

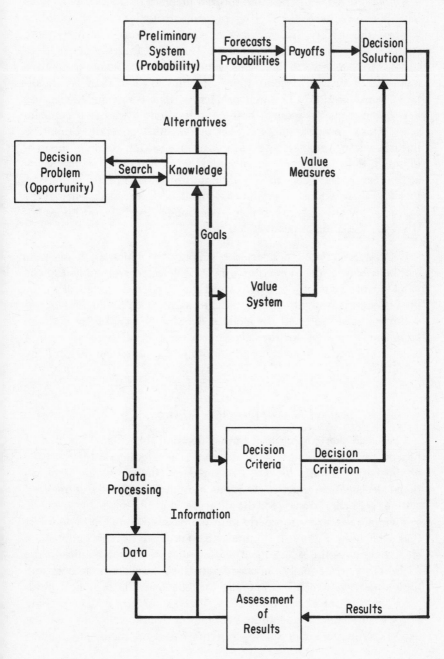

with uncertainty by estimating the probability of future events.

Valuation: After the possible future outcomes of alternative actions have been predicted, the possible outcomes must be ranked according to their desirability. The ranking or valuation process is even more complex than the prediction process. There are four sources of difficulty. First, real-world decisions generally involve some qualitative measures of success. Second, there generally is more than one qualitative consideration; the initial problem is thus compounded because it is not possible to reduce these considerations by using a common scale. Third, the desirability of various outcomes generally cannot be linearly related to objective measures of success; for example, the one-millionth dollar of income to an individual or company has less value at the margin than does the ten-thousandth dollar. Fourth, in the statistical mode, where uncertainty is coped with, the decision maker's attitudes toward risk can become confounded with his attitudes toward the valuation of possible outcomes.

Criteria Selection: To select the strategy by which a set of goals can be achieved, decision criteria must be selected and applied to the valuated products of alternative strategies. Under the classical mode, the criterion is straightforward: the alternative with the highest payoff is automatically selected. In modern decision theory, however, there is no single criterion for the selection of the best strategy. Indeed, in some decision situations, it is optimum to select more than one strategy at random.

3. BEHAVIORISTIC DECISION-MAKING

The basic shortcoming of a formal decision theory analysis, and of box diagram representations in general, is its rigidity. Although each of the basic building blocks is required for the development of rational decisions, in practice decisions are not made by the formalized system we have described. Results are not obtained by a single sequential pass, or even orderly multiple passes, through a system like that shown in Figure 1. Formal decision analysis concentrates on choice activity—the selection of a particular course of action—to the exclusion of two equally important activities, intelligence activity and design activity, which conceptually precede but still must be considered a part of the choice process. Intelligence activity is the searching of the environment for conditions calling for decisions and involves the use of abstractions and sudden insights based on the smallest hints;

the design activity is the creation, development, and analysis of alternatives.

Each phase of decision-making is itself a decision problem of limited scope, but not necessarily difficulty, and each of these subproblems involves the same triumvirate of activities—intelligence, design, and choice. Large problems are broken down into smaller problems; these, in turn, may generate smaller problems. Eventually, one or some can be solved directly, and their solutions are used to climb back up to the next level of problems, until results bearing on the original problem begin to be assembled.

Behavioristic approaches to the study of decisions concentrate on search and design activities. The rapidly growing body of knowledge on this aspect of decision making is known as "artificial intelligence" (dealing with the simulation of human thought). The core of this research activity is the study of heuristic problem solving. According to Gyorgy Polya, the word *heuristic* derives from the Greek word for the branch of study belonging to logic or philosophy, the aim of which was to investigate the methods of discovery and invention. In its present use, *heuristic* is a general name for any aid to the discovery of a device or procedure used to reduce problem-solving effort, particularly any "rule of thumb" used to solve a problem.

While heuristics may not lead to an optimum solution to a particular problem, its great advantage is its economy of decision-making resources and its usefulness in finding good acceptable solutions to recurring problems. The principal characteristic of heuristic problem-solving is its reliance on simple approximate methods of solving numerous subproblems to build up a solution to the whole problem. This approach is in contrast to the application of formally correct, but frequently tedious, methods of mathematical optimization or maximization. Heuristic methods are employed for the solution of ill-structured problems—those which cannot be expressed in mathematical, or possibly even in quantitative, terms.

The conceptual distinction between the two types of decision, well-structured (programmed) and ill-structured (nonprogrammed), is important to an understanding of the future role of mathematics and computers in aiding business decisions. Problems can be programmed to the extent that they are repetitive and routine, to the extent that a definite procedure has been worked out for coping with them. Conversely, problems are nonprogrammed to the extent that they are novel, unstructured, and consequential. There exists no routine method for dealing with such a problem because:

(1) It has not arisen before;
(2) Its nature and structure are elusive; or
(3) It is sufficiently important to require unique attention.

There is a strong association between the degree to which a problem is nonprogrammed and the level within an organization at which it is handled. Problems which are nonprogrammed are generally handled by top-level management. The failure of operations research and computer techniques to penetrate top-level management problems is due to this rational phenomenon. It is the hope of management scientists that significant progress in the field of heuristic problem-solving will initiate this penetration.

C. The Computer as a Decision-Making Aid

The most outstanding feature of computers is that they can do some things better than a human can. The computer can assume those tasks which the human finds tedious, for example, searching out simple recording and mathematical errors. Just as machinery supplanted wearisome manual effort during the industrial revolution, so the computer has supplanted wearisome mental effort.

Computers are used primarily in the solving of problems which are highly programmed. In the computer trade, a program is a detailed set of instructions governing the sequence of steps required to complete a complex task. Thus, those problems for which the solution process can be structured are suitable for computer solution, providing computerization can be justified economically.

1. COMPUTER SUPPORT OF FORMAL DECISION-MAKING

In our analysis of economic computer support of formal decision making, we will review the formal sequence of the elements of the decision problem (Figure 1).

Data: Magnetic tapes and other computer memory devices are an efficient and low-cost method of storing data. The high density of computer memory systems, the increasing ease of recording and transcribing data, and the computers' ability to recall data rapidly have made computers the repository of an increasing amount of the data generated by and required to conduct the day-to-day operations of a business.

Information: Solving most problems requires the analysis of specific data in a particular format. Information can be obtained from data through data processing, the primary activity of computers. The computer generally provides the most economical and swift means of scanning, selecting, arranging, and presenting data which, for a particular problem, becomes information.

Knowledge: Included in the body of knowledge about a particular problem is the solution of other problems with a similar format. The solution techniques for a large number of structured problems have been worked out and have been programmed for computers. Many problems which appear to be different because they involve different variables have similar solution methods. The major portion of the search and creative activity emphasized in behavioristic problem-solving focuses on finding and exploiting these similarities.

During the creative activity, executives and their mathematically trained staff should guard against oversimplification in the use of analogies, similarities, and models. Problem solutions (decision) can be affected by this disease when the problem-solver abstracts from a problem unit a subproblem that is easily solved. The users of the solution then rationalize that the overly abstracted problem was the one which needed to be solved in the first place. All solutions to business problems are affected by this process; one of the major attributes of good business judgment is the ability to recognize the degree of model aphasia in any business problem solution.

Prediction: Forecasting activity may be classified as extrapolative or associative. Extrapolative forecasting relies solely on historical information about the event to be forecast. Associative forecasting uses the historical relationship(s) between the event in question and other events. The other events are forecast, either by extrapolation or association, and the expected relationship between events is used to forecast the event in which the decision-maker is interested.

Computer programs are available which make formal forecasts, using data on events and their relationships with other events. Recent studies indicate the computer-made forecasts are at least as good in most areas as purely judgmental forecasts.

Valuation: The problem of quantifying values, reconciling conflicts between them, and reducing multiple goals to a common measure is the most difficult area of decision-making. The use of the computer as a decision-making aid is severely constrained by this difficulty. Unless the degree to which an objective is achieved is measurable, quantitative methods (and hence the computer) cannot be applied.

Criteria Selection: The computer is of no use in selecting the decision criterion for a particular problem. Selection depends on the current attitude of the decision-maker or organization and the importance of the decision. However, the computer is frequently the least costly means of applying a stated decision criterion to a large number of alternatives with an even larger number of possible outcomes.

An Example of Computer Support of Decision-Making—Portfolio Balancing: Of particular interest to financial executives is the use of the computer to determine the optimum investment portfolio. The underlying complexity of the portfolio selection problem is the result of its combinatorial character. If a financial manager is looking for a portfolio with as few as 10 stocks out of a possible 100 securities, the number of alternative portfolios is more than 17 billion! It is impossible for the human mind to balance the relative advantages and disadvantages of all these alternatives. Faced with a problem of this complexity, all the analyst can do is apply some "rules of thumb" to a number of conventional groupings. This procedure invariably excludes a large number of the possible alternatives from the decision process. Therefore, no matter how successful the portfolio selected is, one cannot help but suspect that a better alternative was not even included in his deliberations.

By combining mathematical analysis and the use of the computer, an investor can select a portfolio which is close to optimal. Risk and expected-earnings information on each security is used to eliminate the alternatives which are clearly nonoptimal, and the remaining portfolios, called "efficient portfolios," are ranked according to their expected returns and relative riskiness. (A portfolio is considered efficient if no other portfolio with the same expected return has less risk or, conversely, if no other portfolio with the same risk has a higher expected return.) Provided with such a ranking, the investor can select a portfolio on the basis of his own investment strategy, including his attitudes toward risk, with the assurance that a more optimal portfolio for that strategy does not exist.

2. COMPUTER SUPPORT OF BEHAVIORISTIC DECISION-MAKING

Human beings, by interacting with their environment, can think, learn, and create. Computers can do only what they are programmed to do; if computers come to think, learn, and create, it will be by virtue of the programs which enable them to. Computer technology does not limit the symbol-manipulating capability of computers to numbers; they can manipulate words just as easily as numbers. Also, the computer's potential for flexible adaptive response to a task environment is the same as that of a human, although we are only beginning to find out how to capitalize on this potential. In its problem-solving capacity, the human mind is governed by programs that organize a myriad of information and knowledge into complex processes that respond and adapt to the problem environment and to the clues that are extracted from that environment as the problem-solving sequences unfold. Several computer programs have been written which simulate this human problem-solving process, but success in this area has been slow, and some seemingly insurmountable barriers have been encountered. Nonetheless, progress continues to be made.

It is a corollary of the hierarchical structure of organizations and the parallel assignment of business problems according to the degree to which they are structured that significant interaction between higher management and the computer in problem-solving endeavors must await significant developments in heuristic problem solving and the simulation of human thought processes. As computers' ability to manipulate less well-structured problems grows, their potential for assisting decisions at higher organizational levels will increase. However, computer-assisted decision-making for highly structured subproblems must be accepted and exploited by top management before developments in artificial intelligence, even at its currently immature stage, can be used effectively in most organizations.

D. The Accuracy of Decisions

It is impossible to assess fully the accuracy of decisions made in the face of uncertainty. Consideration of the formal steps in the decision-making process illustrates this fact.

First, decisions are considered to have been faulty generally on the grounds that the actual future events differed from those which were predicted at the time of the decision. Such judgments are invalid because the very nature of uncertainty and probability assumes that the future will not be exactly as it was predicted—unforeseen events always intervene. A valid criticism might be that the prediction system itself was faulty. One can evaluate the prediction system used to determine whether possible events had been adequately considered and assigned a probability which reflected subsequent history. However, it is not possible to reconstruct the environment, attitudes, and knowledge existing at the time of the decision fully enough to determine whether subsequent actual events should have been assigned a higher probability, i.e., whether the prediction system was, in fact, at fault.

Second, the values placed on actual outcomes are generally inappropriate for the measurement of the soundness of a decision which yielded that particular payoff. Value systems change, and the accuracy of decisions cannot be assessed without recreating the set of values relevant to events predicted at the time of the decision.

Third, the fact that more than one decision criterion may be appropriate makes it difficult to assess the viability of decisions. If the best or the worst of predicted possible outcomes happens, for example, there obviously exists a decision criterion which would have secured the best decision.

Reviewing past decisions is as necessary as making new decisions and forecasts and should be undertaken despite its difficulties. Such reviews constitute a valuable addition to the knowledge supporting future decisions. Also, the ability to pass judgment on decision-making capacity clearly increases with the number of decisions made and reviewed. One of the great advantages of formal, if not computer-aided, decision-making is that all of the principal elements in a decision, including assumptions, are made explicit, thus facilitating the review process.

Applications of Technology

Bross, Irwin D., *Design for Decision*, Macmillan & Co., New York, 1953.

Baumol, Wm. J., *Economic Theory and Operations Research*, Prentice-Hall, Englewood Cliffs, 1961.

McDonough, A. M., *Information Economics and Management Systems*, McGraw-Hill, New York, 1963.

Miller, D. W., and Starr, M. K., *Executive Decisions and Operations Research*, Prentice-Hall, Englewood Cliffs, 1960.

Simon, Herbert, *The New Science of Management Decision*, Harper & Bros., New York, 1960.

CHAPTER 4

Management Practices: A Changing Art/Science

Management Science Versus Management / Effects of Computer Use on the Management Environment of the Future

MANAGEMENT'S USE OF computers and information technology has caused much speculation about the efficacy of the scientific approach to management. Unfortunately, such discussion has caused some confusion about the causes and implications of the shifting boundary between art and science in the practice of management. An understanding of the nature and significance of this shifting is essential to the executive's reacting positively to the changes and potential changes induced by the new computer information technology. This chapter provides an analysis of this phenomenon to aid the executive in answering questions concerning the introduction and use of quantitative methods and computer-based information systems to improve business effectiveness.

A. *Management Science Versus Management*

For most executives, the art of management is characterized by judgment, experience, and intuition; for "management scientists," management tends to be characterized by rational decision-making and the use of formal models. Perhaps the primary source of confusion in the minds of executives about the gap between these two views is the failure of both groups to recognize and make explicit the important distinction between the management of a business function—such as inventory control or corporate accounts—and the management of people.

33

A manager appreciates the benefits of better information and improved understanding of the dynamics of the business function for which he is responsible. However, he also recognizes that, as an executive, he must rely continually on other people. Top-level management establishes the policy (decision rules) which he must follow and by which he is measured; he receives information from and delegates actions to those below him in the corporate structure; and he collaborates with those on either side. Hence, even though he is responsible for the conduct of a quantitatively describable activity, he can learn about the progress of that activity and can exert the desired control over it only through people.

The management scientist's contact with others in the organization is more limited; he deals with people primarily during the implementation stage of the work for which he is responsible, to gain improved information and understanding. The unpredictability and, often, irrationality of "people" actions are the antithesis of all that he is trying to accomplish. Hence, when he refers to the "art of management," he may tend to demean it with such descriptions as "seat of the pants" or "hunch" decision-making.

Management scientists must recognize—and most do—that management art will affect the outcome of their activities. The major source of problems or less-than-optimal utilization in new computer-based systems is the failure to adapt the system to the people who will use it. Mature students of scientific management know that the actual management of an activity may appear less than optimal when viewed as a rational "model", but that it may be more efficient than more rational methods would be, because of its ability to accommodate the human personality. For example, in many small businesses, the most advanced technology used is the telephone. Many of these businesses appear at first to be mismanaged; yet, analysis shows them to be amazingly flexible, fast-reacting, and profitable. Their systems are rational in terms of the activities they are conducting and, more important, in terms of the people who are conducting those activities. Thus, the management of activities depends on a system of people; and, if computer control of an activity is to be effective, the computer system must be modified (possibly even away from the optimal) to accommodate the art of managing people. In short, if the optimum use of people and computing machines is considered jointly, the most productive use of the combination generally implies less than optimum use of either taken alone.

A second source of confusion is the tendency of an executive to judge scientific approaches on the basis of specific applications. When he considers scientific management, he often centers on his own contact with specific incidences of the use of quantitative methods, most of which occurred in areas not directly under his control.

The management scientist, however, considers the scientific approach as detached from any individual applications of it, let alone the "good" or "bad" which resulted. He is concerned with the benefits which might be gained from a careful analysis of the goals and dynamic behavior of a business activity, the formulation of improved methods for achieving improved performance, and the testing and implementation of those methods. He suppresses his own preconceived ideas about which techniques are most appropriate until some preliminary investigations have been made, because experience has taught him that the careful analysis frequently reveals that the crux of many problems is in areas not originally thought to be relevant. Concurrently, the executive thinks about case histories—who got the blame and what the costs were, or who got the credit—the executive or the scientist?

Thus, the executive and the scientist must not only specify the function of the manager (control of activities or people) but must also agree to approaches (not specific tools) and the ground rules for their collaboration if they are to work together successfully. Two important sets of distinctions must be made:

(1) The conceptual distinction between managing as the art of interacting with people and managing as the science of controlling a quantitatively measurable activity; and

(2) The distinction between "good art" (the application of sound judgment based on experience) and "good science" (the application of sound principles); and conversely, "bad art" (hunch or seat-of-the-pants decision-making) and "bad science" (the rush to apply "cookbook" solutions).

B. Effects of Computer Use on the Management Environment of the Future

Once the initial distinctions between management art and management science have been made, the boundary between the two appears rather inviolate. The present manager who is a "good artist" should be, and is, relatively secure in his position. However, he must recognize the significance of the new information technology in the management of activities, its effects on the management of people, and its ramifications for managers in the future.

First, the new automation will reduce the number of people between the executive and the activity for which he is responsible. Computer information systems, independent of any decision-aiding functions, will reduce the cycle time between the gathering and analysis of information and the impact of decisions. Process times associated with activities will become more "machine paced" than "people paced."

Second, the nature of management is conditioned by the character of the system being managed, and the management of activities is rapidly becoming a joint venture of men and machines. The knowledge and training of the managers of the future will reflect this development. Not only will they be strong in their ability to interact with people, for there will always be people within organizations and people in other organizations with whom business must be conducted on a personal basis, but they also will have quantitative training in one or more of the sciences dealing with dynamic systems (systems and control engineers and mathematical economists, for example) so that they can use such systems in the conduct of their business.

Third, as computer use makes the internal operations of a firm more controllable, concern for the external environment will increase dramatically. The average future time horizons of concern to managers also will be lengthened, and the number of problems and the depth at which they are analyzed will be increased greatly. With the computer, a manager can instantly summon data, solution techniques, and simulated results of his decisions. The use of the computer system in this role will be the result of the interaction of the management process and advances in computer technology.

Fourth, since time sharing and remote computer power have become economical, the spatial allocation of computer power has become the business of interstate commerce in information. Current corporate structures will be profoundly affected by decisions of governments, and information utilities dividing the liability and responsibility for information handling among corporations, utilities, and the public. Also, economic considerations dictate that where economies of scale are present in an activity, it will come to be performed by firms partly or wholly devoted to conducting this activity for other firms. Such activities as personnel search, patent search, legal precedent research, technical journal abstracting, and security quotation are already being taken over as central services to the larger corporate community as the direct result of technological advances in computer systems.

B. Practical Application of Computers
to the Management Task

General Managers' Responsibilities for Electronic Data Processing and Information Systems

Introduction / Perspective / Responsibility for Strategic Planning / Responsibility for Management Control / Summary

A. Introduction

THE MANAGER with the most difficult task to do in any business is undoubtedly the general manager. He has to be a jack-of-all-trades, having an understanding of all the activities of the business—personnel, marketing, finance and accounting, production, and research and development. He has to harmonize or coordinate these activities, exercising top-management control in order that corporate short-term objectives will be accomplished: He has to determine long-range objectives and make the decisions necessary to allocate resources to attain these objectives. He sits at the apex of the management pyramid, making decisions on hiring, discharging, promoting, compensating or changing key personnel.

Electronic data processing (EDP) and information systems (IS) activities have become so important, requiring the investment of resources equal in magnitude to some of the other more established activities, e.g., accounting, that the management control and strategic planning of this activity must also be added to the general manager's already complex job.

The purpose of this chapter is to define and then examine the nature of the general manager's responsibility for electronic data processing and the development of systems. We will accomplish this first of all by placing the general manager's responsibility for EDP and IS activities into the perspective of his total top management job, and then examining the strategic planning and management control decisions requiring his direct involvement.

B. Perspective

The overall framework of the general manager's responsibilities for EDP and Systems can be seen in terms of four dimensions which make up a business entity. These are: business activities; levels of management; organization structure; and the basic functions of management.

Business Activities are simplified into six major categories: Finance & Accounting; Marketing, Production, Personnel, Research and Development, and EDP and Informations Systems.

Levels of Management are simplified into three categories, i.e., "top" (including general manager, marketing V.P., financial V.P., etc.), "middle" and "lower" levels of management.

Organization Structure is more difficult to describe in generalities because of its uniqueness to each company. The "general manager" being described in this chapter is meant to be the corporate top manager, whether or not the company is centralized or decentralized, with the added recognition that in a decentralized organization the general manager of a division or profit center is analogous in many of his responsibilities to the general manager described in this chapter.

Basic Functions of Management have been summarized into three categories: (a) strategic planning, which is the process of deciding on the objectives of the organization, the resources to be used to attain these objectives, and the policies that govern the acquisition, use and disposition of these resources; (b) management control, which is the process by which managers ensure that resources are obtained and used effectively in the accomplishment of organizational objectives; (c) operational control, which is the process of ensuring that specific tasks are carried out effectively and efficiently. Some distinctions between the basic functions of management and examples of activities under each heading can be seen in Tables 1 and 2. (For a more com-

Table 1

SOME DISTINCTIONS BETWEEN STRATEGIC PLANNING,
MANAGEMENT CONTROL AND OPERATIONAL CONTROL

Characteristics	Strategic Planning	Management Control	Operational Control
1. Focus of activity	On one aspect at a time	On whole organization	Task or transaction
2. Degree of structure	Unstructured and irregular; each problem different	Rhythmic; prescribed procedures	Highly structured, heavy reliance on prescribed procedures
3. Nature of information	Tailor-made for the problem; more external and predictive; less accurate	Integrated; mostly internal, historical; some external and predictive; usually financial bias	Tailor-made to the operation; often non-financial
4. Persons primarily involved	Staff and top management	Line and top management	Supervisors
5. Mental activity	Creative; analytical	Administrative, persuasive	Follow directions
6. Planning & Control	Planning dominant, but some control	Emphasis on both planning and control	Emphasis on control; a small amount of planning in a restricted area
7. Time horizon	Tends to be long	Tends to be short	Day-to-day
8. End result	Policies and precedents	Action within policies and precedents	Ensuring specific tasks are done

Table 2

EXAMPLE OF ACTIVITIES

Strategic Planning	Management Control	Operational Control
Setting financial policies	Working capital planning	Controlling extension of credit
Setting marketing policies	Formulating advertising programs	Controlling placement of advertisements
Setting personnel policies	Formulating personnel practices	Implementing policies
Planning the organization	Planning staff levels	Controlling hiring
Acquiring a new division	Deciding on plant rearrangement	Scheduling production
Choosing company objectives	Formulating budgets	Operating within budgets

plete description of the basic functions of management see reference 1 at the end of this chapter.)

The interlocking relationships of three of these dimensions can be seen in the dimensions of a cone in Figure 2. The particular point of note is Figure 2c, which relates the basic functions of management to the management levels. It can be seen that strategic planning is the responsibility of very top management; e.g., Board of Directors, Presidents, Vice Presidents, and Comptroller levels, with middle levels of management involved from time to time. Management control is primarily the concern of middle management, although both top and lower levels are involved to some degree. Operational control is the major role of the lower levels of management with some overlap into middle management.

Management control is distinct from operational control in that the time horizon in reporting information is longer, being measured in weeks, months, and years, compared with a day-to-day time horizon for operational control. Also the nature of information is different, the focus being on financial summaries of integrated operations, including information on the future, as well as history, and allowing room for subjective evaluation and decisions. In comparison, operational control information is focused on indices of performance that may not be financial; on single tasks or operations, using historical information and

Figure 2

THE MANAGEMENT PICTURE

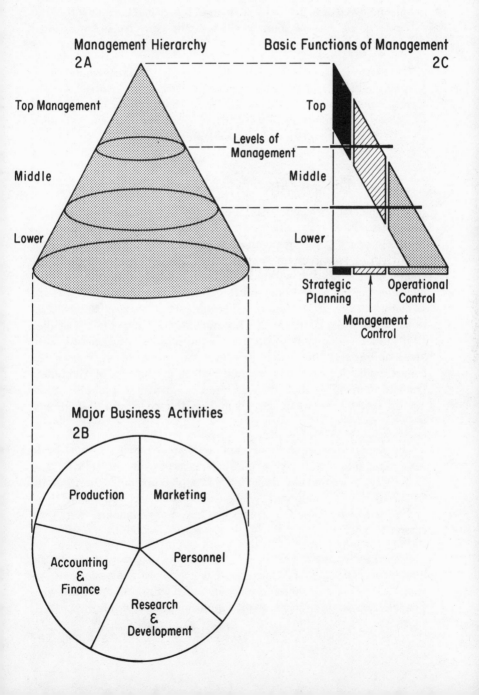

allowing little, if any, room for subjective evaluation and decision. Strategic planning has a much longer time horizon than either management or operational control, and requires much more external and futuristic information specially prepared for a specific problem. The people involved are primarily staff and top management, with little dependence on line personnel, which is the converse of operational and management control.

The general manager is obviously in the "Top Management" category of Figure 2c. Therefore he should be primarily involved in *strategic planning* for the company and its activities including *EDP and IS;* secondly, he should be actively involved in *management control* of all activities, which again includes *EDP and IS.*

C. Responsibility for Strategic Planning

The financial, personnel, and physical resources invested in EDP and systems have grown astronomically in many companies in the space of a few years. Many general managers are fully aware neither of the extent of resources committed nor of the widespread impact that computers have had or will have on their business. Strategic planning decisions governing the rate and direction of growth have been made in many cases by EDP managers, accountants or whoever else is functional head of the EDP activity. Investment of resources in the field of EDP and IS will continue to grow as applications expand to more areas of business, new more powerful and versatile equipment becomes available, managers become skilled in the use of computers (maybe demanding their own desk-top terminal and real-time information system—see reference 4), and as the EDP and IS "empire" grows.

The general manager should not abdicate from his responsibility for making informed decisions on the long-term plans for the EDP and IS activity. If a company has no corporate planning staff, the IS group trying to develop a long-range systems plan lacks top-management guidance and by default becomes the corporate planning staff. (See reference 3.)

We will examine below three of the major decision areas having long-term consequences and involving large commitments of resources: the organizational implications of EDP, equipment and vendor selection, and the selection of computer applications.

1. ORGANIZATIONAL IMPLICATIONS

Long-range planning inevitably involves examining the suitability of the organization structure in the light of expected changes in some aspect of the business. The decisions facing the general manager are:

- How will the growth in EDP and IS affect the organization structure, and
- How will the organization structure affect the technical optimization of EDP and IS.

How EDP and IS will affect the organization structure is still being debated by the organization "experts" with considerable differences of opinion. (See reference 10.) One school of thought, led by Professor Thomas L. Whisler, University of Chicago, suggests (reference 10, pages 16-60, and reference 8) that there is already a significant movement to drop decentralized profit centers and recentralize authority and profit responsibility. The argument for this centralization of control is that EDP and IS provide more information, covering a wider scope of operations, quickly to top management enabling them to make the necessary decisions, thus bypassing the need for profit-center managers to make those decisions. Also the nature of managerial work is changing, much of the logistical (i.e. structured, repetitive or routine) work is being centralized on the computer—purchasing, production planning and control, inventory control, reordering, shipping and invoicing, preparation of payrolls, and accounting. Managers who previously supervised these functions have fewer people reporting to them for the same volume of activity. Professor Whisler quotes substantial evidence including an example where one level of the hierarchy of a division was eliminated because of a shift toward more centralization of control over production, inventories, purchasing and accounting (reference 10, page 31).

Another school of thought, a major contributor being Professor John Dearden, Harvard Business School, while agreeing with the trend toward centralization of logistics systems, does not believe this means a trend toward centralizing organizational control and the elimination of profit centers (reference 10, page 174).

Authority and responsibility are delegated to profit centers because of top management's inability to maintain the required breadth and depth of expertise, and find the time to make all the management control decisions in a large and complex business. The business itself must be capable of being subdivided logically before profit centers are feasible. Dearden argues that the company will still be large and complex, and top management will still lack the breadth and depth of expertise and the time to exercise centralized control, even with computers.

Although the effects of EDP and IS on organizations are not fully agreed upon or even fully recognized, it is safe to say that for many years to come, the organization structure of a business will depend on such factors as the need to motivate people, geographic location, type of business, capabilities of individual managers, etc., and will not be organized per se around the computer. There is likely to be more centralization of routine or logistics systems in horizontally and vertically integrated companies. But there is significant doubt as to the feasibility, or advisability, of centralizing logistic systems of profit centers in companies carrying on dissimilar businesses, such as conglomerates. The general manager should be watchful that EDP and IS technology are not being used to force organizational structures detrimental to managerial initiative. A centralized organization structure may be the best way to disseminate predetermined changes, but a less centralized or decentralized structure may be needed to initiate changes. Also, a corporation's need for professionals with initiative and creativity puts a limit on the degree of centralization. Professionals resist controls and have a strong need to exercise initiative which is more difficult in a centralized company.

The effect of organizational structure on the use of computers is primarily a consideration of centralized versus decentralized data processing. There are three major factors that determine whether to centralize:

- The organization structure, more specifically the degree of decentralized profit responsibility existing already in the company;
- The question of technical optimization in the use of hardware, files, and systems, and
- The availability of skilled personnel to staff more than one computer center.

The centralization of data processing does not necessarily mean the centralization of organizational authority and responsibility. Profit-center managers could not care less how or where the data is processed as long as they obtain what they want, when they want it.

Obviously there is the problem of allocation of costs of a centralized EDP capability, but a profit-center manager can live with this just as he lives with allocation of corporate staff expense (although a better procedure is not to allocate these costs at all but retain and control them at the point where they are incurred and thus where they can be controlled, or, if absolutely necessary, only allocate them on a standard cost basis). Currently, there is a tendency for profit-center managers to want to manage the EDP capability that serves them, but this is only a manifestation of their fear that they cannot get the service they want unless it is under their control. The service comprises routine data processing of logistical applications, presentation of information for management control, and informational retrieval on specific topics of interest to profit-center managers. Once the EDP capability matures to the point where managers and EDP personnel can communicate with one another, understanding needs and problems, then data processing can become more of a service independent of the profit-center manager's immediate sphere of control.

Technical optimization is sacrificed in some cases where data processing capabilities are decentralized. Each situation should be judged on its merits but the above generalization holds true where communication costs are not a significant expense. The problems here are in the use of hardware; the unit cost of data processing diminishes as the size of equipment grows. Also the maintenance of one set of files is far easier than the attempt to maintain several copies of the same file at several decentralized locations. At the present time the most serious consideration in centralizing or decentralizing for many companies is the scarcity of qualified personnel to staff more than one data processing center. One large aerospace company cites this as its major reason for complete centralization, a measure of which can be obtained by knowing that it has over 75,000 tapes in its tape-file library!

Understanding the effects that computers have on the organization structure, and conversely, the effects that the organization structure has on the use of computers, allows more knowledgeable decisions to be made or the number, size and characteristics of equipment to buy and influences the selection and development of computer applications.

2. EQUIPMENT AND VENDOR SELECTION

Procurement decisions often commit a company to a particular manufacturer for five or more years, because the cost of changing manufacturers is high in terms of reprogramming, physical transfer of equipment and the substantial learning curve on getting to know the new equipment. Compatibility among systems of different manufacturers is growing, as will be shown in detail in Chapter 8. Suffice it here to mention that because of the high rate of technological obsolescence, high numbers of possible permutations in equipment configurations and the considerable differences between offerings of vendors in hardware, software and other assistance, it is sometimes advisable for a company to use the services of outside specialists rather than to rely solely on equipment manufacturers or in-house EDP staff. The outside specialist should work with both in-house EDP staff and equipment manufacturers, using his special knowledge gained from previous procurement decisions and his objectivity because of his position as a complete outsider with no product to sell or empire to build, in advising the general manager as to the best course of action. His work too should be reviewed; the general manager needs to consider the several sides of the case. The stakes are high; one large oil company pays over $50 million annual rental on hardware alone; its software costs may easily equal that figure.

3. SELECTION OF APPLICATIONS

Computer applications are becoming more complex, taking on an appearance of integrated systems reaching, in many cases, across divisional and functional boundaries. Some systems, especially the integrated variety, take many man-years to design and program and several years to reach operational status after they are first conceived. All this time, plus the valuable resources of analysts, programmers and equipment, are tied up. It is imperative that the general manager take some responsibility for deciding which applications should have priority in receiving these large investments in scarce EDP resources.

Historically, computer capability has developed under the finance and accounting manager. The early applications were mostly accounting-oriented, later spreading to other logistics systems. The costs and benefits from most of these early applications could be quantified, allowing top management to see real cash savings. Most of the quantifiable applications have been computerized by the more advanced companies. Their problem now is in finding some way to select applications with the best payoff when both the costs and benefits cannot be quantified. An additional problem is that since many applications cannot stand alone, the high cost of equipment and the use of the same files and inputs for several systems not only makes for complex designing and programming, but precludes the possibility of cost/benefit analysis for any one application except on an incremental cost/benefit basis.

The most profitable applications are likely to occur where the capabilities of the computer can be brought to bear on the major problem areas governing the success of a business in its industry. The computer has the capability of performing repetitive operations speedily without getting bored or introducing human error; processing large amounts of information or formulae even from many users at remote locations; producing accurate values consistently; and manipulating many interacting variables. The factors that govern the success of a business are much more difficult to define because they obviously depend on the basic dynamics of the specific business. In one case, control over inventory may be the crucial profitability factor. For example, a large U.S. airline's seat-reservation system—a glorified system for control over the inventory of airline seats—is a significant improvement in customer service which gives that carrier a competitive advantage as well as more information for such tasks as crew scheduling and profitability comparisons of routes and flight times. In a large advertising agency, measuring advertising effectiveness may be the principal area in terms of which media to select in order to get the highest payoff. Computerizing the personnel file or the fixed-assets records in preference to developing the applications in the two examples cited above does not make sense! Richard Werling, an executive of Continental Airlines with many years of experience in the computer field, says that:

> "Identifying opportunities for action-oriented systems involves going directly to the main stream of the business, determining what must be done well for the business to succeed within its industry and for the business to grow." (Reference 11.)

The importance of selecting applications is emphasized by a report that the Board of Directors of one large company, after careful study, decided recently to promote from his post the 34-year-old manager of a division with a $100-million annual sales volume and give him responsibility for directing the company's system-development activity. Yet another Board of a large company formed a committee of the Board to assume responsibility for the development and direction of all management information systems.

To determine the high-payoff areas of the business requires a thorough understanding of all aspects of the business. The general manager is one of the few people in a company with the necessary perspective, experience and authority. Therefore he cannot afford to abdicate his responsibility for guiding the selection of applications.

D. Responsibility for Management Control

The general manager exercises management control over EDP and IS activities just as he does over the activities of personnel, production, marketing, finance and research & development. He has to ensure that the EDP and IS activity operates within the corporation's policies and precedents in accomplishing congruent EDP and corporate objectives.

Besides being interested in the EDP activity's conformance to budget and performance criteria, he is also concerned about two other significant problem areas—namely, standardization and development of integrated systems.

1. USE OF STANDARDS IN EDP SYSTEMS

The importance of standards in data processing is widely recognized, but somehow recognition and use are two very different things. Many are the stories of man-years of programming wasted because of the inability of one programmer to understand and modify the work of another programmer who left the company for greener pastures; and again, of the inability to run an application on another profit center's computer due to the original programming being written for a nonstandard equipment configuration. Besides the standardization of methods for documenting systems and programs, standards or procedures are needed to control

- The handling of input data to insure that documents are not lost before being entered into the computer and that correct information is entered into the system;
- The processing of data and the use of files, programs and output data in order to assure the security of the vast amount of financial, sales, personnel and other valuable information being processed; and
- The organization of responsibilities in the EDP and Systems activity.

In accounting there is a division of duties to safeguard against fraud e.g., separate people will have the duties of preparing payroll, inserting cash into pay envelopes, and physically paying wages. In data processing there needs to be a similar division of duties into, for example, designing systems, handling input documents, processing the data and operation of libraries.

Auditing the financial accounts of a business is becoming very complicated. The traditional "audit trails" by which internal and external auditors could trace transactions through the business are disappearing rapidly with the advent of integrated systems. The audit function will continue, no doubt, but how it will pursue its task, verifying correctness of systems dealing with financial information and adherence to those systems, is subject to great change. The use of standards mentioned earlier is a sound base for internal auditing, but these should be supplemented with validity checks on input data (using editing routines, batch controls, computer anticipations of input data, etc.), on processing (recording unprogrammed halts, recording use of files, etc.), and on output data (using computer generated totals and statistical analysis of sample transactions, for example). Many validity checks can be built into computer programs, but this is often left up to individual programmers who are usually so busy trying to get the system programmed that they don't want to be bothered with embellishments for internal auditing purposes. Before a system is too far along in design, consideration should be given to inserting an audit trail. On completion the system should be tested with real data to verify validity of both the information produced by the system and the audit trail.

Another aspect of standardization is on equipment. The corporate policy of one large oil company (mentioned earlier as having $50 million annual rental for computer hardware) is to buy equipment from only one manufacturer. The company is heavily decentralized into profit centers, many of which have their own EDP capability. In all there are over 50 separate computer installations. The principal reasons for buying from one manufacturer were to obtain compatible equipment, thus providing back-up capability to any division from another division, and allowing the exchange of systems and the joint use of files. The profit center managers acted autonomously within this corporate directive and bought from the same manufacturer. Unfortunately, compatibility has not been achieved. There was no corporate directive as to the standardized equipment configuration to buy (size of central processing unit, types of terminals, etc.), and also there was no directive as to standardized programming languages or methodology, all of which are needed to obtain compatibility.

2. RESPONSIBILITY FOR SYSTEMS

In the early days of data processing top management did not need to interfere in the natural development of computer applications between the using department and the EDP department. But the development of integrated systems, crossing over departmental boundaries and into more than one profit center in a decentralized company, requires authorization and control from top management.

The high investment in equipment and software necessitates designing systems in such a way as to use the data-processing capability to the fullest. To do this means designing files, inputs and sometimes outputs that will serve several different purposes. For example, it is no longer necessary to design an inventory control system with its own files and input documents and then a purchasing system with its own files and input documents. It is possible to design one integrated system comprising subsystems for inventory control, purchasing, expediting purchase orders, and accounts payables using the same set of files and input documents, and servicing more than one profit center simultaneously. To design and program this is difficult, but to obtain an entry into the different profit centers and to different departments is impossible without top management support.

A problem that all managers have is keeping abreast of the availability of new tools that will assist them in managing better. Management styles and decision-making abilities are based on experience and techniques tested and proved over the years. Naturally managers have a great reluctance to abandon such apparatus without very good reasons. It is vitally important for the general manager to keep abreast of developments in computer applications in order to encourage the acceptance of computer applications by his subordinate managers.

Management information systems are a popular topic of interest. They are difficult to understand because of the multitude of different opinions on what is an MIS. For simplicity's sake we can define it for the purpose of this chapter as a "management and operational control system" using the definitions of "management" and "operational control" explained early in this chapter. The general manager cannot abdicate his responsibility to participate heavily in the conceptual design of an MOCS. Whether he likes it or not its design will be determined by the information he asks for. Subordinates tend to ask for information which allows them to answer their superiors' questions. Thus, the top manager perhaps unwittingly provides the overall influence on the nature and content of information flows from the top level on down.

One danger to be aware of in designing an MOCS is the difference in the information threshold of different managers. One top manager may want to get more detail on business operations than did his predecessor. Information threshold is a function of his personality, his prior training in a particular activity before becoming a top manager, and his style of delegating responsibility. The president of a one billion-dollar company examines weekly production reports of five divisions, mainly because he used to be production manager and came up through the production activity. He rarely looks at the financial reports or marketing forecast. He is, in effect, exercising operational control over the production activity, instead of spending his time on strategic planning for the whole corporation. An MOCS will reflect the information needs of the top manager, the levels of data bases and reports will all be designed and geared accordingly. The unfortunate factor here is that the MOCS will probably have to be redesigned as soon as the person in the top management position retires or becomes more aware of his strategic planning responsibility. The time span for designing an MOCS for the company referred to above was approximately four years from conception to implementation, so the amount of investment is substantial.

E. Summary

The purpose of this chapter was to indicate the responsibility that the general manager bears for planning the strategy of and exercising management control over the electronic data processing and systems activity. In strategic planning, the general manager has to consider the effects that an EDP and information systems activity has on the formal corporate organization, and conversely, the effects that the formal organization of the company has on the technical optimization of the use of EDP and IS resources. Also he must concern himself with the selection of equipment and vendors and the selection of applications to be computerized in order that the large investments of corporate resources in EDP and IS are allocated to produce the greatest return.

The general manager must exercise management control over the EDP and IS activity for the same reasons as he exercises management control over other corporate activities such as marketing and finance—he has to ensure that criteria of expense and performance are being met and that each activity's goals are congruent with corporate goals. He must be sure that the quality of work produced by the EDP activity satisfies external reporting requirements as well as the internal needs of the corporation.

The growing trend toward designing integrated systems which cut across the responsibilities of several managers in different profit centers or activities, requires the general manager's authorization and cooperation if these systems are to be adopted by subordinate managers. In particular, in the design of integrated management and operational control systems, he must participate actively in determining the hierarchy of goals to be achieved and the information he needs to evaluate actual performance and take corrective action where appropriate.

The conditions that determine high computer-systems payout can be summarized as

- The need for top managers to take the same interest in return on investment for computer systems as they would for any other kind of business investment;
- The responsible involvement by managers in the development and implementation of systems;
- The focusing of systems effort into the critical problem areas of the business; and
- The employment of systems people with breadth and depth of experience in operating areas of the business, and who also have an understanding of human behavior as well as technical competence in computers and systems.

Many of the underlying factors affecting these conditions have been discussed briefly in this chapter. (For additional discussion of them, see references 3, 5, 6, and 9.) Subsequent chapters will deal in more detail with several of the topics. For example Chapter 6 extends the discussion on applications to a specific example of a management control system for distribution, Chapter 7 discusses the use of computers in the finance and account activities, Chapter 8 discusses organization and procurement in more detail and Chapter 9 is concerned with problems in the implementation of systems.

It is interesting to speculate on the effects that computers will have on the decision-making abilities of the general manager. (See reference 2.) The use of computers can provide the top manager with more choices from which to make a decision. He can operate more like a selector, rather than like a judge sitting in judgment as to the advantages and disadvantages of a single opportunity. He can obtain more thorough analyses of problem areas by coupling the speed of the computer with modern analytical techniques such as network analysis, operations research, decision simulation, etc. The speed of the computer enables him to take more time over decisions because less time is spent in gathering information.

Looking further into the future, we can see an increase in the use of simulation models in exploring alternative courses of action; a reduction in the time required to transmit information between divisions and corporate headquarters due to the growth in data communications and direct input techniques, and the computerized collection and summarizing of pertinent information for top management's use. The greatest impact will still be in large companies, which will continue to lead the way in advancing the state of the art in computer utilization.

References

1) Anthony, R. N., "Planning and Control Systems: A Framework for Analysis," Harvard Business School, Division of Research.

2) Brady, R. H., "Computers in Top-Level Decision-Making," *Harvard Business Review*, July/August 1967.

3) Dearden, J., "How to Organize Information Systems," *Harvard Business Review*, March/April 1965.

4) Dearden, J., "Myth of Real-Time Management Information," *Harvard Business Review*, May/June 1966.

5) Garrity, J. T., "Top Management & Computer Profits," *Harvard Business Review*, July/August 1963.

6) Garrity, J. T., and McNerney, J. P., "EDP: How to Ride the Tiger," *Financial Executive*, September 1963.

7) Head, R. V., "Management Information Systems: A Critical Appraisal," *Datamation*, May 1967.

8) Leavitt, H. J., and Whisler, T. L., "Management in the 1980's," *Harvard Business Review*, November/December 1958.

9) McLaughlin, W. J., "EDP Contribution to a Manufacturing Operation," *Financial Executive*, April 1966.

10) Myers, C. A. (Ed.), *The Impact of Computers on Management.* Cambridge: The MIT Press, 1967.

11) Werling, R., "Action-Oriented Information Systems," *Datamation*, June 1967.

CHAPTER 6

Initiating and Implementing a Computer Program: A Managed Beginning

Introduction / Study of Applications / Staff Selection / Vendor and Equipment Selection / Implementation Plan / Project Implementation

A. Introduction

INTEREST IN THE USE of computers in a corporation can arise in a variety of ways. Individuals with an interest in and knowledge of computers and data processing can attract management's attention and initiate a preliminary evaluation program. Or, top management itself may be dissatisfied with the timeliness, accuracy, and completeness of present report documents and initiate a project to evaluate the potentials of computer use.

The steps taken during this preliminary analysis and as a direct result of it are the most important in the development of an appropriate computer program for a corporation. A carefully considered overall plan, in which the major alternatives have been examined and the consequences of errors considered, is a prerequisite to a "managed beginning." The choice of applications, staffing, and equipment selection determine the course of the entire program. As the program progresses, it becomes more difficult to select different applications, modify organizational arrangements, reassign and change staffs, alter equipment orders, or even change suppliers.

59

B. *Study of Applications*

1. THE PROJECT GROUP

The desire to use computers in an organization usually leads to the appointment of a committee or project group. Its members should be knowledgeable about the business, alert to innovation, and represent the various functions and departments in the company. Ideally, these men would know the general potential of computers and, at least, be familiar with similar businesses' use of data processing. At least one member of the project must know about computer hardware and systems; he can serve as a source of information, offer some tutorial assistance, and provide some perspective on what is and what is not reasonable in data processing.

The function of this project group is to uncover potential applications. The composition of the group, their own preferences as to procedure, and the nature of the business itself will determine how this task is completed. In general, the most thorough and straightforward way is to undertake a review of all the company's operations and, simultaneously, to carry out a program of interviews at all levels of management. Many executives, supervisors, and foremen are aware of problems with present procedures. Discussions with these men will lead to innumerable suggestions for computer applications and for modernizing and unifying seemingly separate functions into integrated systems.

2. ESTIMATE OF BENEFITS

Undoubtedly, the important applications will be in the mainstream of company operations. For example, large distributors will recognize inventory control as an important application, or some manufacturers will recognize maintenance scheduling as an application with high priority. As each potential application is reviewed, some estimate should be made of the likely benefits that will accrue from automation, such as reduced personnel costs, lower inventories or faster turnover, more efficient operations, and more timely information for planning and control. Such benefits as reduced personnel costs will be tangible, others will not be. Any economic justification should be clearly identifiable, and every attempt should be made to arrive at reasonable estimates.

Some of the pitfalls in making estimates of savings are extremely interesting. One company in the Midwest, for example, carried out such a study and carefully determined the personnel savings that would result from computer use. The proposed application was very large, involving several departments, and consequently the anticipated savings in personnel costs were substantial. However, several years of development effort were required before the manual application could be converted to the computer systems, and a second review midway through the development effort showed that more than half the anticipated savings had vanished. A comprehensive analysis indicated that a recession had taken place in the intervening period and that a general tightening of the operating budgets had resulted. Fewer people were doing the same job, therefore, the base on which economic savings were determined was no longer valid.

3. Assistance from Equipment Manufacturers

The manufacturers of equipment can be very helpful during feasibility studies. It is important to remember, however, that at this stage the manufacturers' staffs are concerned primarily with securing an order or letter of intent. Their staffs are an expensive overhead item, which computer manufacturers will use only to the extent necessary. The prospective user, therefore, should not rely entirely on the manufacturers' representatives during the feasibility study; rather, he should provide the necessary staff to do the work, turning to the manufacturers only for guidance and assistance.

4. Management's Role

The importance of management's role during these early studies cannot be overestimated. The results of the feasibility study, including the recommended applications in some order of priority and the preliminary estimates of time and cost, are the basis on which management decisions will be made.

To judge progress and evaluate alternatives successfully, management will need orientation and education. A manager cannot possibly spend enough time to become thoroughly familiar with details about his systems. His subordinates must teach him.

C. Staff Selection

Once the initial feasibility study is completed and management has reviewed and approved the plans, design and implementation begin. The steps of the feasibility study, the recruiting of staff and creation of an organization, and the selection of equipment usually overlap. Some of the staff participating in the feasibility study may remain with the program; likewise, in anticipation of future requirements, some specialists in hardware or software may be hired during the feasibility study. Also, the order for the computer usually is placed before serious systems design begins, particularly if the general features of the computer required are reasonably clear or considerations not directly related to the applications being implemented dictate the choice.

1. STAFF REQUIREMENTS

Normally, the staff is composed of three kinds of skilled professionals, whose functions overlap—systems analysts, programmers, and operations researchers. Staff size depends very much on their competence, on the number, size and complexity of applications, and the approximate time over which the work is planned.

Systems Analysts define the application; they determine and document the inputs, the processing, and the outputs in sufficient detail to permit the programmers to write the instructions for the computer. In a payroll application, for example, the systems analyst determines who collects what information on the hours worked by each employee, where that person collects it, and how the information is prepared for keypunching. Considerable detailed information is then collected about the various wage levels applied to each employee, overtime, various deductions, etc. All these detailed calculations are described in a "flow chart," which is a systematic description of all the relevant and necessary calculations performed. The systems analyst will also consider the files which must be maintained (e.g., an employee file, perhaps in employee number order) and the exact information that each file contains.

A systems analyst relies on the operating personnel of the company for most of the needed information. As he develops the details of the system, he frequently reviews existing procedures with the operating people and suggests changes which will make the procedures more adaptable to computer processing and, perhaps, even more efficient. He also plays a major role during the actual conversion of the application, when the existing procedures and the new system are run side by side before final changeover.

The requirement for constant interaction with the operating personnel indicates that the systems analyst must be sensitive to problems in operating the business. Ultimately, his ability to deal with people, his knowledge of the business, and his skill in organizing the new system can greatly simplify the overall job of the manager of data processing.

Programmers are professionals in the art of writing instructions for computers; they like to work alone and gain great satisfaction from the manipulation of computer language.

The programmer begins with the flow chart the analyst has prepared. He is not concerned with the "why's and wherefore's" of the application, but does know about the computer to be used and the language for that computer. The steps from the flow chart to the computer program are to the analyst straightforward and routine; to the programmer, imaginative and creative. When fed to the computer (or compiled or assembled), his product, a program or set of instructions, will perform, in the most efficient way possible, the functions specified by the analyst in the flow charts.

During the debugging stages, when the programmer tries to find errors in the programs, he works closely with the systems analyst. Each finds the mistakes the other has made; thus, their responsibilities and efforts overlap, and they must work together throughout the implementation of the program.

Operations Researchers are concerned primarily with developing better ways to perform the computer applications and with specifying the rules and generalized descriptions by which they will be performed. Their efforts precede those of the systems analysts and their concern is more with understanding *why* an application is performed in a certain way, rather than *how* it is currently performed.

The operations researcher collects, analyzes, and studies the data necessary to understand the process and to devise a new and better way of running an operation, given certain objectives and constraints.

In this capacity, he can improve the overall quality of the effort and the program and should, therefore, be allowed to concentrate on the applications he believes will benefit most from his techniques and approaches.

2. SOURCE OF STAFF

Staff can be hired or recruited from present company employees. Internal staff will be familiar with the business, but may know little about systems analysis, programming, and operations research; new staff may know nothing of the particular business, but will know a great deal about computer techniques.

Internal staff can be trained in systems analysis and programming, but such training would be unnecessary and time consuming, particularly since qualified programmers are generally available externally. Characteristically, programmers are highly mobile; their allegiance tends to be not to a business or a company, but to computers and computer use. It is this mobility which makes it possible to secure programming staff on reasonably short notice.

It should be noted that growth in computer use has created a shortage of qualified personnel, and computer programmers' salaries reflect this shortage. However, a first-rate programmer produces great amounts of accurate material; the higher salary is quickly offset by savings in debugging and program running times.

. Newspaper advertising is the natural way to recruit systems analysts and programmers. In addition, several employment agencies specialize in computer personnel; a glance through a few journals will reveal the more active agencies in any given geographical area.

Computer and key punch operators are also a vital part of a computer installation. To provide time for the training needed for the particular equipment ordered, they should be recruited shortly before the computer is delivered. The existing supervisory staff should be aware of the requirements, by that time, and able to make the appropriate plans.

3. ORGANIZATIONAL ARRANGEMENTS

Perhaps no step in the planning process will elicit more management interest than the organizational arrangements for the emerging data processing or management information systems activity. To a large extent, the overall performance of the activity will depend on an organizational arrangement appropriate to the needs of the corporation.

No one organizational arrangement is best. The environment in which the new organizational structure is to perform and the people who will make it up determine to a large extent the details of the most desirable organizational arrangements.

Organization Under Controller: Figure 3 illustrates the simplest conventional organizational arrangement; it reflects the fact that the first use of computers was in the accounting functions, which are easily mechanized and provide a readily identifiable economic justification for introducing a computer system. Under this arrangement, a Manager of Data Processing reports to the Controller; reporting to the manager are systems analysts and programmers (or their supervisors) and the operators and key punchers (or their supervisors). Whether systems analysts and programmers are under different supervisors depends on total numbers and the particular application.

Figure 3
ORGANIZATION UNDER CONTROLLER

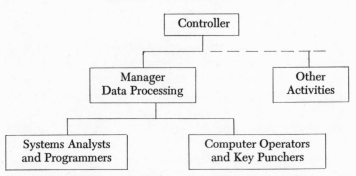

This organization generally is applicable for a small company ($20-50 million gross income). Although under the direction of the Controller's Department, such a system provides for the data processing or information systems needs of the manufacturing, marketing, or engineering departments.

Organization Under Controller—Multilocation Activities: More complex arrangements are generally required when dealing with multilocation computer activities. Consider, for example, a large corporation with three data processing centers—one in the East (New York), one in the Midwest (Oklahoma City), and one in the West (Los Angeles). In this situation, it would be possible to have one manager in charge of systems, one manager in charge of programming, and one manager in charge of operations (Figure 4). Each location would have its own supervisor.

Figure 4

ORGANIZATION UNDER CONTROLLER—MULTILOCATION ACTIVITIES

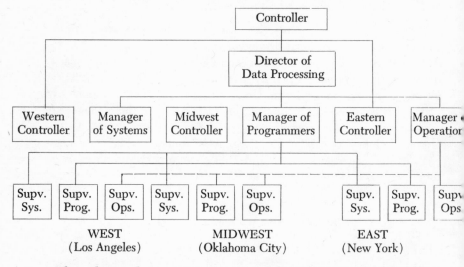

The scheme shown in Figure 4 ensures uniformity in procedures and applications among the various locations since all operations are under the control of one person, the Manager of Systems. However, a disadvantage of this arrangement is that lack of an on-site manager at each location requires the resolution of problems at much higher levels of management than might otherwise be necessary. Designation of on-site overall managers (Figure 5) provides for prompt action on matters affecting a given data center. For example, disagreements between programmers who want machine time and operations personnel who insist no time is available can be resolved at once. Such decisions by on-site management often make the difference between progress and confusion.

In Figure 5, the maintenance of uniformity and the allocation of tasks to the various data centers is the responsibility of the Director of Data Processing. This arrangement is generally satisfactory, since

Figure 5
ORGANIZATION UNDER CONTROLLER—MULTILOCATION ACTIVITIES
WITH AUTONOMOUS MANAGERS

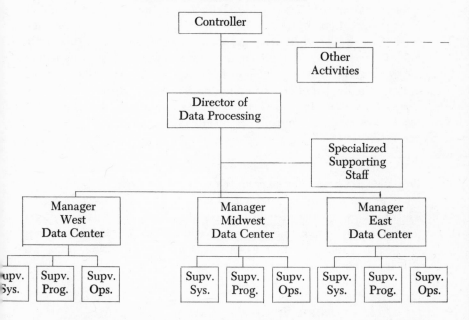

differences between centers and necessary planning can be completed at meetings of the data center managers.

Organization Under a Director of Data Processing: In recent years, as computers have been used in more and more functions which are not related to the controllers' activities, the trend to establish a Director of Data Processing (or Vice President of Information Systems) outside of the controller's activities has gained acceptance. For example, control of a computer system such as American Airlines' SABRE reservation system cannot be construed as a responsibility or "service" of the controller, and illustrates the organizational arrangements under a Director of Data Processing. Computer activities controlled under such a system are typical of those used by corporations with sophisticated information systems.

D. Vendor and Equipment Selection

The prospective user often must select a vendor and his hardware many months before actual delivery and before the detailed system design, which could assist in making the selection, is far along or even begun. Fortunately, in most instances the choice is not difficult, although considerable care should be exercised before a contract is signed.

The eight major vendors of computing equipment are IBM, Control Data Corporation, UNIVAC, Honeywell, General Electric Company, Radio Corporation of America, National Cash Register, and Burroughs. Each markets a full line of computers and such peripheral equipment as printers, card readers and punchers, tape units, and disks. At least a dozen smaller suppliers, including Scientific Data Systems and Electronics Associates, Inc., market a more specialized line, but their comparable processors are fully competitive with those of the major vendors.

Vendor and hardware selection can be approached in two ways. Proposals can be requested from the vendors and, after suitable evaluation of the submitted proposals and other factors, selection made. The study group may decide that certain clearly identifiable criteria justify merely contacting a given vendor and placing the order; nothing is gained by asking several vendors to prepare proposals which will not be considered in any event.

1. PROPOSAL SPECIFICATIONS

If formal proposals are requested from several vendors, it is essential that the vendors have complete and clear specifications upon which to base their bids. The study group must provide a detailed outline of the applications being considered, giving some indication of the size of the files and the volume of activity anticipated. Much of this information should have been gathered during the feasibility study and included, at least in summary form, in the final report to management. If such specifications are not provided, the vendors' proposals will not be comparable and will be very difficult, if not impossible, to evaluate properly.

Depending on the complexity of the system, the vendors may require from a few weeks to several months to prepare their proposals. Vendors try to be responsive to requests and prepare their proposals carefully; they are willing and anxious to reexamine areas where a misunderstanding has led them to an unresponsive proposal. Very likely, the vendor's representatives will want to discuss various details with members of the committee and to review some of the applications being considered.

2. Proposal Evaluation

The proposal evaluation process usually begins with a formal presentation by the vendor of the approach he will take, the combination of hardware and software he will use, the staff support he will provide, and the cost of the proposed system. After the presentation, the proposals are examined by the study group to reveal differences which were not readily apparent during the sales-oriented oral presentation. Adopting specific criteria is useful in analyzing and comparing the proposals; some of the elements necessary for a thorough comparison are discussed below.

Normalization of the Proposed System: Meaningful comparisons can be made only if substantially the same set of specifications were used by the vendors. If information on the number and type of transactions, the overall size of files, frequency of access to files, reliability requirements, outputs, etc. was provided and used by all the vendors, normalization will not be necessary. Otherwise, considerable effort and skill will be required to make the proposals comparable.

Separation of the System into Recognizable Parts: The system proposed will consist of many individual components of hardware and software. The components should be studied individually and collectively to establish their effectiveness in the application.

Consideration of Overall System Organization: Vendors often try to adapt an existing line of equipment to the proposed application. Their ability to do so depends on their understanding of the problem. In evaluating the practicality of a particular vendor's approach, the following factors should be considered

- Has he adequately considered centralized, semi-centralized, or decentralized hardware?
- Are all the costs clearly identified?
- Is there an undue concentration of costs in any one part, such as terminals or multiplexers?
- Has the system's performance been adequately determined?
- Does it degrade gracefully under overloads?
- Is there adequate provision for growth?

After evaluating all the proposals, the study group must consider the vendors themselves. Final vendor selection, which amounts to the formation of a partnership between user and vendor, is usually based on business considerations—a vendor's experience and reputation, his support and servicing of equipment, his knowledge about the operations, or his compatibility with the equipment and programs currently being used.

After the selection is made, the unsuccessful bidders must be notified. In fact, it is useful to plan to review with the unsuccessful vendors the major points of difference and the basic reasons for the final choice. Explicit recognition that such discussions, usually called debriefings, will be carried out introduces a considerable degree of objectivity during the selection process.

3. THE EQUIPMENT ORDER

Because of the long lead time (from 6 to 24 months, depending on the manufacturer, the computer, and the peripherals) needed for current computing equipment, the customer frequently has to order a machine before he knows exactly what use he will make of it and the exact elements that will make up his configuration at time of installation. It has become customary to give the equipment manufacturer a letter of intent, stating the customer's intention to order a machine and inviting the computer manufacturer to assist in the detailed definition of the application areas and of the exact equipment to be ordered. The main purpose of a letter of intent, however, is to place the user on the equipment manufacturer's delivery schedule.

If a letter of intent is signed, the account representative for the equipment manufacturer will arrange for the necessary program to educate the company's staff in the use of the equipment. He will also make available one or more systems engineers, depending on the size of the account, to assist the company's staff in the selection of and preparation for the computer system.

The staff should be aware that certain manufacturers have developed strengths in manufacturing certain items of equipment and that the sales engineers, following the manufacturer's marketing policy, will encourage use of these items. The user must be sure that he orders only those items which will be best for his company's particular job. Also, the manufacturer naturally will try to sell as expensive a system as he can. Therefore, someone on the user's staff must be qualified enough in the technical details of the equipment under consideration to judge the reasonableness of the order being placed.

Because of the long lead time for delivery of hardware, the manufacturer may require the account representative to "production schedule" the machine about nine months before the delivery date. At this time, the customer must order the actual machine and other hardware he needs, on a unit by unit basis. If the exact configuration of the machine still has not been specified, the customer can "over order"; for example, he can order four tape drives if he does not know whether he will need three or four and can cancel the order on one unit as late as 30 days before delivery, if the contract has been set up to allow it.

Timely placement of an order for equipment can be very important. A delay in placing the order may result in a corresponding delay in the installation and the whole program. Lead times, item by item, should be carefully discussed with the vendor and taken into account in the planning. A more important reason for placing a firm order is that a signed contract for equipment with a firm delivery date generally provides a much-needed incentive for systems analysts and programmers to begin serious work.

E. Implementation Plan

In any group preparing for the arrival of a computer system, there are a number of documents purporting to be plans for the project. Seldom, however, is there a single cohesive implementation plan, giving the background, the purposes, and the organization of the program in a way that makes clear, to all personnel, the level of backing being provided by senior management and the interaction of the project leaders with other levels of management. Such plans have three fundamental characteristics.

Plans should be "layered" in detail, with each level designed to meet a specific purpose. Planning documents should be designed to meet the specific needs of each broad group of users. Although considerable detail will eventually be required for the successful completion of the project, to some detailed information will be of little value, and both waste and lack of interest will result if plans are not divided into layers according to the level of detail they will contain.

Generally, three levels of plans are necessary and sufficient. Level One plans are designed for senior management, including boards of directors and those managers who will not participate actively in the implementation program but will benefit from the project and are ultimately responsible for the performance of personnel who will be active participants. Any plan which is to be reviewed and absorbed by this group must be concise and oriented toward encouraging their participation. The plans should be educational, informing senior management about the degree of participation which is desired and the extent to which it will benefit from the project. Such plans would include a general schedule of the program so that the reader can determine the time period during which he may be asked to provide support and the date by which he can anticipate receiving benefits. Also, general descriptions should indicate the organizational structure of the project, the manpower requirements, and summary financial figures. Details of the program implementation (e.g., PERT/time or PERT/cost charts) should not be included, but appropriate references should be provided so that greater detail can be found easily if it is desired.

Level Two plans are designed to satisfy the requirements of the project management and, therefore, should contain detailed PERT charts, the list of participants, summaries of the timing estimates of the various program segments, estimates of man-day requirements for analysis, programming, debugging, etc. This document should not present flow charts, but should contain summary information block diagrams, particularly schematics of any interrelationships between applications. These plans will be the basis for review and evaluation of the project and will provide the guide for day-to-day management of the project.

Level Three plans are extremely detailed and include the complete documentation of the program packages. At this level, the planning merges with actual program documentation, the end product being operational applications.

Plans should be "circular" and dynamic. Each plan should refer to previous plans and experience in the area being considered and should lead to an evaluation procedure. Starting from a given background situation, the plan should indicate intentions, organization, and steps to be taken, and should lead back to a mechanism by which to evaluate the success of the plan so that future plans (or modifications) can be developed in a more efficient manner.

No plan in the area of computer use and information systems will stay fixed for very long. Even the full contents of a Level One plan cannot always be established by the time it should be issued. Thus, plans should be "loose leaf" in nature so that new versions of a section can be inserted, sections not ready at the time the plan is issued can be included later, and small changes can be made without difficulty.

Plans should have a multiple time horizon. Plans are generally concerned with different spans of time. The activity in the near future can be specified in detail, while only the objectives of the distant future can be provided. To provide for this condition, two alternatives are available. First, the full time scale can be incorporated in a single plan, providing those activities which will occur in the near future and can be specified are carefully separated from those which are merely long-term objectives. Second, separate plans can be developed for the short and the long term. A single plan is generally more satisfactory. Frequent updating as time passes brings the plan into conformity with near-term expectations.

F. *Project Implementation*

Perhaps the most difficult phase in the whole program will be the detailed planning, writing, debugging, testing, and documenting of the program. Frustrating to management during this phase—which may extend from many months to a few years—is the fact that it is very difficult to assess accurately the rate of progress and the quality of the work. Implementation usually has to be subdivided into many small parts and only a few individuals (sometimes only one programmer) are familiar enough with particular aspects of the project to judge progress.

Because it is difficult for the Manager of Programming or Director of Data Processing to determine until late in the program whether work is progressing satisfactorily, whether the conversion dates will be met, and whether the machine programs will run efficiently, it is imperative that he establish a PERT network against which progress can be systematically checked. In addition, the manager must meet frequently with his people, taking a serious interest in some of the details of their jobs, and constantly engaging in conversation and asking questions. In this way he can uncover difficulties before they become serious problems.

1. MANAGEMENT'S ROLE

Management's role throughout implementation should remain clear and uncompromising. Perhaps its most important function will be to resolve differences between the various departments and the data processing activity. Invariably these differences will arise, either about the details of a particular system design for a given application or the priorities assigned to various tasks. Management should resolve these problems promptly to avoid delays which can have, a multiplying effect on the whole program. While some delays may be justifiable, any excessive or repetitive postponement of key dates, coupled with general confusion and uncertainty, indicate poor management by project personnel and should be investigated.

Management should resist firmly any suggestion that parallel operations (running the existing procedures side by side with the new system before final changeover) are not required because the new system is completely accurate and running parallel operations will be wasteful of time and money. Management should insist not only that parallel operations can be completed but also that adequate fall-back procedures have been developed and tested. Sooner or later such procedures will be needed, and it can prove costly and embarrassing to everyone concerned if they are unavailable or have not been tested in advance.

2. POST-CONVERSION AUDIT

The final step in the implementation plan is the post-conversion audit. An overall evaluation is not simple, but is worth the time and effort it takes; it is the best means of ensuring improved overall performance through better operations and better planning.

The performance of a computer activity depends on many factors— the accuracy of the work, the overall economies of the applications, the growth and use of their resources throughout the corporation, and the efficiency of the computer operations. Good post-conversion audits depend on establishing and maintaining good records and being able to analyze the performance of each activity. Very often it is impossible to reconstruct this performance and, in particular, to compare plans with results because such records have not been kept. For example, the plans should include detailed estimates of the time required to program the applications being considered. These estimates are used to arrive at manpower estimates and completion dates. If a record of the allocation of manpower as work progresses is not maintained, it will be impossible to compare the outcome with the plans, to isolate the cause for any slippage and, more important, to improve future planning.

A well-defined recording system also provides operating management a sound tool for evaluating the effectiveness of the computing center and a basis for correcting inefficiencies. The information can be used to forecast future workloads and future computing needs and to assess the improvement expected from hardware changes. In multilocation computer centers, good records will assist upper-level management in evaluating use and efficiency at the different centers. In fact, the whole system of cost allocation is often based on careful recording of use and other factors.

Thus, it is important that measures of performance appropriate to the installation be designed and adopted, and that regular review procedures for monitoring performance be established. The following example illustrates how an index of efficiency can be established which provides some measures of machine performance and a basis for historical comparison.

For several years, a major computer manufacturer has been placing meters on its computers. "Metered time" is the time the central processor is actually operating or running. Some of this metered time will (or may) be devoted to reruns; "rerun time" is time spent in running a job a second time because of operator error, program error, or machine malfunction. "Down time" is that time the computer is inoperative because the machine is malfunctioning or customer engineers are providing preventive maintenance. Idle time is that time the computer is neither being used nor worked on. Based on these definitions, a very straightforward index of efficiency might be:

Percent Efficiency =
$$\frac{\text{Metered Time} - \text{Rerun Time}}{\text{Total Manned House} - \text{Down Time} - \text{Idle Time}} \times 100$$

Many other indices based on other measurements are possible. When dealing with complex computer systems, particularly on-line applications and time-shared computers, the measures of systems performance can be quite subtle and complex. Oversimplified performance measures may well obscure the very facts the manager is seeking. Whatever measure is chosen must be reviewed for its worth in actual use. Nevertheless, the development and use of reasonable measures is a prerequisite of efficient operations.

CHAPTER 7

Implementing System Change

*The Parties Involved in Systems Change / Typical
Problems in Information System Change / Basic
Understanding / Steps and Processes Aiding Change /
Factors Affecting Rates of Change / Possibilities for
Change*

IT IS THE COMMON EXPERIENCE in considering management information systems and computers that the technical features of the system receive the focus of attention and the processes by which the organization changes from what it is doing now to what it ought to be doing are given attention as an afterthought. It is the thesis of this chapter that these priorities should be equal, or that the attention given the processes of change should receive the highest priority of attention. Many will object to the thesis. Yet there seem to be important arguments supporting it, and its presentation may serve to reorient and improve the growth and development of management information systems.

This chapter considers the parties involved in making a systems change, reviews some typical problems which have been experienced in the management of systems change, describes steps and processes which may aid changes, reviews factors affecting rates of change, and then summarizes the implications of this view of managing changes in information systems.

A. *The Parties Involved in Systems Change*

The idea that some people are involved in information systems change implies that other people are not involved. Some people involved in the systems change are inside the company or organization making the change, and others are outside the company. Some information systems changes may affect only those portions of people's lives which can legitimately be called the "business" parts of life, but other changes affect the leisure and recreational parts of life, personal matters, and even some very private matters. In effect, involvement in information systems changes varies widely. A narrow view of who is involved and who is not involved probably leads to important oversights in planning and management of the systems change. Several stories can illustrate the degrees and varieties of involvement.

A credit card customer for an oil company may be asked to accept a computer listing of the date, place, and amount of his purchases in place of a copy of the original document which was completed at the time of his purchase.

A checking account customer of a bank may be asked to accept the idea that he be charged an interest rate during the time that his checking account shows a negative balance. The customer in turn may wonder if he should be paid interest while his checking account shows a positive balance.

It is the job of a business clerk in a telephone company office to receive inquiries about last month's bill and requests for changes in telephone service, such as the installation of a new telephone or the addition of an extension. The telephone business clerk is asked to change from preparing a written memorandum describing the customer's new telephone needs, and looking for the customer's bill in a bin of paper records to keying the information about the customer on a typewriter keyboard and displaying either new or old information for the customer's record on a cathode ray tube (television screen).

Airlines reservation agents are changing their jobs from one in which the agent examines a simple count of seats sold or not sold when he is correcting and adjusting a passenger's travel plans to a system in which he maintains passenger name records for each leg of the proposed flight. Space on down-flight legs can now be made available for sale when a passenger fails to show for his trip with an accuracy which was not previously available.

A plant manager is accustomed to receiving monthly reports showing materials in process, raw material inventories, finished product inventories, payroll distributions, and year-to-date costs and budgets. It is proposed that he receive reports only when conditions in inventory or personnel costs deviate significantly from that which can normally be expected. It is further proposed that he receive new reports or exceptional conditions when product delivery commitments cannot be met and when employee absences and resignations are different from what can normally be expected.

A buyer for a women's sportswear department in a department store has been accustomed to learning about sales trends of new items by talking with the sales clerks and by serving some of the customers herself. A new information system proposes to put on her desk each morning a report of the previous day's sales by item with recommended reordering dates and quantities as well as recommended "sale" prices for items which are not being purchased.

Annual income tax reports are put into machine-readable form to facilitate the collation of information from several sources and the checking of reports for accuracy and reasonableness. This file could be used for many purposes such as studies of population migration and potential consumer markets, studies of changes in the composition of families and households, statistical surveys of the economic effects of individual health problems or of rioting and civil disobedience, and yet other important economic and social uses. Should the file be used for these purposes? The policy to the present time, probably wisely, has been that it should not be used.

Medical services can look forward to the time when individual medical histories and descriptions of laboratory and clinical findings as well as therapy can be accumulated. Histories of this kind offer the ultimate potential of career health records which follow migrant Americans from personal physician to personal physician. To whom should medical records of this kind be available? Candidates include the family physician, the physician treating the patient in the family physician's absence, the gynecologist, the ophthalmologist, dentist, psychiatrist, hospital, public school physician, and company physician.

Information systems for public school management can perform student scheduling as one of its services. Who is involved? The student is involved who receives the message that a requested course cannot be offered because the number of students requesting the course in combination with scheduling requirements and priorities for other courses reduced class size to an uneconomic level. The teacher is involved who is asked to teach three different courses in widely separated parts of the school facilities on the same day of the week when each course requires lengthy pre-class preparation. So is the taxpayer whose tax bill may increase because expensive information services are being added to the school district's budget. The taxpayer is involved because scheduling rules which reduce variation in class size from a policy-determined level of 25 students per teacher because the improved scheduling can increase the utilization of classrooms and reduce the number of classes, thereby postponing increases in the size of school facilities and keeping staff requirements near the minimum. The school administration and school board are involved as they determine policy and procedures governing scheduling and course offerings.

Who is uninvolved in information produced by the weather forecasting system?

A systems analyst is involved with others in his company in describing the changes and objectives as a management information system is changed, in preparing system specifications including specifications of input and output and filed, and in planning the order and schedule for the efforts necessary to change the existing management information system to the proposed system.

The manager of an insurance underwriting group is involved in a systems change which will automate most of the functions performed by his underwriting staff, reducing it to a smaller number of people and changing its function from the review and classification of insurance risks using data supplied on forms to a function of reviewing and underwriting exceptions which cannot be automatically processed.

These examples illustrate how customers, personnel at different levels in an organization, and sometimes widely diffused members of the public are in one way or another involved in information systems change. The examples also illustrate how the issues of personal privacy affect information system design and use. Other important problems and issues, such as issues surrounding the protection of ownership of systems technology, particularly software, and issues of the competitive value of information stored in an information system, and issues of the pricing of information services, are not illustrated. Implementation of systems change must consider who is involved and affected by the systems change and how the problems and issues will be studied and resolved.

B. Typical Problems in Information System Change

Those with experience in the design and implementation of information systems change often speak of "resistance" to systems change. They have experienced unanticipated delays in the development and conversion of information systems. They have had reports from the system that become nearly useless because errors in input reduced the meaningfulness of the reports. Reports from a computerized information system have been rejected as out-of-date when they are received or as unusable in the format presented. Nearly every proposal for a system change has met the comment somewhere that "It cannot be done" which can be interpreted as "I do not want to have it done."

To label this "resistance" and attribute it to the exasperating qualities of human nature is an unproductive and frequently harmful view of these problems and experiences. The difficulties in implementing systems change can be addressed more productively by regarding objections and complaints as useful indicators of actual or potential difficulties. An analysis of prior problems in implementing systems change or an analysis of objections to a proposed system change may allow steps which avoid or ameliorate the problems. Several classic problems in implementing information systems change can be identified.

1. The Issues of Development Strategy

Some systems changes are planned as if they were to be a giant step forward. The new system is described as "the next generation." The new system is regarded as distinctly different from the existing system. Massive efforts in system development and in system conversion are foreseen. Significant incremental benefits are anticipated.

Other system changes are regarded as evolutionary. Instead of emphasizing the break with the past, compatibility over time is emphasized. Uncertainty about the future is accepted, and new features in the system are regarded as likely to be short-lived because they may be replaced by something better. Flexibility for making the next change is a design criterion for making the change now being planned.

These contrasting attitudes toward system change can result in very different management of development programs. Recognizing the future as uncertain and describing system changes in evolutionary steps appeals to us as the more accurate description of what has actually happened during the decade of computer utilization. This view may allow smaller changes to be made quickly, to be made with smaller investments, and to be abandoned if necessary. It may allow those involved in the change to regard it as a relatively small step, as a step which probably is more understandable since it is small, and as a change which soon will be followed by other changes. A small change which is found to be lacking in usefulness can be abandoned for the procedures and reports which preceded the change.

2. ISSUES RELATED TO OPERATING OBJECTIVES

Changes in operating objectives to be achieved by changes in the proposed information system range from being unspecified to being unrealistic. We refer to the operating objectives of the information system, not the operating objectives of the organization. Failure to specify operating objectives for the revised information system results in a continuous, time-wasting, energy-wasting search for the specifications of the revised system which can continue during the entire effort. It often results in a revised information system which does not interface effectively with other segments of the organization's information system. Unspecified operating objectives allow people to think their own varied hopes and objectives are project objectives, and this can only result in disappointing most of the people when the project is complete. Unrealistic operating objectives for the revised system usually lead to achievement failure or to unexpected and lengthy delays, either outcome resulting in general disappointment.

It is easy to conclude that operating objectives for the revised information systems should be specified, yet operating objectives are difficult to specify. Very often the operating objectives of the revised information system are only generally specifiable at the beginning of the development process, and are revised and changed during the development process. Information requirements for the future nearly always remain unknown, or at least some portion of the information requirements remain unknown. Therefore, specifying the operating objectives of the revised system is, in some degree, an impossible task. These conditions suggest an approach which specifies the operating objectives of the revised information system as early as possible, sharing the information as widely as possible, and recognizing frankly the areas in which there is uncertainty. This statement of operating objectives will have to be updated during the time that the revised information system is being developed. In this way expectations probably can be adjusted toward realism during the development effort. Those whose information requirements will not be met by the revised system can take whatever action is required to fill the unmet needs or to adjust the organization's operations so that they will be minimally affected by the absence of the anticipated information.

3. Issues Related to Input Supply

It has been common experience in revised information systems to have at least a period of time in which the data input to the system has a noticeable increase in errors. Sometimes the input errors remain high over extended periods of time. There may be several reasons for this experience. Sometimes the input systems make so many demands upon the data suppliers that the opportunity for error increases and the actual errors increase. Sometimes the revised information system eliminates processing steps which were incorporated in the predecessor system and thereby eliminates from the system some of the error-checking and quality control procedures. This will result in an apparent increase in input errors. Sometimes the revised system has a capability for detecting errors which is greater than the capability of the predecessor system, and this condition will result in an apparent increase in errors. Sometimes the revised information system requires that people observe and record information which they cannot reliably observe and record. The system designer, unacquainted with these aspects of information technology, asks for judgments which cannot be made or fails to provide the technology, such as questionnaires or definitions of codes, which will allow the judgments to be accurately recorded. Sometimes the systems designers prepare codes which are efficient for their use of space in machine-readable storage, but are inefficient as languages which data suppliers use to describe in written form what they have observed or to transmit information orally in a conversation. The conversational use of codes and input languages is illustrated by the retail sales clerk who sometimes needs to tell someone else what she just sold because she is leaving the floor to keep on important appointment and another clerk is preparing the sales slip.

Other problems related to input supply include questions of how much and what kinds of information shall be supplied, and questions of who shall be responsible for supplying the information. These problems are closely related to the issues of the operating objectives for the revised information system, discussed above, and the issues related to work reorganization and communication reorganization, discussed below. Sometimes the opportunity for information collection rests in a situation normally handled by one part of the organization, while the need for information comes from another part of the organization. When the work of collecting information lies in different departments, there is often a problem in introducing a change in procedures. When the information required represents an increased or a decreased requirement for observation and recording by the person supplying the information, there may be difficulty in getting the new requirements consistently supplied or the obsolete requirements consistently omitted. These problems are related to the effectiveness with which the data supplier is given cues about the required information, the understanding he has about the need for, and use of, the information, and the trust he has in the revised information system and its capabilities for maintaining operations and services which the organization performs to the standards which he has learned to be satisfactory.

4. ISSUES RELATED TO WORK AND COMMUNICATIONS REORGANIZATION

Revised information systems frequently change the work requirements for individuals and rearrange communication linkages in an organization. Work requirements sometimes can be changed so that it becomes impossible for an individual person to perform a job satisfactorily, not necessarily because that person's capabilities are limited, but rather because the requirements of the new job exceed human capability. In the other direction, work can be redesigned so that it becomes boring and meaningless, unable to hold the attention of the individual performing the task and therefore just as incapable of human performance. Sometimes work is moved from one portion of the organization to another part of the organization, thereby changing perceived importance or influence or control. Sometimes changes in the information system reroute the flow of information and thereby change either the perceived or the actual capabilities for influence and control. To tell a person or a department that the proposed changes in information systems will make no difference in the organization of work and of communications, when in fact they do, will only enlarge the credibility gap. Ignoring the issues will not cause them to disappear. Changing jobs so that they become impossible for people to perform or so that they become uninteresting can only lead to problems. It becomes imperative to examine these aspects of the implications of an information systems change.

5. Issues Related to Use of the System

At least some of the operating objectives of the revised information system usually are apparent, although they may not be well specified. The operating objectives can be assumed to be legitimate. It is nearly always true that the revised information system will have potential secondary uses or effects which are not a part of the apparent and publicly stated operating objectives. People at all levels inside and outside an organization can sense these potential uses and may be concerned about them. They may attribute to the information system uses which it will not have and respond to the information system and its requirements upon them as if those potential uses were real uses.

People have responded negatively to the routinization and depersonalization which the development of information systems has brought, unnecessary and unfortunate as that effect may be. People sense when an information system is designed to "make everything routine" and they also sense when an information system is designed to "release time from the routine so that it may be devoted to the unique and the non-routine." The manager who is also a citizen and a parent and a customer in his other life roles said, "When I want attention, I punch the card full of holes and write on it the message that I want to communicate." Jokes about the silly errors of automated information systems and about the inappropriate responses from such systems have been earned. Designers who fail to become sensitive to these issues are likely to create resistance to their systems; designers who become sensitive to the issues are more likely to create systems which are well received.

Changes in information systems, particularly those which increase the amount and complexity of the information available for use, offer the opportunity for new controls and additional checks on performance. People at all levels sense these opportunities, and as long as the control can be established over "that fellow over there who is a constant source of problems and annoyance to me," the system is acceptable to the speaker. When the information system is used to control and check on him, it is not acceptable. These attitudes are legitimate, and are held whether they are legitimate or not. Sensing these issues and handling them in the design and operation of a revised information system is likely to result in a system which has greater acceptability than one in which issues of this type have been overlooked.

The basic and underlying condition affecting these issues is the style of leadership and influence in the organization as reflected by top management and by management at other levels. A climate in which everyone is checked upon in many ways, communicating a basic attitude of distrust, will create an environment in which changes in information systems which could lead to further checks and controls will be resisted. A climate which encourages the development of controls which are perceived as legitimate and also places open, obvious, real limitations upon uses for information which are perceived as undesirable or illegitimate is one which will foster the early acceptance of proposed changes in information systems. For example, a system which allows input errors to be first presented to the document originator may be more acceptable than a system which presents the error to some other person. A system which presents information about individual performance only to that individual will be more acceptable than a system which shares that information with the individual and with other persons, and the latter system in turn will be more acceptable than a system which fails to share the information about individual job performance with the individual whose job performance is being assessed. The effective design of information systems is no substitute for appropriate organizational and managerial climates, but the insensitive design of information systems can harm what otherwise may be an effective and productive organizational and managerial climate.

As the capacity and scope of information banks is increased, issues of access to and appropriate use of that information become more significant. There are issues related to the access one department may have to information from another department, issues of access to information which may be sensitive for the organization in its public posture, issues of access to information about individuals which may be private or appropriately withheld from other individuals. People are willing to share information about themselves and about situations when they know it can be useful to them personally or help in solving problems in which they have a deep interest. They are understandably reluctant to share information if they feel it will be an annoyance to them or work to their own disadvantage. People have been annoyed when telephone book information or magazine subscription lists have been used for solicitation purposes. Information about errors made in the manufacture of parts, about errors in the recording of reservations for airlines travel, about the accumulated production of a section or department in a company, about individual medical history, about personal income, about judged effectiveness in a job, about performance in school, about complaints and problems in a work environment, about complaints in a neighborhood, about criminal activity, about customer complaints, and about many other things are obviously of critical importance to business, government, and society in general. They are also sensitive items of information. The development of information systems in general, as well as the problems which a specific change in an information system will experience, are closely related to the success with which controls over the use of the information are brought into existence and effectively applied with shared knowledge of the nature and effectiveness of the controls. Proposed changes in information systems experience "resistance" because issues of these types are present without being articulated or without being satisfactorily and openly faced and solved.

C. Basic Understanding

It is essential to understand, or even assume, that every individual in an organization wants to support and aid changes toward improved information systems for his business or organization. To assume otherwise is wrong in most instances, and invites resistance in others because of the effects the assumption has upon the behavior of the person expecting "resistance." The difference in assumptions can be illustrated with several examples.

"You fellows don't like the proposed changes in the information system because it eliminates your job. Therefore the criticisms you make of the proposals are self-protective and without legitimate basis." (The speaker assumes the other fellow does not want an improved information system.)

"Our information system proposes to eliminate certain jobs. We need your criticism and suggestions about the system as it will affect organization performance as well as your own ability to contribute." (The speaker assumes the other fellow wants an improved information system and can contribute to its design.)

"We have concluded that this work must be transferred from Accounting where it is now being done to Marketing where it should be done since they are in frequent contact with the customer. Accepting that as a given, what do you think the problems with the proposed system will be?" (The speaker assumes the other fellow cannot handle the issues and problems concerning the place in the organization where the work should be performed.)

"From where we sit, things indicate that this work should be performed in Marketing in the future instead of being done in Accounting as is now the case. However, we cannot be sure that we see all the issues and problems. What do you think?" (The speaker assumes that the other fellow can handle constructively the issues and problems related to where the work should be located in the organization.)

There are real and important motivations for resisting proposed changes in information systems. We cannot expect people to say that they want to have their job eliminated or to say that they want to have the work for which they traditionally have had responsibility to be moved to the responsibility and control of someone else. These motivations can be accepted as real and as legitimate. It is important to understand at the same time that people with these motivations can and often will contribute constructively to the planning of and conversion to the proposed information system. The assumption that people can and will help is a reasonable and accurate assumption when the problems and issues are openly recognized and treated, even in all their uncertainty. The assumption that people will resist proposed changes in information systems and must be manipulated or removed from effective participation can only increase the probability that the assumption will prove true. It is very likely that managers and systems designers and imaginative persons and innovators of all kinds will influence the response to their proposals by the assumptions they make, either implicitly or explicitly, about the likely reception to the proposals. It is safe to assume that the response to a proposal usually will be based in very large part upon the merits of the proposal as they are understood.

D. Steps and Processes Aiding Change

Probably there are no formulae for steps or techniques which aid the introduction of a systems change and assure its accomplishment as designed and on schedule. There are, however, a number of steps or processes which make the systems change an activity about which any interested person may get information and which may be influenced by people who wish to be active in shaping the characteristics of the proposed system. These steps and processes simply express the desire of those with specific responsibilities for planning the change to have the help and suggestions of anyone who can assist. They also can express the willingness of the organization to face the real and difficult problems associated with systems change for the purpose of resolving the problems as openly and satisfactorily as is possible.

The steps and processes we discuss are related to elements of the systems development work and to the overall objectives of the systems change as well as the management of that change. We discuss aspects of systems development work in which a large number of points of view need to be represented. Many experienced people in system development work respond negatively to the concept of "a system designed by a committee." We are not suggesting processes in which choices are made by voting, nor are we suggesting that a system be designed in response to the needs and interests of those people with the greatest perceived influence. We are urging that systems design be conceived to allow substantial future change, that the proposed new system be tried in concept as well as in actual operation with those who are knowledgeable about present operations and their problems, and that objections to the proposed and pilot systems be used as creative inputs to produce important modifications in the proposed and developing system. Our suggestions about steps and processes aiding systems change describe some points in time and some topics for review which encourage the involvement of a variety of parties of interest in the systems change and provide ideas about important aspects of the proposed systems change.

1. REVIEW OF SYSTEM NEEDS AND OBJECTIVES

Early in the process of considering a systems change it is appropriate to consider and specify the problems or opportunities to which the proposed systems change is responding and the operating objectives which the revised information system will meet. It may be as important to understand what the proposed system will not accomplish as it is to describe the operating objectives which will be accomplished and the problems which will be solved. Drafting these ideas so that they may be presented on paper is an important step, but it can be viewed only as a preliminary step to face-to-face discussions during which the several parties affected by the systems change can query and comment upon the points of view presented in the draft document and make important and substantial changes and restatements of the problems and the objectives. Areas of uncertainty need to be identified. Differences in statements of problems need to be encouraged, for in the differences may be important clues to restatement of the problems which can lead more directly and quickly to satisfactory systems changes.

This process does take time. Risks that changes will be unnecessarily delayed by spending time in this activity need to be balanced against risks that hurried treatment will result in incomplete or inadequate statements of problems or objectives and in later costs and delays in redoing work which was inappropriately conceived. Perhaps the strategy of keeping the product of current systems changes as flexible as possible for future systems changes, and the strategy of making large systems changes in small steps which are conceived and tried in as short a time cycle as possible, will both contribute to reducing to manageable size the problems of longe-range uncertainties and large commitments of funds and resources. Certainly, the early formulation of operating objectives and problems to be solved in the proposed systems change is not an essential step; perhaps the needs are so obvious and the objectives so clear that they are well understood. Perhaps the needs are so ambiguous and the objectives so difficult to specify that some searching time is needed to make even preliminary statements. The step of reviewing system needs and operating objectives as guides for the development of the proposed system changes is one way to bring a variety of points of view to the problem and potentially benefit from the review.

2. REVIEW OF INPUT AND OUTPUT SYSTEMS

The data supplied for the information systems has a primary influence upon the usefulness of the system. Changes in data supply which accompany changes in the information system often include observing and recording new information or adding substantially to the complexity of information previously recorded. Sometimes the point of observation and recording is changed. Often the basic information is transformed into a specialized language, usually called codes, which can be processed efficiently by the information system. The completeness of the desired input is affected by many considerations including the simplicity of the observation-recording task and the design of the aids (forms for recording an observation, languages for describing the observation, reference manuals in complex systems) for supporting the data input system. The quality of data input is an often-criticized part of an information system in system analysis and programming circles, yet the simple checks of elements of the input system which can be made by talking with people who supply the data and letting them try out input devices often go unmade. Use of professional skills and scientific methodologies specifically oriented to the task of developing methods by which people may simply and accurately record their observations or desires is encountered even less frequently than the simple checking procedures. The recognition of codes as languages which grow and change has not yet been achieved.

The possibility that some judgments cannot reliably be made by human judges is lost in the general sense of uneasiness about "input accuracy" without specifically determining the cause of input errors and omissions. These omissions in systems development work which dominate the last decade can be changed, and some things can be changed very easily.

Showing people proposed forms for recording information, getting them to use the forms if only in an experiment, having them look up the codes in a manual, asking key punch operators or automatic reading devices to read the input document, and simple inspections to determine the most frequently experienced difficulty or error are all relatively inexpensive procedures which will disclose the most obvious difficulty in the observation-recording situation. Similar checks can be made of input document flow and other technical features of the input system.

Interest in and arguments about the data to be used as input often have their basis in a desire for particular outputs. The type of outputs to be generated by the proposed system, the ways in which these outputs will be different from the outputs currently available, the distribution of the outputs, the occasions on which outputs are generated, and many other questions fuel interest in the output system. The proposed output system should be discussed with parties who are using similar outputs from the existing information system as well as with parties who have potential interest in the revised system output. Such discussions need to be varied enough in their format and purpose to allow the full range of criticisms and questions related to the proposed system to be expressed. In an organization in which open criticism is an everyday style of operation, these types of discussions will be relatively easy to arrange. In organizations where critics are unrewarded or even punished, the discussions are still possible but may require elaborate and obvious protection for the critic. One such protection is to invite an outside organization to conduct the discussion through individual interviews and summarize the information without reference to its source. Often it will be possible to use simpler approaches, depending in part upon the previous success of information systems changes in the organization as well as the general organizational climate.

The issues related to the use of the changed information systems are relevant to the discussions of both the input and the output systems. These issues are present whether or not they are discussed. Discussion offers the opportunity to identify the difficult issues and work out solutions or protections for the most difficult problems. Failing to address these issues probably increases the likelihood that systems development work will meet many barriers and be delayed or even stopped altogether. Some call these issues "political issues" and feel they are outside the responsibility of those who lead the formulation and development of changes in information systems. Regardless of the allocation of responsibilities for exploring and solving the problems, the issues are there and are necessarily a part of the total work which must be completed in order to aid the implementation of systems changes.

3. REVIEW OF JOB DESIGN AND COMMUNICATIONS

Changes in the input system and in the output system and in the flow of information cause changes in jobs, changes in communications within an organization, and changes in communications between people inside and people outside the organization.

Changes in job design can vary from the complete elimination of a job through the routinization of elements in a job to the enlargement of a job. Elimination of a job may be a change which is more easily accomplished than the other changes, difficult though job elimination may be under some circumstances. Some jobs can be made routine enough that many people will lose interest in the work and performance of the work then deteriorates. This situation sometimes can be adjusted by staffing the job with people whose skills are matched with the changed job requirements. Sometimes additional duties can be added to the job so that the staff skills already available are engaged in interesting work while the routine portions of the work are performed in spare minutes or as a small segment of a larger and more interesting task. Sometimes new jobs make very different demands upon the skills and attention of the jobholder so that the job is necessarily restaffed or so that the job cannot be performed by any person. The latter situation will cause high input error rates, delays in system response time, high turnover rates on the job, high absence rates, general complaints about confusion or fatigue, etc. It is remedied by redesigning the job so it can be performed to adequate standards by skills normally assigned to work of that kind.

Hastily designed or slightly inadequate changes in information flow and communications within the organization will be "corrected" by people who invent informal methods for replacing the necessary parts of the older communications system. This is a desirable outcome since it quickly identifies the needs which are unsatisfied by the new system and may suggest the modifications necessary to improve its performance.

A pre-operation description of the proposed tasks to be performed in each job and the proposed flow of information may allow some of the most obvious changes in job design and communications to be identified and the most obvious problems to be detected before actual pilot operation. For example, major features in the changes of content and distribution of management reports probably can be reviewed by discussion prior to actual operating experience. As another example, changes in the methods of getting data from customers and presenting information to customers may be able to be reviewed by interviewing customers about "what would you think if . . . ," but such changes probably need the test of a simulated or actual pilot operation. As another example, it is likely that only the most obvious problems and benefits of access to customer records in conversational mode with cathode ray tube display and keyboard input system can be reviewed without actual simulated or pilot operation.

4. Review of Organization Performance

Usually the operation of a computerized information system is not the primary service of an organization. Instead, the information system is operated by the organization in order to improve its own performance in providing the service or manufacturing the product which is its primary reason for existing. Proposed changes in information systems can appropriately be reviewed for their potential effect, and even their actual effect, upon the many different kinds of performance of the organization.

In a retail merchandising organization, can the improved information system reduce the risk of a stockout following clear indications of customer acceptance of an item without unnecessarily increasing the risk of excess inventories or the risk of necessary "sales" at reduced profit margins? Can the information system be designed so that it is perceived by the buyers as an aid to their work?

Can an improved information system reduce the inventory of materials in process, lower the cost of production by lowering set-up costs through better choice of batch sizes, improve response to market demand by rescheduling production work to fill an order requiring short delivery time, or provide better profits through improved understanding of the costs which can be controlled?

In an educational institution, will an improved student personnel information system allow more sensitive staffing for the short-term future course, requests of the students, improved individual counselling and educational program planning, lower drop-out rates, improved facilities utilization with a consequent lowering of costs or an increase in enrollment at the same costs, improved performance feedback to students with the consequence of higher student performance and better morale?

In a research and development organization, can an improved information system shorten project duration, reduce variation from expected project completion dates, reduce variation from expected project budgets, increase perceived utilization of personal skills, increase morale, broaden and develop personnel skills and capabilities in shorter times than previously experienced, improve the client-judged quality of research and development services?

It is usually understood that a computerized information system used by an organization is intended to aid it in one or more aspects of its performance. A review of a proposed information systems change for the purpose of anticipating the effects of the change upon aspects of organization performance which it could legitimately be expected to influence may aid in the early formation of a systems change and may aid again in the later stages of pilot operation and early operation following conversion.

5. REVIEW OF SYSTEM DEVELOPMENT MANAGEMENT

The process of conceiving changes to be made in an information system and of developing and implementing those changes is the task of systems development management. A review of the processes by which system development management assesses needs for system changes, develops operating objectives for proposed changes, develops and tests the features of the new information systems, responds to the needs and problems of the organizations and people it serves, and aids the organization in the accomplishments of its performance objectives may uncover opportunities in the management of system development which will further aid the introduction of systems changes.

E. Factors Affecting Rates of Change

Many factors affect an organization's ability to change its computerized information systems, sometimes having a constraining effect upon the rate at which changes in the information systems can be made and sometimes enlarging the opportunity for change. We list several factors affecting the rate of change without intending that the order of presentation indicate in any way the influence the factors may have or the priority they have in affecting rates of change. Our comments seem to us to follow logically from our experience in systems work and from the research literature about organization performance in general and about adaptation and change in particular. While we intend that this summary reflect the current state of knowledge, we understand that little work has directed attention to the effects on organization performance of the presence or absence of specific features in an information system. For this reason, our comments must necessarily be read as subject to empirical study and confirmation.

1. ORGANIZATIONAL CLIMATE AND ADAPTABILITY

An organization which has a recent history of successful adaptations and changes in a variety of its activities, including changes in information systems, is likely to be prepared for further changes in its information systems. An organization with little recent change, but a recognition that the need for change is high as well as a climate which indicates that experimentation is desired and that some failures can easily be accepted, also is likely to be ready for changes in information systems. An organization which encourages change, is interested in change, lets proposals for change originate from many places in the organization, yet does not impose changes when there seem to be reasonable uncertainties about benefits, is likely to be an organization where changes in information systems can be accomplished.

This organizational climate is created in part by management attitude toward changes of all kinds, and in the instance of information systems, toward changes in information systems in particular. However, management alone may not be able to create the climate necessary to encourage change, although they are surely very influential. Customers, employees, and competitors also affect the climate for change.

2. Prior Management of Systems Change

The organization's recent experience in changes in information systems can have an important effect upon its readiness for further change. Changes which have proceeded smoothly toward objectives which were well accepted and which seem to fit naturally into a larger pattern for systems change can aid the climate for further change. Systems changes which have been accompanied by extraordinary problems, clear dislocation and disorientation of the organization's normal performance in support of its major purposes, an image of careless experimentation and inept learning by doing, and other negative prior experience in the management of systems change can reduce the willingness of an organization to accept a new change. Changes which have fallen short of expectations will reduce the probability that further information systems changes can be made easily.

3. Style of Management Support for Change

A management style which supports information systems changes in general and which provides general guidelines by which proposed changes are to be judged probably is most effective in encouraging information systems changes. A management style which champions rather specific changes may lose the possibility for creative proposals in areas which are not receiving management's favorable attention at the moment. A lack of interest by management serves quite effectively as a means for rejecting or discouraging the presentation of proposals for systems change. Management can act quite effectively to discourage proposals for change, and can also be effective in encouraging change by indicating the general areas within which it wishes to entertain proposals for change.

4. Cost Benefit

The sensed relationship between the costs of a proposed change and the benefits which the change brings to the organization is an important factor affecting the acceptability of a particular proposal and, therefore, the probability that a particular proposal will be implemented. "Costs" and "benefits" are often more concepts than they are well-defined aspects of organization performance. Costs in the field of information systems changes have the reputation for being poorly estimated with a bias on the side of being underestimated. Costs have usually concentrated upon the computer programming costs and systems analysis costs and have seldom examined conversion costs, costs for employing more highly skilled personnel, the expectation that development costs will necessarily be amortized over a very short system life, and other features in the cost landscape. Benefits have been bifurcated into those which are called "tangible" and those which are called "intangible," concepts which really divide benefits into the class which can be estimated without very much work and the class which people recognize as real but have few ideas for treating. As a result, both the view of costs and the view of benefits have been foreshortened during the last decade, and the distortion in perception and judgment resulting from these foreshortened views is generally unknown. The rapid growth in the use of computers has occurred despite this imperfect knowledge of cost-benefit relationships. Perhaps it is unrealistic to expect the concepts of cost and benefit to have much influence on the adoption of information system changes in the future, but in a rationalized world for decision-making, they should have some influence.

Both lost opportunities and poorly executed uses have been recognized in the growth of computer usage. This suggests that some improvement in the tools for rational choices in their use may be possible and even welcomed. It has been the frequent experience of organizations using computers that the expected "tangible" reductions in costs have failed to materialize and that the effects of the growth of computer use in the organization, while not meeting fanciful forecasts of some of its prophets, have indeed shifted responsibilities and communications and patterns of operation in an organization in unexpected, sometimes uneasy, and often beneficial ways. This experience urges that new attention be given the benefits which are difficult to assess since they seem to power the growth of computerized information systems, whether they are understood or not. We would like to suggest that the technniques exist for observing and recording organizational performance, for patterning observations so that reasonable deductions can be made about cause-effect relationships, and for examining the interrelationships among complex observations so that some progress can be made in understanding the benefits or lack of benefits from using specific computerized management information technologies.

5. TECHNICAL FEASIBILITY

Throughout the history of digital computers, ideas for using computers in solving practical problems have exceeded the current capabilities of computers and associated hardware and software for handling the problems. The technical feasibility for handling certain applications within specified economic bounds, or even without economic bounds, represents an important factor influencing the rate of information systems change. Searching libraries of documents for answers to a question which has not previously been asked, helping a young student to learn to read, assessing the incremental effects of admitting one more student to a particular field of study in an institution of higher education or admitting one more order for a particular product in a complex manufacturing system, and yet other problems of similar complexity can be conceived but not yet solved in ways which are much beyond the simplest demonstrations of feasibility. The problems go unsolved in their larger and more practical applications because the technologies for storing and retrieving information remain primitive, because the logical and mathematical structures for assessing incremental effects are not yet invented, because the data bases for these systems are not yet operational, or because the computer hardware or economics cannot meet the challenge.

6. RESOURCES

Sometimes shortages in resources of various kinds can limit the rates of information systems change. Shortages in personnel with the appropriate skills and shortages in current income or capital resources which can be allocated to systems development may act as factors constraining the rate of systems change. A less obvious restraint, yet one which is potentially among the more important constraints, is the lack of importation of ideas for system change from outside the organization. While most computerized information systems have been tailored to fit the needs of the organization which sponsored their development, it is likely that an operating system somewhere else and the development of systems concepts somewhere else have affected the design and development of every information system. The means by which these ideas are imported to an organization sometimes can be closed and thereby reduce the rate of information systems change.

7. OTHER FACTORS

There are other factors which can act to limit the rate of information systems change or set some other kind of boundary upon its development. For example, laws regulating the cooperation among banks have had some effect upon the cooperative development of data processing services or the sale of data processing services by larger banks to small banks. Some public utilities have been required to retain unwanted information in their customer bills by rulings of public utilities commissions. While these constraints may operate occasionally, the opportunity for useful changes in information systems usually are relatively unlimited by such constraints.

F. Possibilities for Change

While the attention of those who have studied the ways in which social systems adapt to new requirements and the attention of participants in the management of change in information systems have been drawn to "resistance to change," we suggest that viewing the increased utilization of computers in information systems as a dynamic process of systems change rather than as a static problem in system design can result in more and more goal-orientated changes than have been experienced in the last decade. We argue that the familiar problems need a new framework, that the design and development of computerized information systems should be viewed as a long-range set of small, frequent, developmental steps rather than as a series of relatively large steps from "one generation of information systems to the next." By accepting frequent revision as an essential of the life of any information system, the approach to its design and implementation is changed dramatically from our most common experiences in the last decade. The attitudes and expectations of the participants are different, and the opportunity for more rapid systems change and development probably is enhanced. We can only guess that this is true. While there have been studies from the points of view of the social sciences of the adoptions of innovations in agriculture, new drugs, and education, systematic studies of the adoptions of innovations in management made possible by the computer have been infrequent. Thus, our conclusions about the possibilities for rapidly increased changes in the future remain to be tested, either by practical experience or by systematic studies or by both. We suggest how increased skill in managing information systems changes can be achieved through systematic research as we discuss "Research and the Future of Information Technology" in Chapter 14.

That management's stance toward change in the information system should be one of encouraging exploration and even experiment seems an inescapable conclusion. Management style for accomplishing change and making improvements should be characterized by open communication about the need for change and by a willingness to share responsibility for planning and implementing change.

C. Computers and Corporate Operations

CHAPTER 8

Computer-Aided Management Control Systems in Production

Introduction / Classification of Computer Applications in Production / The Role of the Computer in the Production Organization / Implementation of the Computer System in Production

A. Introduction

ALMOST 40% of the computers in the U.S. are installed in manufacturing organizations. This chapter will provide a brief review of the major management-oriented functions performed by computers in the production process of manufacturing organizations. The next chapter is devoted to the use of computers in the distribution process of manufacturing organizations.

To understand the management-oriented functions of a computer in the production area, it is necessary to be familiar with the operational functions which it performs. Accordingly, the first section of this chapter contains a description of the major functions performed by computers in the operational control of production. The following sections discuss the ways different levels of management interact with the computerized production systems and requirements which such systems impose on management.

The effects of introducing computers to a production activity can be discerned on many levels within an organization. On the broadest level, there is a promise of increased efficiency in the use of inventories, accurate and detailed production accounting information, and a better distribution of work over the whole manufacturing plant. On a more detailed level, there are promises of increased efficiency in the basic production process and higher quality in the product manufactured (numerically controlled machining, computerized process control, etc.).

The following section describes the major applications in greater detail.

B. Classification of Computer Applications in Production

1. ROUTINE PROCESSING AND STATUS REPORTING

The applications discussed in this section deal with routine processing procedures and basic information reporting. This category of computer applications in the production area includes many of the simplest and most commonly found applications in business today. These applications are simple in that they typically only involve gathering together information from several sources, possibly editing or summarizing this data, and then preparing a printed document or recording a result in a computer file. The functions carried out by the computer in these applications are almost exclusively clerical operations. Typically, the implementation of these applications on a computer replaces low-salaried clerical personnel.

(1) a. Computer Order Processing

In many industries, when an order is received from a customer, a number of routine clerical steps must be performed before the order is ready to be submitted to production scheduling or to be sent to the warehouse for filling. Typical operations performed in the order processing procedure are verification of the product code, check of the credit status of the customer, determination of the product price and applicable discounts, look-up of the customer's standard shipping instructions from a customer information file, and other similar operations. In most of these operations, the great majority of the orders can be handled routinely and the computer can readily perform these routine operations. Some small percentage of the orders requires external, manual attention. The computer will divert these orders from the mainstream and give an indication of the nature of the problem encountered. For example, the credit check on an order from a regular customer will only require looking up the customer's credit status in a computer file, but the credit check on an order from a new customer will require a complete credit investigation which cannot be performed by the computer. Therefore, orders from previous customers would be processed routinely but orders from new customers would be signaled for external investigation. Typically, the end result of the routine processing of a customer order is a printed, multi-copy document containing all of the appropriate information which is then distributed to various departments within the organization.

Another less common application which is sometimes implemented in conjunction with the order-processing procedure is the maintenance of an open customer-order file. When an order is initially processed, it is recorded in a computer file which would specify, among other things, the customer name, the date order received, the product numbers and quantities ordered and the promised shipment date. If an order is partially shipped to the customer, this information would be recorded in the appropriate record in the file. When an order is completely shipped to the customer, the record is deleted from the open customer-order file. This file can be used to generate periodic status reports of each individual order and of future commitments by product code and can also be used to generate automatic releases either to production or the warehouse at the appropriate time in advance of the promised shipment date.

The benefit obtained by computerizing routine customer-order processing and maintaining an open customer-order file depends on the volume of orders processed and the normal elapsed time between receipt of the order and shipment to the customer. Computerized order-processing systems should only handle standard situations, and provide that special requirement orders should be detected and signaled for manual processing.

(2) b. Shop/Purchase Order Preparation

The preparation of routine shop orders and purchase orders frequently involves copying a great deal of standard information on a standard order document. In addition to the part number and the quantity required, a typical shop order contains such information as the list of component materials, the tools required, the shop routing and the piece rate or standard production time for each operation. All of this information is standard and can be maintained in computer files. When a shop order is desired, the part number and quantity required are entered into the computer and the shop order form is printed automatically. Similarly, preparation of a purchase order includes such standard information as the vendor name and address, product specifications, quality standards, shipping instructions, etc. This information also can be maintained in a computer file and the purchase order printed automatically whenever a product number and quantity are entered into the computer. Manual procedures would be used to modify or add non-standard information in special situations.

An application which is analogous to the open customer-order file is the maintenance of an open file for shop orders and purchase orders. These files are appropriate when the order remains outstanding for a significant period of time and the status of the order can change between the time that the order is initially generated and the time it is completed. This is a particularly desirable file when a shop order may go through many separate operations in production. When the completion of a shop order is spread over several days or weeks, the open shop-order file can also show the portion of the order which has been completed and the amount still outstanding. For a purchase order, the open purchase-order file is particularly useful to keep track of partial receipt shipments so that the outstanding balance will be known. Periodic reports are generated to show the status of all outstanding shop orders and purchase orders.

These applications are relatively easy to implement although they may require fairly large files for the standard information. The applications are desirable when the number of orders prepared is large and the information content can be standardized. The fact that the information content of purchase orders or shop orders is not now standardized is not sufficient reason to rule out this application. A little study may show that standardization can be readily introduced.

(3) c. Work-in-Process Status

In the previous paragraph we mentioned that an open shop-order file could be used to keep track of work in process. This is a particularly important application in industries in which production involves multiple operations requiring the movement of the product from one production center to another production center. A record is established when the shop order is initially generated which contains the product code, quantity required, production routing and the standard manufacturing time for each operation. This record is then updated routinely to keep track of the progress of the order through the production operations. The record would show the operations completed, the current location of the partially finished lot, the length of time the job has remained in its current queue and the time available until completion is due. At regular intervals, such as daily or weekly, a report would be printed showing the status of the backlog for each production center. If machine loading is done manually, this report would be used to determine the priority of the jobs in the backlog and used to control the flow of order lots through the shop.

If the number of active shop orders is small, the work-in-process file can be maintained manually. The computer is useful when there are many jobs to keep track of simultaneously. The biggest obstacle to successful maintenance of a work-in-process file is the difficulty in getting complete and timely reporting from the production floor. For this purpose, it is possible to install computer terminals right on the production floor which are connected directly to the main computer. When an operation on a job is completed, the job is moved to another location or other action taken; this information can be entered into the floor terminal and recorded instantaneously in the computer file.

/4) d. Bill of Materials Explosion

Bill of materials explosion means the complete listing of all of the components down to the basic purchased components of a finished product or intermediate assembly. Bill of materials explosion may or may not be required, depending on the nature of the business. In a business in which there are many component parts to a finished product, a bill of materials explosion is undoubtedly required in some phase of the operation. If a company normally manufactures to order, an explosion of requirements will usually be triggered by the receipt of a customer order. On the other hand, if a company normally maintains inventory, either of finished products or intermediate assemblies, an explosion of component requirements is needed whenever a shop order is generated for replenishment of inventory.

Bill of materials explosion is rarely performed completely manually, although it is quite common to use a punched-card tabulation procedure. A computer file can be maintained which records the linkage from finished product to assembly to purchased part. This file can be used to obtain a bill of materials listing of any assembly item whenever needed. The biggest difficulties in operating such a computerized bill of materials file is in defining the initial hierarchical coding structure and then in keeping the file up to date. Many computer manufacturers now have available standard bill-of-material systems which makes implementation of such a system quite easy.

(5) e. Inventory Posting

In almost every manufacturing company, records are kept of the inventory balance of finished products, raw materials and maybe even intermediate products. The maintenance of these records requires the posting of all transactions which affect inventory. These transactions consist of withdrawals, receipts, replenishment orders, backorders, returns and adjustments. One of the most common applications of computers in the production area is the maintenance of inventory records. The inventory record can be maintained in the computer file and all transactions which affect this balance entered into the computer. On a periodic basis an inventory status report is generated. This status report shows the current inventory balance, the outstanding replenishment orders and the due date of each order, unfilled customer order commitments, customer orders backordered and any other pertinent information about each individual product. This information is used for reference by sales and production personnel.

The implementation of a computerized inventory posting system is frequently combined with the implementation of an inventory control decision system. (Inventory control decision systems are discussed in a later section of this chapter.) These systems are generally desirable unless there are very few active items in inventory or the level of transaction activity is small.

(6) f. Reports of Operating Status Relative to Plan

A computer application of wide pertinence is the generation of various reports showing current status information relative to plan. One example of such a report might show actual production completed during the course of a month and actual month ending inventory levels as well as the planned production activity and inventory levels for the month. These reports can be used to evaluate operating performance. Another example of such a report would show labor utilization which would compare actual time charges to budget with an allowance made for differences between planned and actual output levels. Still another report could show a comparison of actual cost versus budget, organized either by production center or by job. Obviously, job reporting would only be applicable when there are very large production contracts.

In all of these reports, the plan could either be maintained in a computer file or could be entered in the computer at the time of report preparation. The actual information would have to be entered into the file either at the time of report preparation or gradually accumulated during the course of the performance evaluation period and recorded in a computer file.

(7) g. *Critical Path Method (CPM) Control*

The critical path method is a basic technique for planning, scheduling and controlling projects of all types. A project is broken down into basic activity elements and formulated as a network of connecting links. A time is established for each activity and milestone times determined for various points in the network. If the network and actual progress completions of individual activities are entered into the computer, the computer can generate reports showing the status of the project and the differences between actual and planned completion times for the various points in the project network.

This application is exceedingly useful for controlling very large projects such as occur in the defense industry and the construction industry.

There are numerous package CPM[1] programs available which make implementation quite easy. The difficult part of this application is in preparing the network plan for the project. The definition of the individual tasks or activities, if done in sufficient detail to be useful, takes significant time and effort. The estimation of the time required for each individual task can also be difficult in some applications.

2. EXCEPTION REPORTING

Exception reporting stems from the well known concept of management by exception. Applications in this area are not much more complicated than the routine processing and status reporting applications, but they do involve some elementary decision-making. The decisions made only involve a determination of whether management attention and judgment is needed in a particular situation. In many production-related activities, it is possible to define criteria which specify when a potential problem requiring management attention exists. An exception report is a list of the few situations (products, production centers,

---

[1] A discussion of the critical path method and related network control techniques is given in *Project Management with CPM and PERT* by J. J. Moder and C. R. Phillips. Reinhold, New York, 1964.

cost categories, etc.) out of a large number reviewed by the computer that are found to require external review or attention. The specific applications of exception reporting within the production area frequently depend on the nature of the manufacturing process; however, a few general application areas can be mentioned.

a. Inventory Shortages

Undoubtedly the most common example of exception reporting in the production area is the inventory shortage report. This report is generated from a review of the inventory status records. An item is listed on the inventory status report if the current stock level reaches zero. In some applications, items are also included in the report when the stock level is not zero, but is low and the probability of a stockout is determined to be high. This report is used to draw attention to inventory problem areas so that action can be taken to quickly replenish inventory.

Computer inventory shortage reports are not difficult to implement, but obviously require a computerized inventory file.

b. Past-Due Reports

A series of reports can be generated from the open customer-order file, the open shop-order file and the open purchase-order file which signals when a particular action is past due. For example, a report can be generated to signal when the shipment of a customer order is past due. An order would be listed on this report when it is found that shipment has not been made by the promised shipment date. The report would be used to initiate expediting action on the delayed orders.

A similar report can be prepared for past-due shop orders. The report would be generated in a review of the open shop-order file. Orders would be listed on the report when it is found that shop orders have not been completed by the specified completion date. The report would be used to direct expediting attention to those products on which completion is behind schedule. A past-due purchase-order report can be generated in a review of the open purchase-order file. Purchase orders would be listed on the report when material has not been received by the specified delivery date. Again, this report would be used to draw attention to delinquent vendor orders.

There is little difficulty in generating these reports if the computer files are available. In fact, one of the primary justifications for the maintenance of computerized open transaction files is the control benefit achieved by these past-due reports.

c. Status Exception Reports

Many of the reports mentioned in the previous section on routine processing and status reporting could be designed so that information would only be printed when the current status met certain exceptional conditions. For example, the reports comparing actual performance to plan could be designed so that information would only be printed when there is a significant deviation between actual and planned values. If a comparison between actual and plan shows little deviation, then printing would be suppressed since management is usually not interested in these situations as long as everything is operating satisfactorily. The CPM output report can also be designed so that only the activities which are significantly behind schedule are printed for management attention.

d. Real-Time Information Retrieval

A special type of exception information reporting is possible with the advent of third-generation computer technology. This type of exception reporting does not meet the standard definition which was given at the beginning of this section. Information is not reported because some type of exception condition has been detected, but rather because an external request is made for a specific piece of status information, which may be contained in a very large file. Reporting is not triggered by detection of some special condition in a periodic review of the file, but rather by an external inquiry which may occur at any time. A good example of this type of exception information reporting is an inquiry on the current inventory status of a particular stocked finished product. Another example of this type of inquiry would be a request for the current status of a particular customer order from the information maintained in the open customer-order file.

This type of reporting essentially corresponds to selective status reporting. If real-time information retrieval capability exists, it is not necessary to print complete status reports of an entire file at periodic intervals. When information is desired, a real-time inquiry is made and much more up-to-date information obtained than would be likely to be available with periodic status reporting.

Real-time information retrieval applications obviously require more elaborate computer equipment and more highly sophisticated computer programs. The inquiry terminal may be a typewriter with printed paper output or a visual display (cathode ray) tube with keyboard.

In some industries the availability of up-to-date information is extremely important and real-time inquiry capability is desirable and justified. Airline reservation systems are a good example of an area where there is a critical need for up-to-date status information and are the best known example of successful implementation of real-time exception status reporting systems. In the typical manufacturing situation, however, this type of capability is seldom necessary.

3. PRODUCTION DECISION RULES

The greatest potential benefits from the application of computers in the production area are obtained from applications of mechanized production-decision rules. These applications are intended to determine the optimal strategy for a particular problem in a given situation. The applications are typically more complicated than those previously discussed. In many cases the development of the logic to include in these programs requires an intensive study of company operations. As a result, the implementation of decision-rule systems may be quite costly and may require a great deal of time. Implementation will be discussed further in a later section.

For some decision-rule applications, such as inventory control, the factors which need to be considered for most industries are well understood. Standard models have been developed and are well documented in the literature. It is not within the scope of this book to discuss production decision rules other than to indicate the areas of application to computers. Numerous books have been written on production planning and control decision rules. Several of these books are listed at the end of this chapter and appropriate references are given throughout this discussion.

a. Inventory Control

Inventory control is concerned with the determination of when to replenish inventory of individual products and how much to order when inventory is replenished. Standard formulas are available for the calculation of order points and economic order quantities. (See references 2, 8 and 13.) While these calculations are not complex, they are fairly time-consuming if performed manually for a large product line. The computer is ideally suited for performing these calculations.

The calculation of economic order quantities and order points requires certain input information such as a forecast of expected demand, unit costs, setup costs, inventory carrying costs, a measure of forecast error and a statement of customer service policy. Normally this information will be maintained in regular computer files. Order points and order quantities are updated at regular intervals. The computer routinely reviews the inventory status of each product. When the on-hand inventory plus previous on-order balance is less than the order point, a replenishment order is initiated for an economic order quantity. If shop order/purchase order preparation is also mechanized, the entire procedure from posting of the inventory transactions to printing of the replenishment order is completely automatic.

Numerous companies have implemented inventory control systems that have achieved very substantial savings in inventory carrying costs and production setup costs and, at the same time, markedly increased the level of customer service. For example, a recent study for a manufacturer of electromechanical equipment has shown that implementation of sophisticated inventory control decision rules in a computer system can reduce costs of inventory and production setups on parts and intermediate assemblies by approximately 40% and at the same time increase customer service from about 60% to about 95%. However, it should not always be expected that inventory levels will be reduced by implementing inventory control systems. Some companies find that the biggest advantage of their inventory control system is the ability to control the inventory and customer service levels.

Inventory control systems are usually not difficult to implement. Some study is required to determine the correct form of the inventory control decision rules but, as mentioned previously, standard formulas are applicable in most industries. The most common problem encountered in implementing these systems is in setting up files of the required cost data. Many company accounting systems do not have suitable cost information readily available. A good discussion on costs is given in reference 8.

b. Scheduling and Machine Loading

Scheduling and machine loading is concerned with determining which shop orders are going to be run on a particular machine or production center and with specifying the priority in which these jobs are going to be processed. Of course this is not applicable to assembly line production, but this is an important function when there are numerous production operations or stages in the manufacture of individual products.

Some companies which have multiple production operations pay no attention to the shop order from the time it is entered into the shop until it finally comes out as a finished product. The shop order specifies a routing for the production lot and it is left to the individual production center foremen to see that the lot is processed through their center and transferred to the next operation in the specified routing. The foremen determine their own priority for taking jobs out of the backlog from this center.

The computer can be very helpful in keeping track of the progress of an order through a multi-operation shop. The maintenance of an open shop-order file which records the current status of each order at all times was discussed previously. Reports are submitted by each production center on the completion of each job and these are entered into the computer file to record the progress of the shop order through the scheduled production operations.

In the earlier discussion it was stated that a periodic report could be generated which would be used for manual scheduling and machine loading. However, instead of printing out this report and using a manual procedure for scheduling and loading of the production centers, it is possible to computerize this procedure. In order to implement such a procedure, it is necessary to define explicitly the criterion for determining the priority of processing jobs which are in the backlog for a particular center. This criterion is selected so as to satisfy some particular objective of the effectiveness of the system. Large-scale simulations are usually used to determine the best criterion for satisfying this objective. A review of priority criteria and job-shop scheduling rules is given in references 10 and 12.

Computerized machine loading and scheduling is appropriate for large companies with job-shop-type manufacturing operations. Hughes Aircraft Company has implemented a job-shop loading and scheduling system which has worked quite satisfactorily. (See reference 3.) The design and implementation of the Hughes system took slightly longer than two years. An early evaluation of this system showed that: (1) the percentage of orders completed by their due dates had increased by 10%; (2) the average order cycle time in the shop was reduced about 25%, effecting a significant reduction in work-in-process inventory and simultaneously increasing machine and manpower utilization; and (3) expediting time was reduced by about 60%. The savings in expediting costs alone more than paid for the implementation of the system.

As can be seen from the example above, the implementation of a computerized scheduling and machine-loading system can take a great deal of time and effort and be quite costly. Simpler scheduling and loading systems can be designed which will not require two years to implement, but a substantial investment will be required to implement the system in any case. However, it can also be seen that the potential savings can be great in some applications.

c. Production Planning and Allocation

Production planning and allocation is concerned with the assignment of products (usually in groups) competing to be produced on specific facilities (possibly at several locations) in particular time periods. In the general problem the product categories have different seasonal sales patterns, different production costs on each potential manufacturing facility, and different inventory carrying costs. Frequently, production capacities are limited so that it is necessary to build seasonal inventory in order to satisfy the demand during the peak sales period. There usually is a cost penalty associated with changing the level of production for a production facility and sometimes even for individual product categories. There is a cost associated with carrying inventory which is built up either to satisfy future peak sales or to smooth production. There is an extra cost incurred to transport material made at one plant to satisfy demand in another plant's territory. Production planning and allocation decision rules are intended to determine a production plan giving the level of production of each product category on each facility in each time period which would minimize some or all of these costs and possibly some other similar costs which are unique to particular industries or companies.

Production planning and allocation is a highly sophisticated computer application which has been implemented in only a limited number of companies. One example of such a system has been implemented by a multi-plant manufacturer of building products. The design and complete implementation of this system took about 18 months. (A preliminary version of the system was working within one year.) The model prepares production plans for more than 60 product categories at five manufacturing locations. The production plans cover an 18-month period (to span a full seasonal cycle) and are updated monthly. Forecasts of demand over the next 18 months are input to the model in each updating. The model considers carrying costs on seasonal inventory, variable manufacturing costs and interplant transfer costs. The model has been operating successfully for over a year and has produced some surprising results concerning where certain products should be produced. While exact benefits have not been measured, it is estimated that savings of several million dollars per year will be achieved.

The difficulty in designing and implementing production planning and allocation systems is in developing a suitable model of the relevant costs which can be solved to find the optimum production plan under given conditions. A review of the current state of the art of production planning and allocation models is given in reference 15. There are various levels of complexity of models which can be used. A balance must be achieved between the complexity of the model and the number of parameters included in the model. A simple model which does not realistically represent actual conditions will be of little value and could give deceptive results.

The implementation of a production planning and allocation system can achieve very substantial benefits, but requires a large commitment in terms of time and dollars.

4. MACHINE CONTROL

In most industries, the computer has not yet been applied directly in the production process itself; however, there are some highly specialized applications in which the computer has a role in the manufacturing process. These are in the process industries and the metal-machining industries.

a. Process Control

Analog computers or controllers have been used for many years in the process control field in the conventional feedback-loop application. In such a loop, the sensor (e.g., a bulb measuring the temperature of oil in a heat exchanger) sends a signal to an analog controller. The controller compares the measured temperature signal to a manually set point, which indicates the desired temperature. If an error signal is developed, it is transformed into a control signal that works an automatic valve to control the heating mechanism.

Digital computers are now being directly substituted for conventional analog controllers in process-control instrumentation systems and also are being used in higher control functions such as feed-forward controls, calculated secondary variables and adaptive controls. When a digital computer is substituted for analog controllers, it performs the same control calculations as the individual analog controllers, but on a time-shared basis. A single digital computer can replace an extremely large number of individual analog controllers. In spite of this, however, it is understood that initial applications of digital computers in this area have shown rather poor economic results.

One type of advanced control function which looks more economically promising for digital computers is called "feed-forward." In this application, when the sensor detects an error from the pre-set standard, instead of signaling some type of corrective action at a preceding stage in the production process, the computer instead calculates what type of compensating action should be taken at a later stage in the production process so that there is no lapse in the output of good material. Although analog instrumentation could be used in this application, it appears that digital computers will prove to be more satisfactory, especially when many such controls are involved. Applications of computers to process control are limited to the process industries. The desirability of using digital computers depends on the nature and magnitude of the company operations. A special type of knowledge is required to evaluate these applications. Reference 4 contains a thorough discussion of the process control field.

b. Numerical Control

A numerically controlled machine tool is usually nothing more than a conventional machine tool with a small electronic control mechanism attached. The electronic control mechanism serves to automatically control the positioning and movement of the work piece and/or the cutting tool. Until quite recently, the input to the electronic controller which gives the machining instructions was limited to either punched cards, punched paper tape or magnetic tape.

While the electronic controller is actually a highly specialized electronic computer, this application is not considered meaningful for a typical business computer. However, standard digital computers are used to prepare the input to the electronic controller. At the present time, digital computers are used to prepare the input for nearly all the numerically controlled tools that cut contoured surfaces. (Input for point-to-point system machines, e.g., a drill press, is usually prepared manually.) The digital computer takes relatively simple machining instructions prepared by the engineer and translates these instructions into highly detailed directions which the electronic controller uses for positioning and moving the work table and cutting tool.

As mentioned above, until very recently, the output of the digital computer which contains the detailed directions was either on punched cards, punched paper tape, or magnetic tape. The latest development in this field is to have direct, on-line computer control of the numerically controlled machine—the digital computer is directly connected to the electronic controller, eliminating the intermediate tape or cards. A single digital computer will be capable of controlling several hundred numerically controlled machines simultaneously (see reference 5). The detailed machining directions, which have been translated by the main computer from the engineer's instructions, are stored in a computer file. When the piece is to be machined, the main computer retrieves the directions from the file and transmits these directions to the electronic controller which directs the operation of the machine tool.

Numerical control is another specialized computer application. Currently, numerical control has common application only on machine tools, but eventually it will be used on many different types of manufacturing equipment. Because of the complexity of the instructions required by numerically controlled equipment, the applications of computers will have to grow with the development of the numerical control area.

5. STAFF STUDY ANALYSES

In addition to the applications concerned with the routine operations of a business, the computer can also be a valuable tool in special staff studies of particular production problems. It should be emphasized, however, that in any study of this type, a computer is only a tool which can perform very complicated and time-consuming calculations. The results need to be interpreted and modified to reflect external qualitative factors which cannot be included in the computer analysis.

a. Plant Location and Layout Models

One of the biggest problems which faces production management periodically is where to locate a new production facility and how to lay out the equipment within the plant. These complicated problems involve many considerations. Fairly recently, some mathematical models have been developed which find an optimum or near optimum solution to these problems by considering some of the quantifiable relevant factors. Three different approaches have been taken in the work in this field: analytical modeling, simulation, and heuristic programming. It is beyond the scope of this book to explain these different procedures, but some references have been given of the work in each of the three approaches. References 1 and 9 use the analytical-model approach. References 6 and 14 use the simulation approach and reference 7 uses the heuristic-program approach. In all of these approaches, the solution to any sizable problem requires a digital computer to perform the calculations.

The work in this area is still in the development stage but does offer some help in making good decisions. The computer is a necessary tool in this type of study.

b. Simulation

Simulation can be used to study many different types of problems. In the previous section it was noted that simulation is one approach to help in making plant location and layout decisions. It can be used to study the effects of changing control parameters in a production scheduling and inventory control system. It can be used to study the interaction between levels in a multi-level production operation. It can be used to study the effects of alternative production plans if an optimizing production planning model is not available.

Simulation can be performed manually, but unless the size of the simulation is quite small, this can be very time consuming and expensive. A computerized simulation program will permit making repeated simulation runs under alternative conditions quite inexpensively.

The big problem in computerizing a simulation procedure is in preparing the simulation program. Most computer manufacturers and some independent companies have now developed general-purpose simulator languages which greatly simplify the construction of certain types of simulator programs. These general-purpose simulator languages are particularly applicable to simulating the flow of material through a system. The computer manufacturers also have developed inventory system simulators which are applicable in many situations. However, care should be taken to use a simulation model which realistically represents actual operations. If, instead, a program which does not actually reflect actual conditions is used to save time and money, the results may be worthless.

c. Special Decision Models

Many other decision problems that do not crop up routinely may nevertheless be set up as computerized decision models and used whenever the need arises. One such decision is the determination of whether to stock a product or make it to order. While this decision is typically made intuitively, most of the relevant factors are quantifiable and can be incorporated in a decision model. Usually the classification of products as stock or make-to-order is reviewed infrequently but it could be reviewed on a regular once-a-year basis, or other regular interval, if a computerized decision model were developed.

Another decision which commonly comes up and involves both quantitative and qualitative considerations is whether to make or buy individual products. Many times a company has the option of purchasing a part from an outside vendor or manufacturing the part from a basic raw material. The cost implications can be readily evaluated with a suitable decision model. Other factors, such as quality, must be considered in the decision in a subjective manner. Evaluation of each product individually is an extremely time-consuming procedure and, as a result, is seldom done. A computer model could be developed which would easily make an evaluation of all of the quantifiable factors. Managerial judgment could be exercised in reviewing the computer results.

All of these applications have somewhat of an element of research in them. They are sophisticated applications which should be considered only after the more standard applications have been implemented. The benefits achieved will depend on the individual company's characteristics. What may be a very good application in some companies may be a very bad application in other companies.

C. The Role of the Computer in the Production Organization

1. TOP MANAGEMENT

The primary function of the computer to the top management in the production organization is in providing up-to-date and compre-hensive status and exception reports which can be used to keep close control over production operations. Specifically, the reports which compare the current status and performance relative to plan are of greatest direct interest to top management. These reports enable man-agement to detect when current operations are deviating from plan and help in determining a specific cause of the problem. Status and exception reports provide the information which management uses to control production operations.

Of course, top production management is also interested in produc-tion plans, but its normal role in this area is in a policy making and approval capacity. Top management can, however, take advantage of a computerized production planning system to request that produc-tion plans be generated under various alternative conditions so that it can select the "best" plan in light of the uncertainties faced. If the production planning department generates plans manually, it is costly to obtain several production plans under alternative conditions and may even be impossible because of the time required. The generation of alternative production plans can be used to study the impact of closing down a production facility or eliminating the use of overtime or various other policy decisions which are the responsibility of top production management.

Finally, top production management is also actively concerned in broad scope, one-time studies such as plant location. Again, the use of the computer would enable evaluation of the optimum solution con-sidering selected quantifiable factors. The final decision would still have to be made by top production management, but the information which it would have on which to base this decision would be greatly enhanced by using some of the specialized computer analysis applications.

2. PRODUCTION ANALYSIS STAFF

It is probably true that there is almost never a group called "pro-duction analysis staff" in the production organization; however, there usually is some place in the organization which has the responsibility for performing special one-time studies which pertain to production operations. This responsibility may be assigned to a separate opera-tions research or systems analysis group. It may be assigned to the regular production planning and scheduling group, or to the industrial engineering group as an extra responsibility. In any case, there is a need to perform one-time or seldom repeated studies such as plant location, plant layout, stock or make to order, make or buy, or various types of simulation studies which require the direct effort by some people in the organization. For these people, the computer can be used as a tool to reduce the time required in routine calculations and in some cases may be able to give partial solutions to problems which would be beyond the scope of manual calculation. The computer can evaluate alternatives and perform various data analyses so that staff studies are more complete and illuminating.

3. PRODUCTION PLANNING AND SCHEDULING

The production planning and scheduling department stands to benefit most from the use of a computer by eliminating the routine clerical operations and the routine decisions. Standard decision rules can be applied to many of its tasks. There will, however, always be special situations which do not fit the standard patterns and for which the routine decision rules will not apply, but these will be relatively few. When the routine decisions are handled by the computer, the special situations can be given the attention which they rightfully deserve.

The computer can be used to perform the routine processing steps of bill of materials explosion and shop order preparation. It can also record the status of in-process shop orders in production operations with multiple centers or multiple levels. In more sophisticated computer systems, the computer can make inventory control decisions and automatically initiate the preparation of shop orders. In production operations in which it is appropriate, the computer can be used for automatic production center scheduling and machine loading. Finally, in highly sophisticated systems, the computer can be used for production planning and allocation decisions.

In most industrial situations, there is no need for real-time access capability by the production planning and scheduling department, but in certain special situations this is a desirable feature. Real-time control would be particularly desirable in multi-center production operations when the turnover of jobs in the backlog of a production center is so rapid that normal batch-process updating is not adequate to keep up with the status.

4. DISPATCHING (EXPEDITING)

In a job-shop-type production operation, the dispatchers are responsible for seeing that jobs are properly transferred from one production center to the next center in the prescribed routing of the product. The work-in-process status file and the machine-loading schedule are the key sources of information used in the performance of the dispatching activity. A computerized work-in-process status file and computerized machine loading ensure more reliable, up-to-date information with which the dispatchers can work. Of greater significance to the dispatchers, however, are the inventory-shortage and past-due reports which direct him to potential and existing problem situations.

In manufacturing operations which do not have multiple production centers, the regular dispatching function does not exist, but the inventory shortage report is still valuable for drawing attention to potential and existing problems so that an effort can be made to expedite production and avoid backorders.

5. Supervisory and Operating Personnel

In many companies with job-shop type operations, the production center supervisor or foreman has to prepare his own machine-loading schedule from the backlog of work which he can physically observe. A computerized machine-loading schedule eliminates this responsibility and permits him to concentrate his efforts on obtaining the maximal efficiency from his men and equipment. A computerized schedule has an advantage over a schedule prepared manually by the production scheduling department in that it will usually be more reliable and up-to-date.

In some manufacturing situations where the speed of reporting is critical, production-floor computer input terminals are used. These can take a variety of forms. In some terminals, the production worker inserts a plastic card which contains an identification code and then keys in certain information such as the job number and transaction or status code. In other terminals, input may be a combination of punched cards and typewriter keyboard. These terminals are connected directly to the computer so that the information reported is immediately recorded in the computer files. These terminals are used to report changes in status of individual jobs such as the movement of the lot from one location to another, the start of production in a particular center, or the completion of production at a particular center.

The machine control applications which were discussed earlier have their greatest impact on the jobs performed by the production worker. With the implementation of more sophisticated process control computers and numerically controlled machines, the production worker's responsibility is changed from that of operator to maintenance. The production equipment is more sophisticated and requires greater attention, but the skills required for maintenance of this equipment are far different from the skills of the regular production operator. This necessitates a great deal of training and upgrading of the production personnel.

6. PURCHASING

The purchasing department typically decides when to replenish stock of purchased parts and then prepares a purchase order to be sent to an appropriate vendor. The computer can be used to automatically determine when to replenish inventory and how much to order and can also automatically prepare the purchase order in the required format to be sent to the vendor. The purchase order would show the vendor's name and address, the part number and quantity, the product specifications, quality standards and shipping instructions, as well as desired delivery date. The purchasing department would have to review this information and make modifications, if necessary, because of special conditions.

The purchasing department would also be supplied with a report showing purchase orders on which delivery was past due so that it can contact the vendor and expedite the completion of a shipment.

D. *Implementation of the Computer System in Production*

The task of designing and installing a computer system for production activities should be accorded a large amount of management attention. Extreme care should be taken in selecting personnel to be associated with the project since they will profoundly affect the rate of progress and the degree of success. Contrary to widespread notions, it is unnecessary to demand proficiency and experience in mathematics as a prerequisite for participation in such a project. More important are qualities such as experience with the intricacies of the manufacturing process, an ability to communicate effectively with representatives of other departments, and the type of mind which finds pleasure in solving elementary logical problems. Also needed, of course, are several individuals with direct experience in the design of computer systems and in the mathematical theory of control systems, but they would typically be members of the company's systems and operations research staff or their counterparts from a consulting firm.

A foreign aircraft manufacturer recently made the decision to install computer systems in one of its assembly plants. As a first step, two programs were immediately initiated. One program started with the formation of a steering committee, consisting of departmental representatives and systems designers, whose tasks were to define the goals of the project, establish priorities, and then to provide overall direction in its implementation. The second program was initiated independently by the systems department. Its aim was to describe how information (as contained, for example, in paper work and personal communications) moved from one point in the plant to another in day-to-day manufacturing activities. Previously, there had been no descriptions of the various procedures whereby different departments communicated with each other. Individual managers and supervisors had a knowledge of what was required to perform their roles successfully, but no attempts had been made to record this knowledge in writing. Training of junior personnel had been carried out by spontaneous explanation and demonstration, with little or no emphasis on how the various procedures fitted into plant-wide systems.

The descriptions generated by this program were designed to reveal three major aspects of how information was communicated within the plant

- the major flows of information from initiating source through the various departments
- the major decisions which were taken on the basis of the information at various points along the flow
- additions or modification to the information which took place at various points.

This program was initiated since it was evident that this type of systems documentation would be required at all stages of the design process of the computer system. Without a full description of the flows, the decisions, and the processing functions available to the steering committee and the designers, there could be no common factual basis for discussing alternative approaches to the system.

The systems documentation program led to other benefits for the computer project. The basic factual material was obtained by interviews with operating personnel. By the very nature of the questions asked in these interviews, operating personnel were forced to take a systems approach in viewing their tasks. This was an important first step in training them to eventually interact with a computer.

The program carried out by the steering committee was, at first, one of defining objectives. Some members of the committee had little familiarity with the capabilities of the computers and were, therefore, assigned to one- or two-week-long computer orientation courses which provided them with a sufficient background to communicate effectively with the systems designers on the committee.

The chairmanship of the committee was assigned to a senior systems specialist to minimize departmental bias in committee operations. Departmental representation, however, was essential for the identification of goals. Furthermore, through the informal communication between a departmental representative and other members of his department, these other members of the department could keep abreast of progress and develop a preliminary identification with the system.

The only contact with computers at this plant had been the preparation of payroll punched cards in-house. These were shipped to the main plant (some 100 miles away) for payroll distribution and reporting on the central computer system. As a first step in developing a computer system for production activities, it was decided to develop basic files covering inventories and assembly requirements, and also the procedures to maintain these files. By using the punched card equipment at the plant, it was possible to *create* the basic files in computer readable form. All processing of the punched cards by computer took place at the corporate headquarters. In slightly different circumstances, this could just as easily have been done at a local computer service bureau. Similarly, information to update the files was prepared at the plant on punched cards and shipped to the computer for updating the files.

In this first phase, there were no strict time requirements on the information produced by the computer. A "turn-around" time of 2-3 days from sending the cards to receiving computer reports was acceptable. To create an inventory file covering over 50,000 parts required three months of inventory-taking and an additional month to reduce the error level from an initial 11% to an acceptable level of about 1%. During this process, the operating personnel learned the procedures required to maintain a large computerized inventory file and gradually developed confidence in the value and potential of the computerized system.

The training of the staff began as soon as the design of the initial system was established. A series of one-hour training seminars was held for supervisory and senior clerical staff—for the first time in the history of the company. Given the opportunity, the primary interest of this staff was to learn about computers. This was in fact done, but all examples of computer applications were related to the system to be implemented. By allowing the trainees to operate keypunches and observe the other punched card equipment in the performance of limited problems which they understood, advances were made in educating them in the potential of automatic data processing and its vulnerability to human error. Eventually, a straightforward systems approach could be taken in the seminars and the proposed system was fully described. Throughout the latter sessions, recurring emphasis was given to the basic trade-off which a computer system would impose on the clerical staff: the favorable reduction of routine clerical work versus an entirely new effort aimed at detecting and correcting errors in the system. This latter point, the shift from traditional clerical activities to error-correction activities, was extremely important in properly orienting the clerical force towards its new tasks.

An additional benefit of the training seminars was that, by allowing the clerical staff to participate in small-scale punched card exercises, it was soon possible to identify those individuals who displayed the requisite ability to take leading roles during later stages of developing the computer system.

The basic philosophy of the steering committee was to proceed in small steps, with speedy implementation, in building-block fashion. It had been found through experience at the main plant that results were significantly diminished if an overly long interval occurred between the design of the system and its implementation. Especially in the early stages, when individuals operated without a clear systems approach, the basic clerical operating procedures tended to change before the computer system became operational. By proceeding in small steps, it was possible to take advantage of short-term feedback from operating personnel to the system designers.

The modular approach of developing the system in small, clearly defined steps resulted in perceptible benefits for the operation of the system, but tended to impose severe design problems. It was frequently difficult to define a series of implementation steps which would result in a widespread, efficient system. This was because there tended to be so many interrelationships between the production departments that one could hardly implement part of the system in one department. Furthermore, in order to utilize programming sources efficiently, it was desirable for each incremental step to include real advances in computerization rather than a modification of past advances. Occasionally some of the programming required to achieve one step would have to be discarded and redone to achieve the following step. From an overall point of view, however, it was judged better to increase the efforts of a few systems designers and programmers than to forego the benefits of introducing the system to the operating staff in a coherent step-by-step fashion.

References

1) Baumol, W. J., and Wolfe, P., "A Warehouse Location Problem," *Operations Research*, 6, 252-263 (1958).

2) Brown, R. G., *Decision Rules for Inventory Management*. New York: Holt, Rinehart and Winston, 1967.

3) Bulkin, M. H., Colley, J. L., and Steinhoff, H. W., Jr., "Load Forecasting, Priority Sequencing and Simulation in a Job Shop Control System," *Management Science*, 13, B29-B51 (1966).

4) Coughanowr, D. R., and Koppel, L. B., *Process Systems Analysis and Control*. New York: McGraw-Hill, 1965.

5) Feinberg, B., "Goodbye to Tape?" *Tool and Manufacturing Engineer*, May 1968, pp. 18-21.

6) Gerson, M. L., and Maffei, R. B., "Technical Characteristics of Distribution Simulators," *Management Science*, 10, 62-69 (1963).

7) Kuehn, A. A., and Hamburger, M. J., "A Heuristic Program for Locating Warehouses," *Management Science*, 11, 213-235 (1964).

8) Magee, J. F., and Boodman, D. M., *Production Planning and Inventory Control*, 2d ed., New York: McGraw-Hill, 1967.

9) Manne, A. S., "Plant Location Under Economies of Scale, Decentralization and Computation," *Management Science*, 11, 213-235 (1964).

10) Mellor, P., "A Review of Job Shop Scheduling," *Operational Research Quarterly*, 17, 161-171 (1966).

11) Moder, J. J., and Phillips, C. R., *Project Management with CPM and PERT*, New York: Reinhold, 1964.

12) Moore, J. M., and Wilson, R. C., "A Review of Simulation Research in Job Shop Scheduling," *Journal of the American Production and Inventory Control Society*, January 1967, 1-10.

13) Prichard, J. W., and Eagle, R. H., *Modern Inventory Management*, New York: John Wiley and Sons, Inc., 1965.

14) Shycon, H. N., and Maffei, R. B., "Simulation—Tool for Better Distribution," *Harvard Business Review*, November/December 1960, 65-75.

15) Silver, E. A., "A Tutorial on Production Smoothing and Work Force Balancing," *Operations Research*, 15, 985-1010 (1967).

C. Computers and Corporate Operations

r-Aided Management Control
ᵧᴄems in Distribution

*Introduction / The Distribution Function / The
Wholesale Drug Problem: Distribution in a Diversified
Market / Inventory Management in Drug Distribution /
Marketing Management in Drug Distribution*

A. Introduction

THE COMPLEXITY of distribution function demands a wide
variety of management skills. This chapter examines the management
functions required in distribution operations and the role of the high-
speed digital computer in obtaining effective control over the physical
distribution and marketing activities critical to the success of distribution operations. The general methods and results obtained in wholesale drug distribution are used as an illustration, because the results
obtained in this application are believed to be typical of those available to other firms whose operations provide them with detailed data
on item demand rates and customer orders.

Efficient processing of the item-demand data, combined with appropriate decision rules for selecting quantity and timing of orders, makes
highly refined control over inventories possible. Similarly, customer-
order data, combined with carefully analyzed distribution costs, can
be used to develop more effective price and service schedules to improve marketing operations. To achieve this degree of refined control,
the computer is used not only to sort and process the item-demand and
customer-order data, but also to apply the carefully developed decision rules, which incorporate management policies on service and
which reflect the cost of operations.

131

B. *The Distribution Function*

In an industrial system, distribution is the activity which receives finished products from a production operation and puts them in the hands of the user. Associated with this distribution activity is the promotion, selection, acquisition, storage, sorting, and delivery of these products. The distribution function separates logically into *physical distribution:* those operations involving the movement of the finished product to the consumer; and *marketing:* those operations concerned with the generation or stimulation of demand for the product. This combined activity is a highly complex and very important component of our industrial system, both in consumer goods and in industrial supplies. It is also an expensive component of the system. The physical distribution costs alone for primary metals, chemicals, and petroleum are estimated at 25% of the sales dollar; and for goods manufacturing, 30%. (Reference 7.) One writer states that physical distribution costs are "estimated by some to represent the third largest component of the total cost of business operation." (Reference 3.)

The efficiency of distribution, whether performed by a division of the firm or by an independent wholesaler, is of concern to the economy as a whole. For most commodities, a variety of distribution channels compete for the distribution job; that channel which can perform the total distribution task at the lowest total cost can be expected to win the competition.

1. FUNCTIONS OF THE WHOLESALER

The wholesaler has traditionally served as the intermediary between manufacturer and retailer. In attempting to serve a large number of retail customers spread over broad areas, manufacturers need a means to provide concentrated sales coverage at the local level, to maintain stocks locally for quick delivery to the retailer, and to support the retailer on the manufacturer's behalf by providing various services, for example, issuing credit to retailers.

The economic function of the wholesaler is to buy in large quantities from a large number of manufacturers, to stock the merchandise, and to sell it in smaller, mixed quantities to retail outlets. To perform this function, the wholesaler must undertake several activities.

2. THE WHOLESALING PROCESS

Figure 6 outlines the flow of orders through a typical wholesale firm. First, the wholesaler must buy the merchandise. The buying function includes the steps of stock checking, ordering, and scheduling delivery. Goods, when they are received, are checked and then stocked in the warehouse where they are held until they are sold. Some goods must be unpacked and put on shelves until they are sold.

At the same time, salesmen are calling regularly on existing and potential customers to solicit orders. In some wholesale firms, these efforts are supplemented by periodic telephone calls to take orders between the salesman's calls. Occasionally, an order is written for a customer by a representative of the manufacturer and is turned over to the wholesaler. Advertising and promotion efforts, including catalog, mailings, and display room visits, add to the total sales effort.

When the retailer places his order, it usually is written up on a standard form and recorded by the wholesaler. The order is then submitted to the warehouse to be filled. (Occasionally, the wholesaler will order for the customer and request the manufacturer to ship goods directly to the customer.) The order is split into two sections at this point, one covering case-lot merchandise, the other covering shelf-stock (broken-case) merchandise. Some firms split large orders into two or more additional sections. Although the full-case and shelf-stock sections of the order take different routes through the warehouse, the functions performed for each are the same.

After the order enters the warehouse, the merchandise to fill it is picked from the shelf or case storage area and assembled. When an item is picked, the order data are compiled by picking prepunched cards or writing the price of the item on the order. The accuracy of the picking job is checked, sometimes only on a spot basis.

In most firms, the supporting documents, including label or bill of lading, are prepared while the order is in the billing process. These documents meet the order at the shipping area, where the merchandise is loaded onto either a regularly scheduled delivery vehicle or a common carrier, for delivery to the customer.

At the end of the billing period, a bill covering all purchases by the customer during that period is prepared and submitted to him. When the bill is paid, the process has been completed.

Figure 6
THE WHOLESALING PROCESS

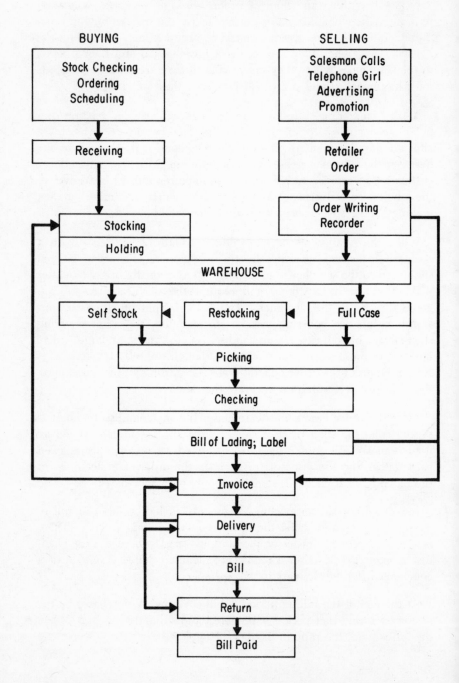

Three to five per cent of all sales are returned to the wholesaler because of damage, improper order filling, errors in order placing, outdated merchandise, etc. The return process is almost exactly the reverse of the order filling process. The goods are delivered to the wholesaler; the necessary documentation of the return is performed; and the material is either discarded, placed back in stock, or returned to the manufacturer. When the return is approved, the customer's account is appropriately credited.

3. MANAGEMENT OF DISTRIBUTION

The managers of a distribution activity try to maximize the return on the resources invested in the distribution activity. Distribution management must consider alternative methods of accomplishing the distribution operations, evaluating them in terms of how well they perform the wholesaling process, and then formulating the distribution policies which can guide intermediate levels of management in making the decisions required in their individual operations. With these policies to guide them, the managers of the various functions attempt to direct and control the operations within their purview in a way which will achieve the corporate objective. (It is beyond the scope of this book to discuss the problems of policy formulation in distribution. Suffice it to say that the objectives of the separate departments of the firm are frequently in conflict with each other. Unless the consequences of the policies of the separate departments are examined for the firm as a whole, there is a danger of suboptimization, i.e., achieving high performance in one department at the expense of one, or more, of the others. See, for example, Reference 5.)

The balance sheet of almost any wholesale distributor will show that the two largest portions of his investable assets are employed as merchandise inventories and (if he is a full-service wholesaler who extends credit to his customers) receivables. In any full-service wholesale houses, some two-thirds of current assets is in the form of inventory, and most of the remaining one-third is in the form of receivables. Therefore, if we consider that receivables are simply a more liquid form of inventory (the wholesaler's goods on the retailer's shelves), we can say that the principal concerns of the wholesaler are his control of inventory and the market strategy he employs to move that inventory. He seeks control over inventory which enables him to meet a high proportion of demand with as small an investment in inventory as possible, and he prices his goods and extends credit and provides other services in what he hopes is a profitable way.

4. COMPUTER AS A MANAGEMENT TOOL IN DISTRIBUTION ACTIVITIES

Distribution operations generate large amounts of detailed information: internal information on inventory movement and external information on customer purchases and other customer characteristics. This information is necessary for the conduct of current business, and it is useful in the planning of future operations. To the extent that the past describes the future, the information on rates of inventory movement can be used to forecast future item demand for stock control, and the information on customer characteristics can be used to develop a marketing strategy that generates and stimulates profitable demand. The degree of refinement achievable in inventory and marketing management is limited only by the effort available to capture, process, and interpret this available data.

Stored-program digital computers have greatly increased a firm's capability to handle the data-processing task. The data processing and computational power of these machines provide even the smaller distribution firms the opportunity to combine routine accounting applications, such as payroll, receivables, and payables, with control-systems applications required in inventory and market management. In addition to files of data on inventory and customers, the control-systems application requires decision rules developed from economic models of inventory and marketing operations which can be programmed for those computers. The data and the decision rules together permit the machine to take over the routine decision-making responsibilities of the inventory and marketing managers, thereby allowing them to concentrate on nonroutine decisions, the skillful handling of which is their very reason for being.

In the sections which follow, the management tasks currently facing the full-service wholesale drug firm are described and the control systems that have been developed for the management of the inventory and marketing functions are outlined to illustrate the methods and application of systems principles. The particular problems currently faced by this industry make these advanced forms of computer-aided control of special value.

C. The Wholesale Drug Problem: Distribution in a Diversified Market

The position of the wholesale distributor in the United States is a delicate one. For the most part, the vendors whose products he distributes consider the wholesaler an unreliable sales representative; the retailers he serves consider him an expensive distribution channel; and the average consumer, unaware of the distributor's economic role, considers him an unnecessary part of the industrial system and as something bordering on the parasitic. From both above and below his position in the distribution system, there are pressures to control him and, if possible, eventually eliminate him.

The wholesaler's sole defense against these pressures is continued effectiveness and efficiency in the distribution role. The wholesale distributor must respond efficiently and effectively to changes in the producing and consuming ends of the distribution channels and in the means of moving the goods through the channels.

Since World War II, a number of upheavals in distribution have have had profound impact on the wholesale trade. The most notable change, of course, has been in food distribution; the cooperatives and the large food chains have assumed responsibility for the wholesaling function, almost eliminating the independent food wholesaler. Similar, but less complete, transformations have occurred in soft goods, hardware, and many other lines of commodities handled by the mass merchandisers.

During this period of rapid change, the wholesale drug industry has been of interest to the student of distribution. The apparent similarities in the requirements of food and drug distribution suggested to many that the drug distribution network would eventually undergo a similar contraction, with the eventual elimination of the wholesaler, or at least a drastic reduction of his role in the distribution process. Contrary to these expectations, the postwar period to 1960 was, for the drug wholesaler, a period of expansion and growth. The most noticeable changes were a slight broadening of the wholesaler's product line and the modernization of warehouse operations and procedures. The full-line, full-service drug wholesaler's experience through 1960 appeared to be the final verification of Edwin Lewis's claim in an earlier *Harvard Business Review* article (reference 2) on the importance of the wholesaler's role in commodity distribution.

Following the experiences of the 1950's, however, a number of changes seemed to be conspiring with the conditions that had been evolving over the early postwar years in drug distribution, with which the full-service drug wholesaler seemed unable to cope and which seemed to foretell of hard days ahead. The years 1960 to 1965 were, in fact, periods of diminished profits. The net after-tax profits for the full-service drug house dropped from a pre-1960 level of 2 to 4% of sales to 1.76% in 1960, 1.55% in 1961, 1.54% in 1962, and 1.51% in 1963. They improved only slightly in 1964 to 1.59% and in 1965 to 1.66%. (See reference 6.) Continuing difficulty seemed likely in view of the problems the industry faced. These problems were:

Changes in the Structure of the Retail Drug Market. With an increasing share of the retail drug market going to the leased departments of mass merchandisers and to chains, the independent retail druggist became more sensitive to price and more reliant on the services offered him by his wholesalers. He divided his purchases among more wholesalers, hoping to find special features of each which he could exploit.

Reduced Discounts from Manufacturers. Noting some of the profits earned by the full-service drug wholesaler during the 1950's and feeling a need to handle more of their own sales efforts, drug manufacturers in the early 1960's reduced their discounts to the drug wholesalers, in some cases to cover the costs of their own selling efforts and in other cases to put themselves in a better position to compete with the wholesaler through direct distribution to the retailers. (An interesting case study is presented in reference 9.)

Increased Costs of Distribution. During the postwar period, the costs of distribution have continued to rise. Labor costs have increased significantly, as have delivery and other costs.

Intertype Competition. In addition to the direct-selling manufacturers, others sought to serve the distribution needs of the drug market. Some distributed only the high-volume items; some sold on a "cash and carry" basis; some organized cooperative buying groups; some offered buying plans which restricted delivery service, specified minimum order quantities, and required prompt payment for goods.

Intratype Competition. As pressures on profits increased, compensation was sought through increased sales volumes. Marketing strategies based on price competition were developed to produce the additional sales volume. Pricing policies were frequently developed without an adequate understanding of distribution costs; rarely did the added volume cover the lost margin. The policy of competing distributors was frequently simply that of imitation: competition was met by adopting a similar pricing policy in overlapping territories.

A typical drug wholesaler buys from about 1000 vendors and sells to about 1000 retailers. His function is to assemble goods, break bulk, reassemble orders, and deliver the orders to the retailers on demand (Figure 6). He maintains an outside and an inside sales force, and he maintains a substantial inventory of the 20,000 or more items demanded by his retail accounts. He supplies his customers with credit and assistance in the form of store design, layout, and promotion. Because of the commodity he sells, he must deliver merchandise to the retailer within approximately two hours of order receipt, and he must accept return goods, not all of which are returnable to the vendor. He provides these services and gains his profits out of a gross margin now reduced to 17% of his selling price.

In summary, today's full-line drug wholesaler must find a way to deal with a diversified market in the face of diversified competition. He needs efficient physical distribution to lower his operating cost and to enable him to meet demand with as low an investment in inventory as possible; his marketing strategy must enable him to price his goods and extend his services to his customers in ways that bring him profitable business.

D. Inventory Management in Drug Distribution

In general, an inventory manager seeks to operate his inventory at the lowest total cost consistent with company policy on service to customers and investment in merchandise. The objective of inventory management is to provide goods, in the quantity and at the time demanded, at the least total cost of acquiring and storing these goods. To achieve these objectives, the inventory manager controls the quantities of his purchases and the timing of these purchases. In making purchasing decisions, he is guided by his understanding of the following cost considerations:

Ordering cost. The placement of a replenishment order imposes a cost on the firm; specifically, the direct marginal labor and material costs associated with the release of a purchase order and the receipt and inspection of goods. As such, the smaller the quantity in each order, the larger the number of orders and, hence, the larger the ordering cost of inventory operations.

Ownership costs. The ownership of goods imposes costs associated with the legal and physical possession of the goods, including the cost of the storage facilities, the capital costs of the resources tied up in inventory, insurance, taxes, and other costs that vary directly with the size of the inventory. The smaller the quantity in each order is, the smaller the average inventory held, and the smaller the ownership costs will be. Thus, a low ordering cost results in a high ownership cost, and vice versa.

Service costs. A reserve, or buffer, inventory must be maintained to meet unforeseeable increases in demand. While it is not possible to meet all such increases, some portion of them can be stocked for. The cost of providing such service is the ownership cost of the buffer stock. The amount of buffer stock needed depends on the degree of variability in demand for the item and the risk the firm is willing to take in running out of stock. The acceptable stock-out risk is an expression of the firm's service policy and reflects an estimate of the cost of a stock-out, i.e., the loss in profit due to failure to meet demand. Investments in safety stock are justified up to the point at which its added cost exceeds the cost of the stock-out.

Ideal inventory control maintains a level of stock of each item which minimizes the totals of inventory ownership and ordering costs, subject to the service requirements. The orders are timed a replenishment lead time in advance of stock depletion, based on an estimate of the maximum demand likely to arise over this lead time.

The possible refinements in a manual control system are limited by the ability to monitor item movement. Typically, a full-service drug house stocks over 20,000 items of pharmaceuticals, proprietaries, health and beauty aids, and, perhaps, a line of animal-care products. Retailers require rapid and complete service and will, of necessity, go to an alternative source if their regular supplier is out of stock. Historically, to provide this service, the distributor maintained close watch on stocks, reviewing his stock status frequently, watching item movement from period to period, and forecasting future demand subjectively. He usually provided for a safety stock by reordering when stock dropped to a time supply somewhat larger than the replenishment lead time. Under such control, sophisticated treatment of the aforementioned cost considerations was not possible. A compromise had to be struck between service and inventory investment, with the result that approximately $1 of inventory was required to support $5 of annual sales in response to approximately $6 of demand.

Advanced forms of inventory management systems have been applied with notable success in the distribution industries, particularly in drugs. These systems maintain stock records, monitor item usage, prepare forecasts based on usage, compute forecast error to determine safety stock, and compute the order quantity, recognizing the various forms of discount to be considered in making the purchase (quantity discount, free goods, prepaid transportation, dated payment, etc.). These functions are performed routinely with the aid of algorithms for the computational routines (order-quantity calculations, forecasts, etc.) in the form of stored programs in the computer. (See Figure 7.) In addition to properly timed replenishment orders, the output of the computer system includes exception reports to the buyers, which indicate greater-than-expected departures in item demand behavior. The computer system maintains files on stock status, current demand forecasts, order quantities, and order points (the stock level at which a replenishment order is issued).

The decision-making apparatus programmed into the computer computes order quantities by combining the following factors and data in a decision rule, which is basically of the form of the Wilson lot-size formula. (See reference 4.)

- Usage rate (annual, semiannual, or other period aggregate),
- Order cost,
- Ownership cost (storage, capital, taxes, insurance, etc.), and
- Cost of goods (including any form of applicable discount related to quantity of purchase).

In making the decision implied in the question in Figure 7, "Is now time to order?", a current order point is compared with stock status (stock on hand plus stock on order). This order point is set by combining information on

- Forecast of future demand,
- Forecast error, and
- Safety factor.

A forecast sub-routine provides the first two pieces of information; the service policy of the firm establishes the third. These forecasts and their errors can be conveniently derived by any of a variety of smoothing or averaging processes, which project past demand into the future; providing a moving average or a weighted average, such as exponential smoothing. The computation of the order point from these

Figure 7
ADVANCED INVENTORY CONTROL, LOGIC DIAGRAM

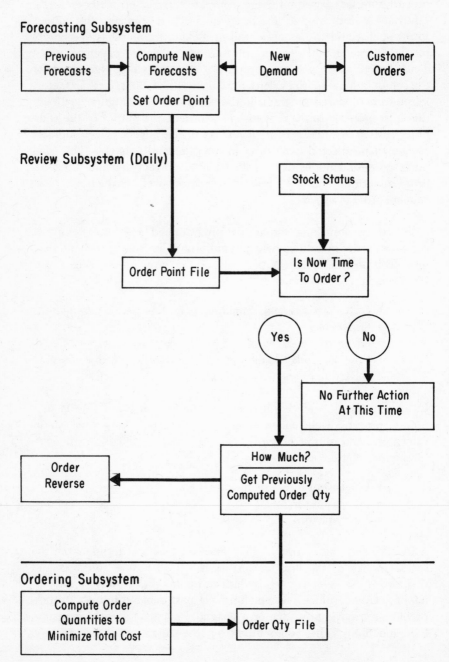

Forecasting Subsystem

| Previous Forecasts | Compute New Forecasts — Set Order Point | New Demand | Customer Orders |

Review Subsystem (Daily)

Stock Status

Order Point File

Is Now Time To Order?

Yes   No

No Further Action At This Time

How Much? — Get Previously Computed Order Qty

Order Reverse

Ordering Subsystem

Compute Order Quantities to Minimize Total Cost

Order Qty File

smoothed demand data, their error history, and the safety factor is described in reference 1.

Control systems of this form have been applied to drug distribution with great success in terms of improved utilization of inventory resources—see, for example, reference 8. With no perceptible change in ordering costs, inventory investments have been reduced by as much as 25%, and inventory service has been raised to 98-99%. Under this tighter form of control, one dollar of inventory supports $8-9 sales, with only a small portion of demand unsatisfied. The full value of such refined control in terms of long-run profitability to the drug distributor is difficult to assess or express in dollars. The retailer served by the distributor is himself in a difficult inventory situation and, therefore, prefers to deal with the supplier who can satisfy his needs most fully and most promptly. Efficient inventory operation is, therefore, also of marketing value to the distributor because it enables him to compete with the various forms of competition he faces.

E. Marketing Management in Drug Distribution

In confronting the problem of drug distribution in a diversified market, the distributor must not only buy wisely to provide a high level of inventory service with a low investment and operating cost; he must also sell wisely to continue to provide services to his customers which some of his competitors eschew in order to lower prices. Because many of these services are expensive, it is necessary for marketing management to know how the costs of distribution are generated and to develop a marketing strategy that either controls these expenditures or directs them at the customers whose trade is profitable enough to justify them.

As mentioned, the market in drug distribution is highly diversified in terms of competition and customers. One of the basic elements of this diversity is the size distribution of the retail drug firm in the United States, as illustrated in Figure 8. The total annual sales distribution of the drug retailer is shown by the straight line; the boxed points scattered about the line show the size distribution of all retail business in the United States, as indicated in the Department of Commerce Census of Business.

The variation in business volume of drug retailers is typical of all retailers. Since the volume of purchase is likely to vary in similar fashion and since the costs of distribution may be out of proportion to the volume of business done with the retailer, the profitability of the sales to that retailer may vary widely. That profitability does, in fact, vary is illustrated in Table 3, which shows the purchasing characteristics of several dozen customers, each drawn from the records of six drug wholesalers operating in various parts of the United States. Volumes of purchases, returns, credit usage, and order size varied widely, with substantial consequences for net profitability.

This variability suggests that wise selling requires a marketing strategy in the form of a price/service schedule, which provides inducements for profitable purchasing by customers. These inducements necessarily take the form of price differentials or their equivalent in services extended to the retail customer. To meet the requirements of the antitrust laws, the inducements must be cost-justifiable, i.e., based on demonstrable differences in the cost of doing business with the individual customer.

The least rational form of response to difficulties in a diversified market is a program of arbitrary price cutting, aimed at building volume in hopes of increasing profits. Price competition that does not take into account the variations in distribution costs will quite likely produce only a temporary advantage to the price cutter and will eventually reestablish a market equilibrium at lower levels of profitability. The more rational response is a marketing strategy—a schedule of prices and services for customers in the market, based on a detailed understanding of distribution costs and the customers' responses to such a marketing strategy. A marketing strategy based on functional costs and an appreciation of customer responses can move the wholesaler toward greater profit totals and higher levels of return on investment in complete conformity with the requirements of Robinson/Patman legislation.

What is required is, first of all, a functional-cost analysis—a careful analysis of the operations of the wholesaler, an identification of all his distribution costs, and an allocation of these costs to the segments of the diversified market he serves on a net-profit basis. Following this step, an examination of his market is required to determine how it will respond to possible new marketing policies and thereby generate different volume totals of distribution costs and produce different levels of profitability.

Table 3

MARKET DIVERSITY

(Results Based on 1962-1963 Operating Data for a Sample of Wholesalers)

		Wholesaler					
		I	II	III	IV	V	VI
Customer Sample Analyzed		40	45	26	25	38	21
Monthly Purchases	Low	350	100	75	956	125	190
($/month)	High	11,400	15,600	7,100	12,000	9,000	7,000
Returns (% of sales)	Low	0	0	0.15	0	0.07	0
	High	17.22	26.50	9.79	23.40	10.19	10.88
Receivables	Low	0.33	0.07	0.36	0	0.82	0.30
(in months)	High	12.58	8.91	18.30	3.94	3.60	2.97
Line Extension	Low	1.89	1.40	1.53	1.74	1.65	2.06
($/order-line)	High	10.59	28.12	15.36	9.39	20.67	7.47
Net Pretax Profit	Low	(9.39)	(35.29)	(11.11)	(1.98)	(12.93)	(14.21)
(% of sales)	High	7.34	8.65	8.48	8.95	7.51	2.30
	Average	3.99	5.06	3.46	6.48	3.23	(0.94)

Figure 8
DISTRIBUTION OF VOLUME OF ALL RETAILERS (375)

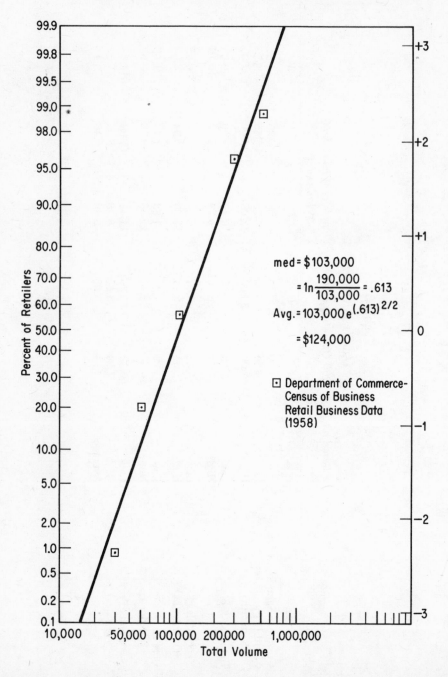

$med = \$103,000$

$= \ln\dfrac{190,000}{103,000} = .613$

$Avg. = 103,000\,e^{(.613)^2/2}$

$= \$124,000$

☐ Department of Commerce-
Census of Business
Retail Business Data
(1958)

1. FUNCTIONAL COSTING

The functional-costing process translates the natural expenses of the firm into cost rates associated with the operations of the firm. Figure 9 illustrates the means by which the natural expenses, such as rent, wages, supplies, and taxes, can be converted into the functional expenses of the firm's operation.

It is necessary first to identify the functional activities of the distribution firm: selling, warehousing, delivery, finance, credit, promotion, returns, and any other cost-generating activity in which the firm engages to serve its customers. Careful separation of the natural expenses into the functional categories is required to develop cost totals for the various functions. For example, within the totals of natural expenses, there are expenses associated with the delivery function, including wages for the transportation manager and the drivers, and the cost of gas and oil, vehicle repairs, insurance, registration, depreciation, and garage space for the vehicles. To develop a total cost for the delivery operation, these expenses must be calculated. Similar totals are developed for all the functions of the distribution firm.

The next step of the process is the conversion of the totals into cost rates which can be allocated to the individual segments of the diversified market in a manner which clearly associates a portion of the total cost with a customer's characteristic or a characteristic of the market segment being analyzed. The delivery cost, for example, would be allocated to a customer according to the number of deliveries made to the customer and the distance of the customer from the warehouse. Clearly, the cost of delivery would vary with both number of deliveries and customer distance from warehouse. Similar bases of allocation can be found for the apportionment of all other functional-cost totals to the segment of the business being analyzed.

It is emphasized that the distribution expenses being tabulated are based on a full allocation of costs, rather than on marginal costs, and that a net profit of the customer is being determined, rather than a contribution margin. Not only is such an analysis required to justify the cost of any differential pricing policy which may be instituted by the firm, but also, on an economic basis, such an analysis is required in order to formulate marketing policies which will have long-term effectiveness.

Such an analysis usually reveals some interesting facts about cus-

Figure 9

MARKETING MANAGEMENT PROCESS

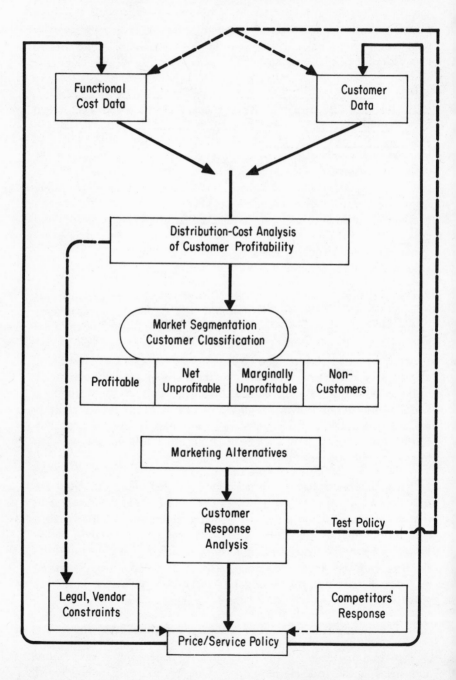

tomer profitability. Typically, the findings are similar to those illustrated in Figure 10. The profitability as a percent of monthly sales shows a marked variation with a characteristic of the customer—in this case, volume of purchases. There is a net loss of accounts of less than approximately $800 per month; above this level, percent profitability begins to improve, and it rises rapidly with increasing sales volume to a plateau of approximately 10%, a level fixed by the total variable cost of distribution in the firm. The implications of such profitability behavior with volume are immediate. In dealing with a market described by the results of Figure 10, it seems apparent that differential prices can be justified by taking account of the variation in percent profitability with sales volume. In essence, the distribution can legally

Figure 10

CUSTOMER PROFITABILITY

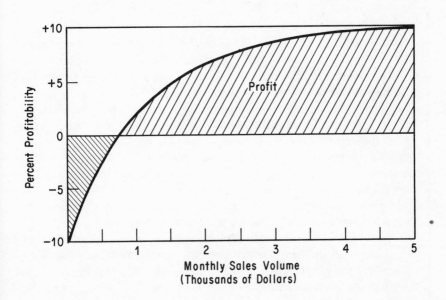

return a portion of his profit differential to his market in the form of price differential or its dollar equivalent in services. How can he do this effectively, in a way which will provide a return on his investment higher than that achieved with his present marketing policy?

2. THE MARKETING MANAGEMENT PROCESS

The real challenge for marketing management in the distribution industries is the rational development of a marketing policy which recognizes the varying levels of profitability in selling to a diverse market. The challenge is one of logically and deliberately developing a legal and effective marketing policy through the combination of the cost data obtained and the data on the distributors' market normally available to the distributor.

Every distributor who has dealt with this problem has applied, in one form or another, the logical sequence described in Figure 9. The principal weakness of approaches used in the past has been that they have been based almost completely on instinct and, in some cases, on the prevailing myths of the industry, rather than on measured cost and measured market behavior. The availability of a functional-cost analysis on the wholesaler's distribution operations makes it possible for him to proceed through this logical process in a quantitative way and to estimate the effectiveness of the new policy prior to its application. He can introduce his policy with a greater degree of assurance of its success than he could if it were an intuitively derived marketing policy.

The process shown in Figure 9 combines the functional-cost data with the customer data needed for the allocation of cost totals to individual customers. The results of such cost analyses make possible a customer classification for market segmentation, i.e., a grouping of the components of the diversified market by common characteristics. In Figure 9, for example, customers are grouped by profitability levels. Using the results of such an analysis, and considering any legal or vendor's constraints and any responses likely to be produced by the competition, the marketing manager can evaluate the various alternatives for their effects on the distributor's profit level. There is usually a variety of alternatives, some of which drastically alter the nature of the distributor's business, and others which simply put his marketing practices on a different basis. By consistently applying estimates of the changes in customer purchases, purchasing behavior, demands for service, and other cost-generating factors to a sample of customers, the manager can estimate the market's reaction to a particular strategy; and, by looping back through the previously made cost analysis with the new customer data and any new cost rates generated as a result of changes in customer behavior, the effects of this policy on the firm's profits can be determined. The policy chosen obviously will be the one believed to yield the highest long-term level of return to the distributor.

The development of a new marketing policy obviously requires the reprocessing of vast amounts of customer data. A complete profitability analysis would require the following data on individual retail customers

- Total purchases,
- Number of orders submitted,
- Number of shelf-stock and full-case order items,
- Location of customer,
- Number of deliveries,
- Method of delivery,
- Type of merchandise purchased,
- Method of payment (accounts receivable),
- Sales costs (promotional assistance), and
- Amount of returns.

These data can be collected, for the most part, from customer records maintained in the data-processing system and can be combined with the cost rates obtained from a periodic distribution costs analysis. One form of the profitability analysis in use is that shown in Figure 11.

Having segmented his market into profitability classes, the drug distributor must determine the alternative price and service schedules he could offer to his market which would produce profitable selling (see Figure 12). These are of many forms and no general prescription for a best policy can be set down; however, the policy which generally proves to be most effective is that which adjusts price through a schedule of discounts on purchases following any of the basic forms described in Figure 12. The accelerating discount rate encourages customers to concentrate their purchasing with the suppliers granting such discounts. Each distributor must consider his own special market features in establishing price and service schedules. For example, he can deal with the various classes of unprofitable customers by:

- Refusing to do business with them;
- Charging them for services;
- Increasing markup to cover their costs or to equalize profitability; or
- Granting discounts.

The various forms of discount shown in Figure 12 are based on volume of purchases made during a period; discounts can be based on any other profit-dependent variable found in the customer analysis described in Figure 9. The precise form of the strategy is a matter to be worked out by management. The important point is that the data

Figure 11

CUSTOMER PROFITABILITY—SAMPLE COMPUTER PRINTOUT

DATE 06/28/6:
NO. OF MONTHS

SALES $8,310.09

DIRECT CHARGES

COST OF GOODS		$6,815.26
TRADE DISCOUNT		20.80
PURCHASE ALLOWANCE		.00
CASH DISCOUNT		126.66
DISCOUNT CHARGEBACK		211.59CR
SERVICE FEE		.00CR
SERVICE CHARGE		1.00CR
FREIGHT OUT		.00
RETURN GOODS EXTENSION		122.26
CLAIMS EXTENSION		13.54
CASH DISCOUNT & PURCHASE ALLOWANCES	$.0220	149.94CR
RETURN GOODS AT COST VALUE	.8300	101.48CR
TOTAL DIRECT CHARGES		$6,634.51

ALLOCATED COSTS

COST PER ACCOUNT	9.96	$ 79.68
COST ON DOLLAR SALES	.0106	88.09
INVENTORY COST OF GOODS	.0251	171.06
RETURNS HANDLING COST	.0612	7.48
ACCOUNTS RECEIVABLE COST	.0700	55.98
NOTE INTEREST—GAIN OR LOSS		.00
SALESMAN CALLING COST		.00
SALESMAN TRAVEL COST		.00
ORDER HANDLING COST	0.221	35.36
CASE LINES HANDLING COST	.3873	5.81
SHELF LINES HANDLING COST	.1226	207.19
DELIVERY COST	1.155	142.07
TOTAL ALLOCATED COSTS		$ 792.72
NON-ASSIGNED COSTS	.0544	43.12

TOTAL COSTS—DIRECT CHARGES, ALLOCATED COSTS,

NON-ASSIGNED COSTS $7,470.35

NET PROFIT BEFORE TAXES 839.74

% OF NET PROFIT BEFORE TAXES 10.11%

Figure 12
BASIC FORMS OF VOLUME DISCOUNT FORMULAS

A.

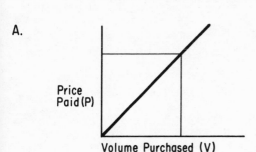

Price Paid (P)

Volume Purchased (V)

No Discount

B.

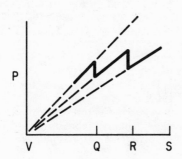

P

V   Q   R   S

Overall Rate Stepped on Volume
No discount for purchases under Q. Discount all purchases at rate r, if purchases between Q and R; at rate s, if between R and S, etc.

C.

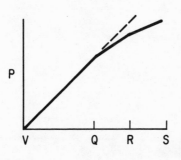

P

V   Q   R   S

Incremental Rate Stepped on Volume
As in B. except that discount applies to purchases in excess of Q and R, etc.

D.

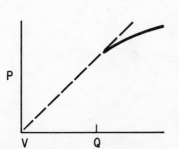

P

V   Q

Accelerating Rate
Discount rate increases as purchases increase.

processing and computational power of today's business machines provide distribution management with aids to his management decision-making responsibilities that can greatly improve the quality of this decision-making.

References

1) Brown, R. G., *Statistical Forecasting for Inventory Control.* New York: McGraw-Hill, 1959.

2) Lewis, E. H., "Comeback of the Wholesaler," *Harvard Business Review,* November/December 1955, 115-125.

3) Magee, J. F., "The Logistics of Distribution," *Harvard Business Review,* July/August 1960, 84-101.

4) Magee, J. F., and Boodman, D. M., *Production Planning and Inventory Control,* 2d. ed. New York: McGraw-Hill, 1967. Pp. 53-79.

5) Meal, H. C., "The Formulation of Distribution Policy," *Transportation and Distribution Magazine,* 1965.

6) National Wholesale Druggists' Association, *Annual Operating Survey,* 1966. 22 East 42nd St., New York City, N. Y. 10017.

7) Neuschel, R. P., "Physical Distribution—Forgotten Frontier," *Harvard Business Review,* March/April 1967, 125-134.

8) Vallario, A. A., "An Inventory Control System with Profitable By-Products," *Management Services,* January/February 1967, 31-36.

9) Warshaw, M. R., *Effective Selling through Wholesalers.* Ann Arbor: University of Michigan, 1961.

CHAPTER 10

Computer-Aided Information Systems for Accounting and Finance

Introduction / Computer Use in Custodianship of Corporate Assets / Management Reporting / Funds Management / Impact of the Computer on the Financial Manager's Role in the Organization

A. Introduction

OF ALL THE functional managers, the financial officer has been most affected by the development of the computer. Except in companies which use computers purely for scientific work, the data processing operation has traditionally gravitated to the financial manager, primarily because the original applications for most computers were in the accounting area. The financial manager controls four primary activities: accounting, custodianship of corporate assets, informing management of the financial progress of a venture, and providing funds to support operations. Each of these four tasks can be subdivided into many categories, and in each area the computer is used to a greater or lesser extent.

To understand the situation financial management faces today, we must trace the development of the computer activity to date and consider its future course, uses, and ramifications for the whole corporation.

Except for some esoteric scientific uses, the computer was originally viewed as a very fast accounting machine, suited to applications having certain characteristics. It was considered another of the progression of mechanical aids used in clerical operations—an improvement over desk calculators, electronic billing machines, punched-card (unit-record) equipment, etc. The only obvious differences between electronic

155

accounting machines and computers were their use of internal program storage rather than hand-wired program boards and, of course, their higher cost.

Because computers had much greater speed than existing equipment, accountants considered their volume applications to determine whether acquisition of a computer would be cost-effective. The evaluation criteria were generally

- *Volume*—The application must require many calculations either many records or many steps to be performed on each record,
- *Accuracy*—Answers must be precisely calculated,
- *Recurrent Processing*—The cost of programming must be amortized over many similar runs, and
- *Need for Logic*—Records must be processed in different ways. The unique capability of the digital computer is its ability to alter, internally, the program being followed. Although the internal speed of the machine was much greater than that of unit-record equipment, it might not be much faster on a particular application, since the speed on an application might be limited by the operations of the card reader and the I/O printer. However, for an application which required that records be processed in different ways, depending on factors found in the input data, great improvements were possible.

Most companies chose payroll calculation as their initial application for the computer, since it complied with each of the criteria. However, payroll applications did not require all of the computer's time, so managers sought billing or other revenue accounting applications which would justify the costs of the computer by savings in clerical costs.

As computer use increased, it was recognized that important collateral benefits were accruing: errors were reduced, enhancing employee and customer goodwill; earlier billing resulted in earlier collections; and information which it was previously impractical to collect for management was now available at negligible additional cost. Except in those few, but painful, instances where inadequate training or preparation were undertaken, the computer as an accounting tool was successful. The projected cost savings were eaten up by higher than expected costs, usually in systems design and programming, but the other benefits of the computer were considered to be worth the reduction in return on investment.

As technology progressed from cards to tape, from vacuum tubes to transistors to integrated circuits, and printing speeds increased, the time available on the machine stayed ahead of the time required for accounting applications, and the data processing manager was motivated to let other departments use the machine and share the cost. Soon the users of the marginal time began to compete with the accounting department for available machine time, creating serious organizational stresses. In such situations, whether the computer remains the province of the financial manager depends on his ability to relieve these stresses, coordinating within his department all computer activities, including those four for which he has traditionally been responsible.

1. Computer Use in Accounting

The range of accounting tasks which have been computerized is tremendous. Almost every company with a computer uses it for payroll and billing; from that point computer use branches out to cover other areas of interest to the managers of the individual corporations. A review of literature and company practices indicates that the following are the most common accounting applications

- Payroll and labor distribution,
- Billing,
- Finished-goods inventory accounting,
- Accounts-receivable ledger maintenance,
- Accounts-payable vouchers,
- Accounts-payable ledger maintenance,
- Check reconciliation,
- Fixed-asset catalogs,
- Work-in-process cost recording, and
- Operating-expense recording.

As the list indicates, almost all clerical tasks have been programmed; the difficult problem is to decide what applications should be automated, what benefits are available, what problems occur, and what costs are incurred. Although we cannot answer these questions specifically, we can point out conditions which may help individual managers decide what computer applications they should develop.

Economy. When a large volume of records must be processed, each involving complex calculations, computer use cuts clerical costs considerably. Payroll, mailing-label printing for a mass marketer, and billing for a public utility or an insurance company are examples.

Error Reduction. Once a clean master file is available and a program has been debugged, a computer is much more accurate than manual methods. Maintenance of accounts receivable ledgers or demand deposit accounting in a bank are good examples.

Improvements in Response Time. In the absence of cost savings, many applications have been justified on the grounds of improved response time. Typical examples are real-time access to customer complaint status for a public utility (to avoid sending two crews to correct one fault when two calls are received), or daily posting of accounts-receivable information in companies dealing with the public.

Improving Management Information. It is certainly of benefit to a corporation to be able to present management with key facts, accurately and quickly. However, to be of value, the data presented must, at least potentially, affect decisions. We suspect that many of the applications justified on this basis actually impede corporate progress by creating "information overload."

2. PROGRAMMING OF THE ENTIRE ACCOUNTING PROCESS

Since almost all the active accounts have been computerized, the question naturally arises: Why not program the whole accounting process? A few companies have been heading in this direction, but we know of no company which has computerized the entire journal-ledger-statement cycle. There are two major reasons why such a program has not been undertaken.

First, the time since technology has made such a goal feasible has been too short to do all the work required. Many companies want to have the entire accounting process machine-maintained and are working toward that goal.

Second, the present system of double-entry bookkeeping was designed for people, not computers. Bookkeeping, as we now know it, is a batch process for collecting historical information. To eliminate errors in the posting and footing of ledgers in manual systems, an "audit trail" of documents must appear before and after each operation. The accounting system designed by a systems analyst for the computer alone, on the other hand, works in real time, features terminals, disc storage, and displays rather than written records, and traces sources and applications of resources rather than traditional accounts. Such a system is confusing to auditors, interesting to the manager who previously waited several weeks for key information from the manual system, and no doubt efficient for the machine.

In deciding to program the entire accounting function, the financial manager must consider other factors than the opportunity for economy, reduction of error, and improvement in response time offered by specific applications. Several of the questions which must be answered by the financial manager before such a decision is made are considered below.

(1) *What is the value of real-time information in my business?* It is apparent that the value of real-time presentation varies from industry to industry, as well as from account to account within a firm. For example, the value of knowing, in real time, the cost of fixed assets employed in a textile mill is considerably less than that of being able to determine, if you are a record manufacturer, whether the latest hit record is in inventory.

(2) *Do I have the authority and/or power to consolidate all corporate information in my department?* A total system requires a knowledge of everything which relates to resource strengths and their costs. If this condition is achieved, such information is always current and addressable in the system, and any systems or files in other departments are redundant.

(3) *Can the system be audited, or, more important, can I, as financial manager, vouch for the accuracy of the income statement and balance sheet produced by the system?* If transactions are entered to the books of account directly at their source, can errors or fraud be prevented; is it possible to trace balances in accounts to their source in order to check accuracy and authorization?

Auditing of computer operations today is generally done in one of two ways: tracing transactions from input through audit-trail documents to the ledger and statement (or the reverse), or putting a "test deck" problem through the program. Either way, the computer is treated as a "black box." In real-time systems it is infeasible to leave an audit trail of printed documents; the sorting and printing requirements would be prohibitive. Likewise, it would be virtually impossible to create a "test deck" which would test all possible conditions in the system.

The only feasible audit program is to understand the internal workings of the program, to control strictly program changes, and to ensure through console logs that only authorized programs are run, that mass storage and memory alterations are controlled and approved and that transactions are authorized and accurate. In short, except for machine failure, which can be detected and handled, proper input will yield accurate statements. In accordance with the well-known GIGO theory (garbage-in, garbage-out), the place to catch errors is at their source. The systems in existence expend a great deal of effort in checking, screening, and editing input precisely for this purpose.

(4) *How can a system recover from failure?* Machine failures resulting in undetected errors are rare and will become even rarer; but shutdowns will occur, as a result of component wear, external power failure, operator error, etc. Therefore, a manager must have a means of recreating the data in storage if we are to trust the system. The most feasible way is to copy the contents of all files on tape at some periodic point, for example at a specific time each day when transaction volume is zero or minimal. During the day each transaction will likewise be recorded-unsorted as it arrives, making it possible to re-create the files after any malfunction or error as long as the tapes are kept.

(5) *How adaptable to change will the system be?* No matter how carefully a system is designed, it will have to adapt to almost constant change and to periodic revolution. In the accounting area, change is an ever-present factor; as the business develops, new transactions require special treatment. Even a simple payroll program changes substantially when, for example, federal income tax withholding changes from a fixed to a progressive percentage of gross pay less exemptions, or when a new deduction for union dues, community fund, Blue Cross, or group insurance is authorized.

The agent of periodic revolution is technology. To date, three generations of computers have been developed. With each successive generation, the manager has had to decide whether to install the equipment or to continue with his present system. From the functional viewpoint of many financial managers, retaining present equipment is probably the lowest cost course of action, but other factors must be considered.

In many business applications, the opportunity for increased processing speeds does not justify expenditures on new equipment, because the operations are limited by the capacity of the input or output units (I/O bound), particularly for tape sorting (a major element of accounting applications); but, the old system may be loaded to, or near, capacity, and the decision to change may be forced by the "need" to put more accounting applications on the machine. (Parkinson's Law definitely applies to computers and can be restated to: "Applications increase to fill the capacity of the most capable machine available in the generally suitable price category.")

The manager also realizes that, unless past programs have been written in COBOL or similar language, a long and costly reprogramming effort will be required to adapt existing programs to the new system. Emulators can alleviate the problem somewhat by making it possible to use the new machine during the conversion process, though inefficiently. Eventually, each program has to be recoded, debugged, and tested. Use of COBOL eliminates major reprogramming (versions for each machine are slightly different, so changes of differing degrees of complexity are required), but it may be considerably less efficient than a well-written program, coded in machine or assembler language.

In short, change is possible; it is frustrating and costly; and it is continual. To date, machines have not been used for the life originally forecast; therefore, system introduction costs, which are usually treated as nonrecurring costs, actually do recur with painful frequency and, therefore, should be considered in systems planning.

(6) *Can complete automation of accounting applications be cost-justified?* American industry has judged overwhelmingly that computers are worth the cost, but few companies have saved money by using them. This paradox is particularly acute to the accounting manager. By automating billing and payroll, he eliminates clerks, but must replace at least half of them with machine operators, input control clerks, keypunchers, systems analysts, and programmers. The computer is a "factory with a very high capital investment in fixed costs and very low variable costs. As a result, its economics are based on maximum productivity" (F. Wallace, *Appraising the Economics of Computers*, Controllership Foundation, 1956).

Obviously, programming the entire accounting process increases productivity. Still, the cost savings earned by accounting uses of the computer alone do not often justify the computer cost (exceptions may be banks', insurance companies', and utilities' use of computers for statementing and billing), and the pressure to spread costs over as many hours of utilization as possible has led to the use of computers for other than basic accounting functions and has placed the financial manager in his new critical role in the corporate organization.

B. Computer Use in Custodianship of Corporate Assets

The computer is often not a cost-effective means of maintaining custodial records; however, much custodial record keeping is done as a by-product of other, more significant accounting tasks. Conventional manual ledgers for items, such as investments, insurance policies, and intangibles, are easily and inexpensively maintained. For volume records, such as fixed assets, where there are relatively few transactions, unit-record equipment is generally adequate, even for the largest companies, although there are successful applications of computers in these tasks. Only in the area of inventory accounting might a computer be useful, and then only when the volume of transactions is sufficient to outrun the capabilities of card-handling equipment.

C. Management Reporting

In modern business, one of the major duties of financial management is to provide all levels of line and staff management with the financial information needed to carry out their assignments. The financial manager must classify, analyze, and present the information in its most useful form. The computer can aid the financial manager in this function by drastically reducing the time required to perform special studies; however, in many companies, the requests for information have mushroomed out of control.

The types of financial reports prepared can be divided into four categories: formal financial statements, budget reports, periodic statistical analyses, and special studies.

1. FORMAL FINANCIAL STATEMENTS

While the computer can be used to produce required financial statements, such applications are not particularly appropriate since they use the computer only as a report generator, a task done less expensively by unit-record equipment.

The computer may be essential to maintain the detail of some general ledger, but final ledger balances require a large number of adjustments and closing entries. Some entries are identical or similar each period; others are individually computed for the particular set of reports. The need for manual adjustments (for taxes, deferrals, etc.) defeats the purposes of the computer.

2. Budgeting

The time delay inherent in periodic computation of variable budgets was a significant factor in inhibiting adoption of this useful technique— by the time the budgets and variance were calculated manually, it was too late to take meaningful action. The computer has proved valuable in this area because it can store historical statistics and cost-volume relationships and can compute the budget figures, as well as interperiod comparisons, as soon as volume figures are available.

3. Periodic Statistical Analyses

Many routine analyses which provide the information base for management decision-making are now available as by-products of the accounting process. In fact, a manager now has difficulty reading all the available information. He is provided with analyses of sales by product, branch, or salesman; inventory status by plant and/or product; payroll distribution for service organizations; accounts receivable agings; and product costs.

Financial managers have failed to be very helpful in the area of data management for executives. Today's computers can generate enough useful information to clog completely the decision-making channels. The task of the financial manager is to evaluate the information and forward to a manager only the key information on which he can act. For example, once a budget is accepted, it makes little sense to report actual costs which are within the predefined limits of budget. Similarly, transmitting detailed operating statements to other than operations managers is unnecessary—summary reports suffice.

The computer, with its capabilities to sort and perform logical operations, can solve the data management problem it created. However, much study is required to determine just what information a manager needs to perform his function properly. Two factors must be considered in designing a periodic management reporting system

- Each manager should be provided the information he thinks he needs; but
- Without uniformity and reasonable provisions against constant change, management reporting by the computer cannot be economical.

These two factors must be reconciled before management reporting can be efficient and economic. In addition, the person in the organization who will decide which requests for information are valid must be specified.

4. SPECIAL STUDIES

The financial manager is responsible for the preparation of numerous special studies which measure the impact on profits of price changes, capital investments, new products, plant location, alternative tax treatments, etc. In many companies, more sophisticated techniques are now being used to prepare these studies. Some of the techniques (e.g., present value) are not closely related to the computer; others (e.g., simulation, linear programming, and queuing) are closely related to the growth in computer use. The latter techniques are not new; the computer has merely made feasible the time required to apply them to solve problems. The impetus for using such modern tools has generally come not from the upper levels of management but from middle- or lower-management levels which understand the techniques and their potential ramifications for the future.

The financial manager must be aware of the various mathematical tools available to solve practical problems so that he can be reasonably sure his staff has applied the best tools to the problem at hand. The characteristics of a particular study will determine whether computerization can be justified in terms of cost. In three situations, in particular, computerization has generally proven valuable

- When a generalized program can be used repetitively to solve similar problems; examples are a capital expenditure evaluation routine and a corporate financial simulation for forecasting or planning,
- When the decision involves a sizable expenditure and the

particular problem cannot be solved accurately without using techniques which require a computer (e.g., linear programming), and

- When the decision involves a sizable expenditure and some key parameters are highly uncertain, a computer model can be run repetitively to determine the sensitivity of one value (e.g., return on investment) to various assumed values of some input parameters.

D. Funds Management

Two of the primary tasks of the financial manager are to provide the funds necessary to accomplish corporate objectives and to invest wisely any excess funds which are generated. The bases of fund management are the long- and short-range cash forecasts, which are closely tied to the budgeting and management reporting systems discussed above. It is surprising that many companies which use computers for the budgeting and reporting functions do not extend the system to cash forecasting, a seemingly logical extension. In fact, of all the areas of the corporation, the treasurer's office seems to be the one least affected by the computer.

Because the basic requirements of funds management are known and the attractiveness of various financial instruments changes rapidly, the computer could be of substantial aid to the corporate treasurer. For example, the computer could match investible cash against returns available from treasury stock purchases, time deposits, cash orders, government bills, notes and bonds, etc. Similarly, if a cash shortage is indicated, the ramifications of common or preferred stock, short- or long-term debt, or lease financing could be evaluated.

E. Impact of the Computer on the Financial Manager's Role in the Organization

Over the past two decades, the financial executive has won an important voice in the councils of management because he has been uniquely able to cope with the increasingly complex nature of modern business. Because the information-processing activity has been centralized in his department, he has been able to provide management with the abstract information needed to replace personal observation of the factory, which is no longer possible in the modern multiplant, multimarket corporation. Whether the centralization of information will lead to centralized management and decision making is not clear. It is clear, however, that traditional functional management distinctions tend to blur as the computer centralizes information and that one begins to view management functions in terms of managing and controlling the following classes of resources

- Supplies,
- Material inventories,
- Employees,
- Plant and equipment,
- Work-in-process inventory,
- Finished-goods inventory,
- Customers, and
- New product development.

As the computer becomes inevitably more central to the management process, the role of the financial manager will change. If the computer function is established independently, the importance of the financial function probably will return to the historical bookkeeping role, the computer executive taking over the management reporting and economic studies functions, which are the keys to the financial manager's status.

The financial manager's efficient use of the computer will determine whether the computer function remains his responsibility. If he fails to develop the computer function to serve well all functional areas of the organization, does not develop all possible ways to use the computer and the techniques closely associated with it (in a broad sense, operations research), an autonomous computer organization probably will evolve.

Taking advantage of the computer's capabilities will be difficult for today's managers, since the computer introduces many alien concepts and requires the development and coordination of skills which the financial man has not been trained to understand, much less appreciate. As the applications of other departments become equal in importance to financial work, unless good service is available, in terms of systems analysis, programming and operations, there will be pressures to establish an independent data processing department or to develop departmental capabilities, a potentially inefficient and costly undertaking. The reaction of the financial manager to the challenge posed by the computer will determine whether the corporate planning and development activities do, in fact, develop within his department.

CHAPTER 11

Manpower Information Systems

*Introduction / Functions of Manpower Management /
Functions for the Manpower Information System /
Benefits and Costs of Manpower Information
Systems / Development of Manpower Information
Systems / A Suggested System Architecture*

A. Introduction

ANY PORTION of the keeping of records or the general flow of information in a business organization which is about individual employees can be considered to be an information element in a manpower information system. The system may extend to include people in the labor market from whom employees may be drawn, or people who have left the company's employ. Under special circumstances it may include still other people. Examples of manpower information systems are a company's information about employees, a professional organization's information about its members, a school's information about its students as well as its information about its staff, a physician's information about his patients, and a motor vehicle licensing agency's information about license holders. The functions to be performed with the aid of these several manpower information systems are somewhat different from each other. This discussion will consider the functions to be performed by a manpower information system maintained by an employer, although some of our discussion will apply to other types of manpower information systems too.

The manpower information system relates to other information systems in a company. It relates to the financial information system in many payroll and salary administration functions. It relates to the manufacturing system as the work time by individuals is being related to a project or a product batch or a departmental payroll. The manpower information system relates to the sales information as each sales-

167

man's name is associated with a sales order or as a group of salesmen are associated with a sales experience in a territory. The manpower information system is used to produce reports to local, state and federal governments as well as to make reports to stockholders and sometimes customers. The data in the manpower information system may also be related to a variety of other information systems maintained by the company about its internal operations and about its markets and other environments.

B. Functions of Manpower Management

The manpower information system should be designed to support the functions of manpower management. As a practical matter, it probably is designed to satisfy the people who have responsibilities of varying kinds for manpower management.

Major functions of manpower management and the common activities in support of those functions are related to each other in Table 4. Seven major functions are shown in the table and described in greater detail in the following paragraphs.

1. *Organize human effort in a way which is economically and socially useful.* The purpose of a business organization and of many kinds of organizations is to organize the effort of people so that the effects of their efforts are useful. In performing this function the work of the organization is divided into departments and ultimately into jobs and positions. This organization is influenced by the work functions to be performed, by machinery and other aids to performing the work, by human skills and their limits, and by human preferences and tradition.

2. *Prepare and maintain a climate in which company and individual goals can be developed and resolved.* Company work objectives and individual developmental and career objectives need to fit with each other in order to achieve both the organization's goals and the individual's goals. Since the objectives for each are subject to frequent changes, the processes by which individual and company goals are arranged to complement each other must function continuously.

3. *Stimulate growth in corporate and individual capabilities.* Many companies, though not all, wish to grow in the markets which they serve, or develop new products and markets in order to grow. The

Table 4

Relationships Between Major Functions and Activities in Manpower Management

Major Functions / *Activities*

Major Functions	Organize work & design jobs	Do individual & team training	Administer projects & other work	Recruit, select, assign, transfer, terminate	Survey salaries, benefit plans, etc.	Budget & administer wages & salaries	Budget & administer benefit plans	Do payroll	Prepare job performance descriptions & conduct reviews	Sense absences, grievances, turnover, & other indicators of morale	Conduct labor negotiations	Conduct medical & safety work	Do research
1. Organize human effort in a way which is economically and socially useful.	X		X	X		X							X
2. Prepare and maintain a climate in which company goals and individual goals can be developed and resolved.		X				X	X	X	X		X	X	X
3. Stimulate growth in corporate and individual capabilities.	X	X		X									X
4. Anticipate and meet company needs for personnel.	X		X	X	X	X	X		X	X			X
5. Detect, diagnose, and remedy personnel problems.	X	X			X	X			X	X	X	X	X
6. Satisfy responsibilities for reporting to employees, government, stockholders, and other groups.						X	X	X			X		X
7. Improve manpower management.	X				X					X			X

An X indicates that the activity represented by the column heading usually is conducted to support the major function of manpower management represented by the row heading. The absence of an X indicates the activity usually has little relationship to the major function.

company's requirements for skills will change as growth occurs. Opportunities for individuals within the company are generated as the company grows, and the individual whose skills and experience have been developed to assume new functions and responsibilities can realize some of his own goals as the company experiences change. The company can identify its own needs for the future and help individuals identify their capabilities and opportunities for growth.

4. *Anticipate and meet company needs for personnel.* Company needs to acquire skills in short supply and reduce or modify skills in excess supply require periodic examination on a current, near-future and long-range-future basis.

5. *Detect, diagnose, and remedy personnel problems.* Sensing personnel problems, determining their causes, and inventing both short and long-range solutions to the problems is one of the functions of manpower management.

6. *Satisfy responsibilities for reporting to employees, government, stockholders, and other groups.* A variety of reporting to government and to other groups is required by law. A company usually chooses to make other kinds of public reports in addition to those required by law, and it generates many reports for a variety of uses by its own employees.

7. *Improve manpower management.* Manpower management usually is improved in a company through its own research and development activities in these areas, through the education of its management on topics of manpower management, through the importation of new personnel to important roles in manpower management, and through periodic reviews of its manpower management processes.

A variety of activities is undertaken by a company in support of these major functions in manpower management. Table 4 describes how these activities typically are related to the major functions. The description of major functions and activities provides an overview of manpower management. The description is not intended to imply that all of these functions and activities are conducted by the personnel department. Instead, they typically are shared responsibilities among many jobs and roles in a company. Clearly members of management throughout the company have important responsibilities for these major functions.

C. Functions for the Manpower Information System

The manpower information system should be designed and operated to support the manpower management functions. In supporting those functions the manpower information system will capture information, transmit it, store it, transform it into appropriate summaries or patterns, and display it for human use. These functions of the information system are common to the functions of all information systems. Yet the information captured, the distribution of that information to various files, the organization of the files, the methods for summarizing or patterning the data, and the ultimate display of the information are all affected by the manpower management functions.

Data capture for the manpower information system, like other information systems, is adapted to both the kind of information being captured and to the events which produce changes in information or occasions for data capture. The completion of a batch of items in the job shop is an occasion for capturing information about the increase in finished inventory as well as information about the work done by a particular machine operator. The occasion for a change in salary is the time to capture information which will both update the employee's salary record and change his department's monthly payroll commitment. The event of an absence from work is an occasion to update the individual's absence record and to assign that cost to an overhead account for absence instead of the project accounts on which the individual normally works. The event of any employment application is the occasion for capturing a variety of information about the applicant which, in the event he becomes an employee, is transferred to employee records. This may include home address and telephone number as well as educational background, prior employment experience, and a variety of other information. The occasion is the primary influence upon the information elements to be captured and upon the method used to capture the information.

Information distribution is primarily determined by the content of the information. A mailing address for an employee may be available because he just became an employee, because he moved his residence, or because the street on which he lives has been renamed. Regardless of the occasion for the change, the distribution of the mailing address in the manpower information system is controlled by the content of the information. New home mailing addresses must be available for specified uses, and the distribution of the information is controlled in accordance with the new information content so that information of that type is available for all of its uses.

Data storage in manpower information systems is affected both by costs and by actual and potential uses for the data. Storage and retrieval costs increase as the size of the files increases. The usefulness of the files and the reports generated from it probably increase as the size of the files increases. The presence of the computer in manpower information systems, as in other kinds of management information systems, focuses attention on the costs and sometimes on the benefits of the files and the reports generated from them in the manpower information system. Questions about storage and retrieval costs usually are solved by the process of discussion and review of the problem within the company. Little serious and sophisticated effort has been focused upon the difficult cost-benefit questions highlighted by the issues of file content and size for the manpower information system. Most resolutions of this problem in our experience have been in favor of short, relatively simple files which support current operating functions in manpower management but give little support to long-range planning or even to the daily operating functions which require sophistication beyond the simplest of clerical functions.

Data transformation and display usually involve the selection of some sub-population of employees from the master file and then may require anything from the simple display of information about individual employees to moderately complex summaries of information. Often codes used to minimize the data storage requirements need to be transformed into words and symbols which are meaningful to the reader of the report. Data stored in machine-readable form invariably must be re-formatted before it can be read by the human user. Typically, computerized manpower information systems have been implemented by writing separate computer programs or separate legs in a periodic computer program which are dedicated to the preparation of "a report." These computer programs perform the retrieval, decoding, re-formatting, and eventual display functions. While we know of instances in which computerized manpower information systems have been conceived, in which these functions are identified, we have seen no instance in which the general flexibility of this approach to manpower information system design has been achieved with a computerized system. Flexibility in re-formatting data from the files has been a feature of clerical manpower information systems as long as they have existed, although the cost of retrieving and processing information from the paper files usually has prevented any significant and frequent use of this feature of the clerical systems. The flexibility of generalized retrieval, transformation, and formatting or display programs allows the manager with problem-solving responsibilities to conceive of special reports which would assist him in his problem definition and solution and cause these reports to be generated. The very flexibility of the manpower information system may contribute to the flexibility of manpower management.

D. Benefits and Costs of Manpower Information Systems

Benefits and costs of manpower information systems are largely unknown. As a consequence, the existence of manpower information systems is founded primarily upon preparing the payroll, preparing reports required by law, administering the rules associated with personnel policies, doing things that are associated with some mystique like "tradition" or "being new," and the influence of the people who have keen interest in and management responsibility for manpower management. The principal boundaries limiting the size and nature of present-day manpower information systems are legal requirements, operating needs, tradition, and managements' judgments about what is feasible and desirable.

With the advent of computers in the last ten years, changes in manpower information systems have been examined for the effects they may have in reducing the clerical work required to operate the systems. Participants in this form of assessing the benefits of *changes* in the manpower information system usually have understood that there were "intangible" effects realized with a computerized information system. This meant that the justification for changing the system was larger than could be estimated only by considering the clerical work which could be eliminated or the growth in the amount of clerical work which could be stemmed. In organizations where manpower management receives only modest attention and where manpower information systems are simple, there is little clerical work from which savings can be realized and, therefore, little incentive to change the manpower information system based upon this estimate of the benefits.

Occasionally, a manpower information system will be developed by surveying the needs for manpower information within the company and the requirements for information outside the company. This approach to information systems development acknowledges the requirement that the system serve its users. The approach may or may not assist the company in accomplishing actual changes in its information system, depending upon the way in which the survey is conducted and the participants and amount of involvement of members in the company in the survey. The approach is criticized because it is reputed to develop unbridled expressions of needs for information. The criticism probably is justified since little has been done to relate the characteristics of manpower information systems to the company's manpower management performance or its total performance.

Other approaches to justifying changes in the manpower information system and in manpower management processes have been tried. The cost of finding, selecting, and hiring an employee sometimes is estimated to form a guideline by which development costs and operating costs for new recruiting and selection processes can be gauged. These kinds of changes usually require changes in the manpower information system as well as in other aspects of manpower management. The cost of waste or of low quality products sometimes is estimated to provide the guidelines for judging the appropriateness of development and program costs for training aimed at reducing waste or defective products. Evaluation of such a program may include changes in the manpower information system as well as in the production and quality control information available to the company. In these occasional attempts to assess benefits and costs for changes in manpower management processes or the manpower information system, the justification usually examines incremental costs and incremental benefits. We estimate the use of this approach to justifying changes in the manpower information system to be rare.

It seems likely that the most useful estimates of benefits from changes in manpower information systems, or from other changes in manpower management processes, are likely to be derived from basic statements of the objectives of manpower management which are then expressed in some quantifiable measures of how well the objectives are being met. In an important way, this situation seems circular. The benefits of an effective manpower information system can only be assessed when an effective manpower information system is in operation. Although this is true, the self-sustaining nature of this circular relationship can be entered to get it started. It requires some initial formulation of the objectives of manpower management in terms which are compatible with and supportive of the other economic and social objectives of business enterprise. Then, rough measures of the effectiveness with which these objectives are being met can be constructed. The first construction of these measures needs to be inexpensive. The measures need to be only sensitive enough to detect changes in the effectiveness of manpower management. Given basic tools of this kind, changes in manpower management including changes in manpower information systems can be introduced on an experimental basis to determine their effects.

Some improvements in the manpower information system are likely to lead to improved effectiveness of manpower management, and in this way the circular and self-correcting relationship between measures of manpower management effectiveness and the introduction of changes in manpower management—including changes in the information system—can be energized. It will continue to be important that the change-and-measure loop be entered by management judgments reached through their humanistic sense of the course of their business enterprise and through their exposure to problems and successes in other companies.

In effect, the measures of manpower management effectiveness cannot be taken as complete and perfect at any time so that the loop by which manpower management is improved becomes a closed loop dependent upon the comprehensiveness of the measures of effectiveness. The process by which manpower information systems are improved is an iterative, step-by-step sequence of changes which represent an information-influenced, dynamically changing manpower management portion of the total management activities.

Since our notions of the way in which benefits from improved manpower information systems can be determined requires that measures of the effectiveness of manpower management be available, it seems appropriate to suggest in broad outline several objectives of manpower management which need to be translated into methods for measuring effectiveness in each organizational environment.

1. *The productivity of the business enterprise in its single or several activities needs to increase over time, both with respect to its own past performance and with respect to its competitors' performance.* Some will argue that productivity is a function of many corporate actions other than manpower management activity, and that is true. Yet, other actions by a company are the consequence of actions and choices by management and employees of that company. In some sense, all company actions over time reflect the company's capability for developing its leadership and other human resources to achieve those actions.

2. *The capability of the company to adopt new enterprises and*

phase out old enterprises needs to be demonstrated. This adaptation is related to the long-term survival capabilities of the organization and is closely related to the way in which its own human resources are developed and utilized.

3. *The skills of individuals, and the skills of groups of people within the company, need to be fully utilized.* One indication of the success with which this objective is achieved is reports from individuals that their work is interesting to them and that they feel challenged to do a good job. Another indication that the skills of a group of people are being effectively utilized is that individuals in the group report their own work to be supported and improved by the work of other individuals in the group and that their working relationships as a group with other groups inside or outside the company are effective working relationships.

4. *Individual skills should change significantly in a one- to three-year time frame in the direction of acquisition of new skills and capabilities.* Information about changes in individual skills can come from the individual himself and from people who are working closely with him in the job setting.

5. *The "waste" or "damage" rates should be low.* Indices of industrial safety and workmen's compensation rates are two examples of common indicators of effectiveness in this objective of manpower management. These indicators are relatively limited in their meaning, however. Terminations in employment which occur so that the terminee's needs for, and expectations of, new employment are not met is an instance of "waste" which needs to be reflected in an indicator. Instances of mental and social ill health such as mental illness, divorce, convictions for crime, and other indications in the employee and in employee family populations are potential indicators. Employment terminations for all causes can be actuarially adjusted to provide an indicator. While employers obviously are not directly responsible for many of these events, the employment environment needs to be managed so that it makes minimum contribution to these events.

Admittedly, these objectives are difficult to define and measure. In spite of the difficulty, it is clear that an organization can develop approximate measures of effectiveness in achieving these objectives. Experience suggests that the wisest strategy is to develop several indicators of the achievements of each objective. This will result in conflicting signals from different indicators, one indicator saying that things are improving while another says that things are getting worse. While this may be confusing for inexperienced management, it avoids the risks and errors involved in using a single indicator of performance effectiveness. By analogy, the knowledgeable motorist probably is more comfortable with ammeter, water temperature gauge, oil pressure gauge, and fuel gauge as indicators of the near-term future performance of his automobile than he would be if he had only one of these indicators, such as the water temperature gauge alone.

Mechanization of manpower information systems has seen steady progress during the last decade. It is likely that increased mechanization will occur without understanding in greater depth either the benefits or the costs of manpower information systems. While additional reduction of the cost of computing undoubtedly will increase the mechanization of manpower information systems, along with the mechanization of other kinds of management information systems, a significant change in the rate at which manpower information systems are being mechanized could occur if the benefits and costs were better understood. In our judgment, the payment from well designed manpower information systems is much larger than has been commonly understood to the present time. The payout can be achieved only through improvements in data capture methods and in concepts forming the basis for the content and display of information for the user at the same time that the information transmission, storage, retrieval, and re-formatting capabilities are being improved. Improvements throughout the system may seem like a difficult requirement, and they are in the sense that the development costs are likely to be high. Nevertheless, the technical feasibility of all portions of these improvements has already been demonstrated.

E. Development of Manpower Information Systems

Manpower information systems exist and are in operation today. The manpower information systems we see for the future and regard as feasible in terms of today's technology are vastly different from the manpower information systems now in existence. By what routes will the systems in existence today evolve to the systems which can be foreseen and which probably have favorable benefits/cost ratios?

There are some conditions which affect the development rate, and we would like to speculate about what those conditions are. We are convinced that the development will be evolutionary, although the evolution may occur through any one of several strategies. One of the most important conditions for making each evolutionary step will be sponsorship of its development. Since development may be expensive in many instances, the methods for assembling sponsorship may be critically important in manpower information systems development. We would like to describe some potential solutions to the problem of adequate sponsorship for systems development. Considerations affecting the implementation of systems changes in general are discussed at greater length in Chapter 7.

There are a variety of conditions which will aid the development of manpower information systems. Certain conditions may be necessary for their development.

a. *Output from the system should receive wide use.* This idea suggests that at least some of the outputs of the manpower information system be of wide interest and receive wide distribution.

b. *Individuals about whom information is stored should receive information feedback from the manpower information system.* The simplest feedback is a display to the individual of his own record. A more meaningful feedback would include information about how his record is being used. For example, if employees knew that their record was being retrieved for detailed examination in searches for people to fill new job assignments it is likely that their attitudes and effort in maintaining the record will be more responsible than if they have no information about its use.

c. *There should be appropriate controls over access to the records and use of the records.* Information being collected so that the name of the source of the information is not known to the consumer of the information should be clearly labeled as being collected under these conditions. Employees need to know how agreements of this kind will be administered so that they may assess for themselves the risks of misuse of the information and guide their answers appropriately.

d. *Objectives for the manpower information system, and perhaps benefit/cost ratios, should be developed.* Lacking these, system development can occur which will be judged after the fact to have been misdirected effort.

e. *The design of the manpower information system should allow significant changes in the content and variety of the input and con-*

siderable flexibility in the types of output. Users generally are not acquainted with the uses of manpower information and their exposure to it will result in changing needs. It will be essential that the system be easily adapted to the new requirements.

f. _The sponsorship for the development of manpower information systems should be shared_. It is likely that the cost of adequate system development will be high with comprehensive systems requiring several million dollars for their design, development, testing, and training for first use. It is true that some portions of a comprehensive manpower information system can be developed and put to use for budgets in the range of $30,000 to $300,000. Many of the systems now in existence have grown with sponsorship at this level. The resulting systems have been limited in their capabilities although they may perform specialized functions very well. They have been proprietary in the narrowest sense of that term, requiring even non-competing organizations to duplicate the development investment in order to achieve a similar capability. The need for sponsorship strategies in addition to the self-help ("We will develop our own manpower information system for our own use") strategy seems apparent.

Sponsorship for the development of manpower information systems can be achieved in several ways. They are:

1. Own use—proprietary
2. Shared use—proprietary
3. Public use—voluntary
4. Public use—required

Manpower information systems are developing under each of these strategies, particularly under the first, third, and fourth. Manpower information systems in use today have largely been developed by the organization which uses it, whether the system is predominantly clerical or predominantly mechanized or a mix of both methods. Government, particularly the Federal government, has sponsored the development of portions of manpower information systems which are available for voluntary use or may be required. Tests of human abilities for use in the selection of new personnel and their placement in jobs they can perform well has been undertaken and maintained by the Federal government for use in employment services offered through state governments. The employer may or may not use the information resulting from these data capture methods. On the other hand, Federal income tax reporting and tax withholding for individuals is required by the Federal government for all except the smallest employers. This reporting is done by social security number. It seems likely that all of these means for sponsoring manpower information system development will continue to be used in the future.

Since development costs for comprehensive, mechanized manpower information systems are high and will continue to grow, it seems to us that the joint development of a proprietary system for shared use by the developers, or for sale to new users, is a means for development which can and should receive greater attention. Systems developed under multiple sponsorship must necessarily meet the different operating requirements of the several sponsors. This requires that generalized, flexible basic systems be developed. If several such shared system development efforts were undertaken, it seems to us that companies and other organizations could avoid the risks and illegalities of joint efforts with competing organizations and that, in the long range, our economy would benefit from the competitive development of several systems.

Under any sponsorship, there are several strategies which can be chosen for manpower information system development. It is our view that system development must be evolutionary. Improvements made today will be replaced by further improvements at some time in the future, probably in the relatively near future. It seems very unlikely that any single, ultimate design for a manpower information system exists or that the several good designs can be conceived in their major outlines, not to mention their detail, at the present time. Thus, the strategic choice of how large a step forward to take at any one time is a choice between small steps and moderate steps. A change to the "ultimate" solution is not possible. We feel it is important that running sub-systems be available for use within time spans acceptable to the sponsors. A great deal can be learned from actual operating experience, so there are important advantages to making small changes and getting actual operating experience as quickly as possible. More sophisticated uses may require changes which cannot be made in less than a year or two, and some developments may require these moderate-sized steps in system improvement.

The development of systems generally requires some choice between the development of small systems which respond to specific needs and the development of more generalized systems which respond to a broader spectrum of needs. The planners for manpower information systems development face this strategic choice also. It seems to us that there is some advantage to having always in view a structure of a general purpose system so that sub-systems can be pieced together into a larger system. It is likely, however, that both the sub-systems and the general purpose system will change in concept as pieces of the comprehensive system are developed and operating experience is achieved. In effect, the choice to develop problem-oriented sub-systems and the choice to develop a comprehensive, general purpose system must both be embraced simultaneously. While sub-systems must be developed and made operational, they must also be compatible with a larger comprehensive system. While a comprehensive system must be conceived to guide the development of sub-systems, its architecture will change as new information content and sub-systems are accepted as a part of the comprehensive manpower information system.

F. A Suggested System Architecture

The manpower information system which exists between data capture and data use can be conceived as having five parts. The design of a system in these parts can lead to a flexible system which is adaptable to new situations and changing demands. The parts are:

a. *Data capture.* The methods by which data captured and recorded are governed largely by the events which occasion new information. In designing data capture methods, consideration needs to be given to the methods which aid and encourage the capture of the required information content which must be captured in order to produce output that is relevant to ultimate uses.

b. *Edit.* Captured information needs to be examined for its self-consistency and for its consistency with respect to previously stored information. Ideally, the costs of editing would be compared with the costs and risks of inaccurate information so that the editing effort can be appropriate for the ultimate use of the information. Some quality control of the information input is essential.

c. *Distribute, update, store, and delete.* The organization of files, the distribution channels and timing, updating procedures, and the eventual erosion of stored information through deletion must be developed. Information distribution timing will affect the response time of the total system. Retention time as well as information content will affect the sophistication of the outputs. Capability for reconstructing history (doing file maintenance backwards) affects the utility of the manpower information system for the examination of trends and for long-range planning. File size affects operating costs. The organization of multiple files affects retrieval costs and the cost of preparing a particular output. By making appropriate observations of system use, it seems to us that it is possible to reorganize files from time to time in accordance with the changing use of the system. System design is changed by this method in accordance with actual operating experience. A system with these capabilities at least would have the characteristics associated with "learning" if not the heuristic characteristics of "problem solving".

d. *Retrieve.* Nearly all reports and other outputs begin by retrieving particular information about all people in the file or by retrieving data about people who meet certain specifications or by performing both kinds of retrieval tasks concurrently. The retrieved matrix of information is then operated upon to produce the finished report. The flexibility of outputs depends upon the file content, the power and flexibility of this retrieval capability, and upon the capability for manipulating the retrieved matrix of information. Thus, the retrieval capability is an important element affecting output flexibility.

e. *Summarize, format, display, and distribute.* It may be more difficult to design and effect flexible methods for summarizing, formatting, and displaying manpower information than to design any other portion of the system. The reason, of course, is that output needs are closely related to the individual skills and needs of the user. However, some generalizations can be made from past experience. The displayed information needs to be read by the user as nearly as possible without benefit of a decoding manual. A report printed in code will go unused. The design of the system will elect either to provide decoding capabilities for output preparation or will elect to carry information "in English" in the record. Flexibility in summarizing the data is important for the use of manpower information in planning and problem solving. This flexibility can be achieved in large part through flexibility in retrieval and through flexibility in combining data treatments for retrieved information. This can be achieved through availability of tabulation and statistical routines which can be used to operate upon the retrieved data, through the use of a report generating programming language by management and staff personnel who are frequent users of manpower information, and possibly through the chaining of retrieval, sorting, and statistical routines. Many of the frequently requested outputs (such as "who do we have

who can fill these requirements?") will be satisfied by computer programs specially tailored to those requirements. This will be true for
outputs which are prepared periodically for wide distribution, for
management reports which are prepared periodically or prepared
when exceptions occur, and for frequently requested reports which are
sought as needs arise. Distribution of reports is an important feature.

Information about employees, particularly information collected
about different topics and for new purposes such as has been stimu-
lated by the social sciences during the last decade or two, is being
collected under a variety of commitments about information use, either
stated or implied. Public and private attitudes about the use of manpower information are changing. It is essential that policy about the
use of the information be developed and that means for administering
the policy be reliable. Lacking such a policy, the development of manpower information systems can continue so long as the person supplying information is confident that it will be used under conditions
which appropriately protect him and other people around him, such
as people in his department or division or company. Lacking that confidence, the basic information essential to the system's validity will
be difficult to obtain.

Periodic reviews of system performance, particularly determining
that its benefits are in favorable ratio to its costs, are seldom a part
of management practice and yet seem to be essential to guide the
appropriate growth of manpower information systems. Management
can and must consider individual, company, and social goals as it
develops the objectives and reviews the performance of its manpower
information system. It is argued by some that the unique characteristics of individual people cannot be described and should not be
reduced to descriptions which can be recorded on paper or stored in a
computer. While the enormous variability and complex nature of human characteristics have not been captured in all their complexity in
scientific descriptions, it is possible to utilize the technologies presently available to make more human use of human resources. In our
view, managements have the responsibility to stimulate the definition
of the goals of manpower information systems and periodically to review the goals, benefits, and costs of the manpower information system
in the routine exercise of management responsibility.

CHAPTER 12

Computer-Aided Engineering Systems

Introduction   /   Technology Descriptors

A. *Introduction*

COMPUTERS are directly applicable to the administration of engineering efforts, the running of engineering departments as well as to the actual performance of engineering tasks. As companies have grown and technology has advanced, the administration of the engineering effort itself becomes a formidable undertaking, particularly so in recent years as engineering disciplines have multiplied and become more diverse and as the need for including diverse scientific and engineering disciplines on specific tasks has become more common. The organization of engineering effort around projects has complicated the administrative accounting for engineering effort and the accumulation of costs by project and the control of cost by project in an engineering department carrying on hundreds of projects at the same time is a very natural application for the computer. The prompt reporting of cost information over the course of the project and the analysis of progress versus cost by project and by activity within projects are both greatly facilitated by modern data-processing techniques. In fact, the practical application of PERT and critical-path scheduling and project control is often made practical by the computer alone.

The development of a product or process normally involves the following phases:

1. Preliminary design
2. Design
3. Prototype development (bread or brass board)
4. Prototype test
5. Final design
6. Hardware manufacturing and production
7. Hardware test, quality control, process control

185

Computers are now being used extensively in parts 1, 2, 3, and 4 in the following usage applications

- Theoretical analysis
- Design concepts by graphic input devices
- Design procedure by storage information and data banks
- Test data reduction or process control by analog digital processing, and digital-analog reprocessing of data

Programs to perform these tasks and engineering applications are being developed by computer manufacturers, in software houses, are being, identified by library organizations and implemented by low-cost programmers. This trend is likely to have several effects upon product development and design economics. First, engineering man-hours per product can be expected to decrease. Sophisticated analytical techniques will be more available to firms without extensive research and development capabilities at low cost. Extensive cataloguing of OEM equipment will be far more readily accessible. Finally, test data will be automatically reduced and made available to the designer inexpensively in graphic form. All of these trends will have measurable effects only over fairly long periods of time. For the same problem—large time requirements—exists in the application of computers to engineering tasks as in the application of computers in marketing and production functions. Engineers, as people trained in technical subjects, can be expected to have less bias against the use of the computer in their personal duties than people lacking much technical training, and so will be more likely to put the computer to use in doing work that is already highly quantitative. It is rather the possibility that adoption of computer systems will result in restructuring of the engineering work itself, and the reallocation of duties, authorities and responsibilities, and even more important, the very large software development task that causes the delay in wider application of computers in engineering. Even so, the computer has been applied widely in such diverse fields as thermodynamics, linear programming, structural mechanics, and statistical analyses.

A good example of the ambitious use of the computer in engineering is a system now under development for the computer design in detail of the whole structure of naval ships. This system starts with information about member sizes and configurations and design requirements as given in the contract scantlings and arrangement plans and specifications. All of this information must be coded and converted to a computer form to establish a computer representation of the hull structure. The system will then proceed with the functions of detail design, including the positioning of reenforcing members such as stiffeners, straking of plate sections, detailing of intersections and connections, the determination of welding requirements, and the detailed lofting procedures used to establish all of the minor cutouts and allowances which must be made in cutting plates. The computer system will generate graphics representing working plans and APT programs which can be used to operate numerically controlled flame cutters to cut out parts from plates. Other outputs will include consolidated bills of materials, reflecting the nesting of parts on stock plates, templates to assist in forming curved plates, and weight and centroid summaries. It should be evident from this example that, as this system is developed and perfected, the economics pertaining to ship design will change radically, as will the time requirements for building a ship.

What in effect is happening in this case is the making of a very large capital investment over time which will eliminate the need both for clerical workers and for draftsmen of various kinds in the construction of at least certain types of ships. But it is hardly to be doubted that, as the system is developed for computer-aided design of ships, so will similar systems be developed for computer-aided design of buildings, bridges, and other large structures. Capital intensification of a whole process of construction of such works would seem to follow inevitably, with marked effects upon organization of the industries involved, kinds of competition, and size and kinds of competitors.

Initially, it would seem that companies engaged in such projects for construction will be reduced in number as money and technology mastery requirements increase for the designer. The programs once developed will not be static, but should be subject to improvement. Although in the case just described the owner of the design program will be the Federal government, private industry in time will develop similarly ambitious programs. But this single example serves as any such single example would as much to distort as to describe engineering applications of computer systems, so broad is the spectrum of technology across which such systems have been, are being and will be developed.

Engineering and scientific applications of computers fall into certain categories that may be described by the following factors

• *Discipline*—The major areas of activity are recognized by academic training, professional societies, etc.

- *Technique*—The computational or operating modes in which a digital computer is used in an application.
- *User*—General characteristics of the organization in which the application occurs.
- *Equipment*—The computer used.
- *State-of-the-art*—The degree of sophistication, development, frequency of use, and importance within a discipline.

Thus, examples of discipline are physics, chemistry, electrical engineering, etc. Examples of a technique are arithmetic, statistical, simulation, etc. Examples of a user are university, aerospace industry, Army, etc. Examples of state-of-the-art are concept, practical, etc. The process of categorizing an application then consists of determining for that application which descriptor should be used for each of the five factors. If we view the factors as axes in the descriptors as coordinates, this amounts to locating an application as a point in a five-dimensional space.

The reason for explaining this method for categorizing engineering applications in the use of computers is simply the vast number of such applications that have already been developed. A recent survey of the field indicates that there are at least 5000 and possibly closer to 10,000 applications which have already been developed in engineering tasks for the computer. The next section lists the so-called technique descriptors, and gives some appreciation of the diversity in technique alone. A scanning of the section should suggest the broad applicability of the computer to engineering functions. A few moments' reflection while scanning should suggest also the force for change which the computer has already become in the engineering field, and the practical consequences of the computer in the organization of workload within an engineering department (the development of narrow specializations in solving certain classes of problems, for example).

In a very real sense, the engineering department becomes the heartland for computer applications to business organizations. But the mere planning of computer applications in an existing engineering department imposes the need for very long-range planning, not only with respect to the computer and the development of software, but just as importantly with respect to the initial selection and training of engineering staff members. The implications are vast also for the development of engineering education itself, so that among the larger companies at least some attention should be given to future needs in engineering professional education and the communication of the perceived needs directly and through professional societies to the leading institutes of technology and schools of engineering. For example, a more generalized engineering training is needed than can be had in conventional discipline areas such as physics, biology, or chemical engineering.

But the more immediate need for most companies is to develop a strategy for applying the computer within their current business and for laying the groundwork so that capital investments in computer hardware, in programming, in computer personnel training will not be washed out by successive generations of computers or by transfers of personnel into and out of engineering in the course of their careers, or the loss of engineers to other enterprises. Critical to this foundation being established is the initiation of rigorously maintained and updated program libraries, the development of detailed computer applications plans, and the selection of computer system development projects according to an overall rationale. Unless this is all done under the most competent technical leadership and management, general management can expect to have continuing problems in applying the computer creatively to its engineering workload as well as in preventing the costs of computer use to be under the most marginal control, if controlled at all. Most seriously, unless general management knows the true nature of the costs which it is incurring in the development of its software as between those programs which have long-range suitability and application for the company's operations and are in fact of a capital nature, and those programs which are designed to answer one-of-a-kind questions and problems, it can well find itself in a position of controlling engineering costs associated with the computer hardly at all.

The computer's use in engineering is not restricted to those cases where it conducts its work without human intervention. Probably its most fruitful applications will come to be those in which it is joined in direct partnership with the individual engineer. Here man's particular talent for ideas and "conceptual" thought are linked together with the machine's extraordinary power over calculations, detail and error. Engineering design is precisely the point at which man and machine can work creatively on a trial-and-error basis to optimize the most complex design jobs. Certainly, all the effort now being devoted to developing input/output devices to facilitate the man/machine relationship is well spent. A number of devices now exist that make it practical for the professional engineering staff to use the company's computer in the day-to-day jobs. As new programs are developed, and as the input/output devices are provided, the effectiveness of the computer in engineering design will be clearly inaugurated. The costs associated with providing for powerful computer systems to the individual engineer are trending downward rapidly. Use of time-sharing and telephone-line access to the computer is within the reach of even the smallest company for engineering design work.

B. Technique Descriptors

1. MATHEMATICS

Techniques classified as being mathematical include analytical techniques, such as differentiation or power series expansions, and numerical techniques, such as numerical integration or finite difference methods used to approximate the continuous analytical techniques. The following describes these briefly.

a. *Combinatorial Analysis*—Permutation and related techniques used for the analysis of various combinations of conditions, entities, etc.

b. *Complex Numbers*—All techniques which fall within the scope of complex analysis, function theory, complex integrals, etc.

c. *Curve Fitting*—Includes all techniques used to develop functional approximations to data, whether based on least squares or some other measure of deviation.

d. *Differential Equations*—All types of ordinary differential equations, linear or non-linear, and with fixed and variable coefficients.

e. *Eigenvalue Methods*—Includes all types of eigenvalue or characteristic value techniques, whether in finite dimensional vector spaces, differential equations or integral equations.

f. *Error Analysis*—Techniques which develop or use approximations, whether to functions which cannot be specified or are just too complicated to be computed exactly.

g. *Euclidean Transformations*—All techniques related to finite dimensional vector spaces, except those included in Matrices and Determinants and Simultaneous Equations.

h. *Extremals*—This class includes all techniques related to the determination of maximum, minimum or otherwise extremal values. It is more general than the class of optimization techniques.

i. *Finite Differences*—Techniques used to approximate and numerically solve differential and partial differential equations. Forward and backward difference techniques are also included in this class.

j. *Harmonic Analysis*—All techniques used to study a mathematical function as a sum of components. When these components are sinusoidal functions, these are generally called Fourier Analysis; however, the component functions may be any orthogonal set.

k. *Integral Equations*—Includes the analytical and numerical techniques used to solve systems of integral equations where these may be Fredholm, Volterra or other types.

l. *Iterative Techniques*—Computational techniques which are primarily iterative in nature, as exemplified by most root solving methods. From an initial approximation, successively more correct solutions are determined.

m. *Interpolation*—Includes all techniques used to determine the values of a function expressed in tabular form.

n. *Logic*—Techniques related to the methods of mathematical logic.

o. *Matrices and Determinants*—All techniques for constructing and manipulating matrices and determinants, except those related to eigenvalues and simultaneous linear equations which are classified elsewhere.

p. *Non-Linear Equations*—All techniques, such as gradient methods, used to solve single or multiple non-linear equations.

q. *Numerical Integration*—Includes all methods of numerical integration except those which are better characterized as Finite Differences. The Numerical Integration technique is used instead of either the Differential or Integral Equations technique descriptor whenever the application emphasizes the numerical integration aspects at the expense of the analytic formulation of the differential or integral equations.

r. *Orthogonal Functions*—In a strict sense, the techniques in this class are a subset of Harmonic Analysis and are applicable when dealing with systems of orthogonal functions but with no or little emphasis upon their use as components of other functions.

s. *Partial Differential Equations*—Includes all techniques, analytical or numerical, related to all types of partial differential equations, except those techniques which can be more precisely identified as numerical integration, finite difference methods, or relaxation methods.

t. *Perturbation Methods*—Includes techniques used to obtain numerical or analytical solutions to partial differential and other equations by an analysis of small perturbations.

u. *Programming*—Includes classical optimization techniques such as linear programming and other mathematical programming methods. It forms a subset of optimization methods and is used whenever the optimization technique can be identified as a programming method.

v. *Relaxation Methods*—Includes the set of techniques used for the numerical solution of partial differential equations in which successive computations are used to obtain "averaged" values.

w. *Simultaneous Equations*—Includes all of the various reduction methods used to solve simultaneous *linear* equations. Such techniques may be viewed as forming a subset of the class of Matrix and Determinant techniques.

x. *Special Functions*—Includes all techniques involving or associated with special functions, such as Bessel functions, Chevychev functions, etc., including methods used to evaluate these functions and their use in the solution of integral and differential equations.

y. *Vector Analysis*—Includes those aspects of Euclidean techniques which are formalized as vector analysis. Examples include techniques such as vector products (dot and curl), gradient methods and special formulations such as the divergence theorems.

2. STATISTICS

The following descriptors should be used to characterize the techniques used in statistical applications. In some cases, and particularly regression studies, the boundary line between the statistical and mathematical techniques may appear to be poorly defined. However, the intent has been to use statistical techniques in applications involving an analysis of stochastic phenomena, while mathematical techniques would be reserved for non-stochastic cases.

a. *General*—Used whenever the application clearly involves a statistical technique but either does not provide enough information to determine the technique or the technique is not one of those described below.

b. *Correlation*—That class of techniques which are related to the computation and interpretation of multiple, single and partial correlations.

c. *Experimental Design*—Includes all techniques associated with the analysis or design of experiments, except those identified as separate techniques, such as Analysis of Variance or Factor-Discriminant Analysis.

d. *Hypothesis Testing*—Probably the most loosely defined of the statistical techniques; however, it is to be used for applications of a statistical nature in which the objective is to apply statistical tests to some hypothesis and for which none of the other statistical technique descriptors are applicable.

e. *Factor and Discriminant Analysis*—Describes the general class of techniques used to determine statistically the combination of factors which contribute most significantly to observed results, with the emphasis here being on the *combination* of factors. The principal techniques of this type are those known as factor analysis and discriminant analysis.

f. *Variance*—Includes all aspects of the technique generally known as analysis of variance.

g. *Probability Calculations*—Includes all the techniques used for the computation of discrete probabilities or probabilities associated with various statistical distributions or events. In particular, the evaluation of partial probabilities obtained by integrating a distribution function would be included.

h. *Regression*—Includes all types of regression techniques, single or multiple, linear and non-linear. In a sense, these may be viewed as special types of curve-fitting techniques; however, they are differentiated here since they are applied to statistical phenomena and consider a distribution of deviations as well as the fitting surface.

i. *Sampling*—Includes all techniques used for the determination of sampling procedures and the analysis of samples so obtained.

3. PROBLEM-ORIENTED SOFTWARE

This technique is characterized by applications which emphasize the development or use of software which is particularly oriented towards a general class of problems. Examples would be program languages such as COGO or STRESS, which are compiler systems and are particularly suited for coordinate geometry and stress analysis problems.

4. DATA REDUCTION, TABULATION AND ANALYSIS

A technique of this type would be specified whenever the emphasis in an application is on the processing of quantities of scientific or engineering data. Such processing may involve certain computations; however, the characteristics of the application is the large quantity of data processed.

    a. *Analysis*—Applies to applications performing the most basic data reduction operations, such as the computation of elementary statistical characteristics of a large mass of data. Such routine analyses would not be viewed as being statistical techniques, since they are more of the genre of data processing methods.

    b. *Continuous Data Analysis*—Used to further characterize applications in which the data reduction techniques concern data which occurs naturally in a continuous or analog form but has been digitized for computer processing.

    c. *Correction*—Applies to applications in which the primary objective is to modify or alter data in some way so as to correct for or subtract certain effects.

    d. *Determination of Parameters*—Used in applications where quantities of data are reduced in order to arrive at parametric values for use in mathematical models.

    e. *Discrete Data Analysis*—Analogous to the sub-technique Continuous, this technique applies to data reduction applications in which the raw data occurs naturally in a discrete form, such as discrete measurements or counts.

    f. *Editing*—Used in applications emphasizing the checking, editing, or validation of data. Various criteria may be used, such as statistical tolerances or others having a more discipline-oriented foundation.

    g. *Functional Evaluation*—Applicable to situations in which certain mathematical functions are evaluated repeatedly for a large number of sets of data.

h. *General*—Used for applications in which data reduction is an important factor but not enough can be determined to assign any of the other descriptors.

i. *Sorting and Classification*—This technique is used for data reduction applications which primarily sort or categorize data.

j. *Statistical*—For applications using data reduction techniques reported as being "statistical" in nature and which appear to be more sophisticated than just the bare minimum (in which case they would have been categorized as as Data Reduction—Analysis) and not sufficiently statistically oriented to identify a statistical technique.

k. *Table Generation*—Further identifies applications in which the objective of the data reduction is to generate tables through either functional evaluation, correction of data, editing, etc.

5. Design Systems

Techniques of this type are used whenever an application is an essential or major component in the design of some object. Applications which simply "motorize" the computations of certain performance analyses would *not* be categorized as using techniques of Design Systems. The application must be of a fairly broad scope and perform a number of non-elementary calculations.

a. *Automated Design Engineering*—Identifies the use of a comprehensive system of design algorithms and documentation procedures, as characterized by IBM's concept of this same name.

b. *Design Analysis*—The emphasis is on determining the system's response to a set of loading or boundary conditions.

c. *Design Automation*—The Design Systems technique in which a number of design functions, such as analysis and detailing, are integrated into one system.

d. *Design Checking*—Identifies the techniques used when the primary function of the computer application is to validate or check designs which were developed by some earlier operations.

e. *Design Computations*—Identifies design applications which are sophisticated because of the design areas to which they are applied but which otherwise use only straightforward computational methods.

f. *Design Documentation and Data Processing*—Characterizes design systems in which the emphasis is upon the generation of documentation (forms, worksheets, etc. but not drawings) related to the design work or results.

g. *Design Optimization*—Describes the use of techniques in design systems which permit the application to improve and possibly optimize a design with respect to some criteria.

h. *Design Synthesis*—This technique is employed in design systems when a computer application is able to formulate or synthesize an initial design from certain initial data, such as functions and performance requirements.

6. INPUT-OUTPUT

This category of techniques is used whenever the input-output operations in an application are particularly significant.

a. *Digital-to-Analog Conversion*—Includes all techniques, except those of a graphic nature, used for digital-to-analog or analog-to-digital conversion, whether on-line or off-line.

b. *Graphics*—Includes all on-line or off-line input or output techniques involving graphical representations in any way, such as the preparation of engineering drawings and other schematics.

c. *Remote Consoles—Time Sharing*—Identifies the computer techniques in any system using shared time or multi-processing.

7. SIMULATION

This class of techniques applies to applications in which the computer is used to simulate certain processes, devices, or phenomena.

a. *General*—This descriptor is used for applications which are clearly simulations but are not specified in sufficient detail to assign some other simulation technique descriptor.

b. *Heuristic*—Identifies simulations in which the program itself develops the logical rules for subsequent stages of a simulation.

c. *Human*—Identifies simulations in which a human generates certain inputs to the computer which represent his reactions to previous outputs.

d. *Mechanical Systems*—This technique is used for simulations of that name, i.e., systems made up of a number of devices or components which have to operate together.

e. *Model Development*—Used to further characterize simulations in which the goal is to *develop* the basic *form* of a model.

f. *Model Evaluation and Testing*—Describes simulations in which the basic model has been determined with all its parameters and is now being used to perform simulations, but the application is not specified sufficiently to determine whether it should appear under a heading such as Monte Carlo or Mechanical Systems.

g. *Monte Carlo*—Identifies simulations which have certain elements of statistical randomness.

h. *Physical System*—Used to further identify simulations in which some process or physical phenomenon is being simulated.

i. *Projective*—Identifies simulations in which generated data is used to determine how a system might perform.

j. *Retrospective*—In contrast with Projective Simulations, Retrospective Simulations use historical data to determine "What would have happened if, etc."

8. Systems Used with Experiments

This category of techniques is used to identify applications in which the computer is integrated with an experimental configuration. Generally, it will serve as a controlling or monitoring device and the mode of operation will be real-time.

a. *Automatic Data Analysis*—Identifies those applications in which the data is collected and analyzed, but there is no feedback to control the experiment.

b. *Automatic Data Collection*—Characterizes applications in which the computer is merely used to monitor, or compile, data.

c. *Automatic Diagnosis*—Identifies more sophisticated applications in which the data is analyzed and interpreted by the computer to determine whether equipment is functioning properly or not.

d. *Control of Experiments*—This is the most sophisticated technique within this category and identifies applications in which the real-time machine analysis of data provides the basis for the computer directing some change in the operation being observed.

9. DISCIPLINE

This descriptor is used whenever the techniques appear to be intrinsic to a discipline and cannot be readily identified by one of the technique categories 1-8. An example would be a case in which the mathematical formulation of an application is peculiar to the discipline and far more important than the computational procedure.

10. SPECIAL

This is analogous to the Discipline technique except that it is used for specialized approaches which are naturally a part of disciplines other than that in which the application occurs.

11. METHOD

Used to identify abstracts which describe computational methods or analytical methods which will lead to computations. The application must be directed towards a specific problem application or technique, rather than being just a general analysis, either mathematical or otherwise.

12. SOURCE

Identifies abstracts which appear to be sources of applications other than those reported in the abstract itself.

13. REVIEW

Identifies abstracts reporting on a review of certain problems within a discipline.

14. CITATION

Identifies the abstract as one which is significant for the survey purposes but for which only a title is reported.

15. CONCEPT

Characterizes abstracts which report on concepts or approaches to computer solutions of problems.

D. Computer Hardware Past, Present and Future

CHAPTER 13

The Development of Computer Technology

Introduction / Computer "Hardware" / Computer "Software" / Computer Systems

A. *Introduction*

WE HAVE DISCUSSED the role of the computer within the context of information technology and the theoretical aspects of business enterprise and management, and have illustrated several points in the previous chapters on the use and implementation of computer systems. This chapter considers the development of the computer itself. The "physical" aspects of information technology fall naturally into two categories: "hardware" (machines), and "software" (programs). We discuss each in turn and briefly survey their development.

B. *Computer "Hardware"*

From a hesitant start with a few experimental computers in the late 1940's, information technology has led to the installation of well over 44,000 electronic computers by mid-1968 (see Figure 13) and has created more than 500,000 jobs in the United States alone. It has been an industrial phenomenon equal in its significance to the mass-production methods of Henry Ford, the steam engine of James Watt, and use of interchangeable parts by Eli Whitney. In the late 1940's and early 1950's computers were used at a few universities, primarily as research tools. Now, their use has spread through government and business, and, while they continue to be used in research, they have taken on accounting tasks as well. More important, they have found broad use in management. We have shown that they have given new powers and opportunities to corporate management in business, government, and other areas in which men engage in large common effort.

Figure 13
NUMBER OF OPERATIONAL GENERAL-PURPOSE
COMPUTERS VERSUS YEARS

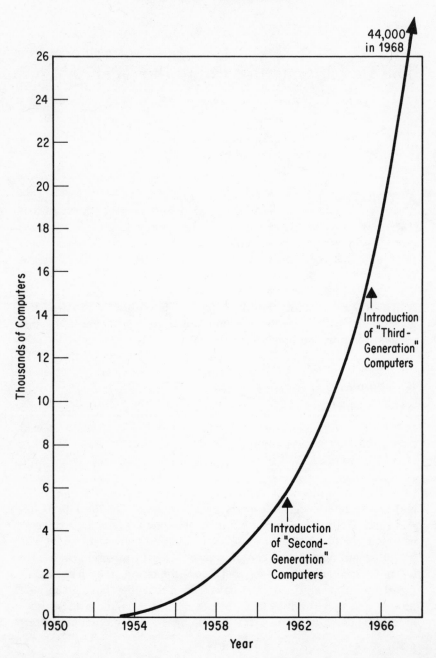

The initial impact of the new technology on government, industry and many individuals has been vast. Eventually the impact of this technology will be felt even more widely by society as a whole; but, the most direct beneficiary will remain not the individual but the organization.

With the spread of electronic computers new professions have developed, such as computer designers, computer operators, and computer maintenance personnel. Such special professions as programmers, system analysts, and data controllers have also developed as a result of the special nature of the new technology. They are the appliers of the technology and, as such, are becoming a new professional force.

Information technology is a force for change. It has promised major changes in corporations, in government agencies, and in individual jobs. This young technology will have further impact on our way of life in times to come.

1. The Basic Structure of the Computer

In basic concept, computers are very simple, capable principally of addition, substraction, storage of data for later retrieval, and, most important, deciding whether one number is larger or smaller than another. A good clerk with a desk calculator can do all the tasks a computer can do. The main advantages of the computer are its tremendous speed and, with perfect instruction, its perfect accuracy. The operational speed of a computer is such that multiplication can be performed as a series of multiple additions (and was in the early computer generations), and yet the action is completed in just a few microseconds. For example, the multiplication 3 x 18 as done by a computer has been $18 + 18 + 18 = 54$. This approach is now being eclipsed.

Computers are made up of three main modules—an input/output (I/O) module, an arithmetic control or central processing unit (CPU) module, and a memory module.

a. The Input/Output Module

The I/O module is the part of the computer which handles all input and output. Input can be in physical forms such as punched cards, punched paper tape, or direct typewriter signals; in magnetic forms, such as magnetic tapes, disks, drums, or bulk storage; or in plain signal form from normal telephone or other communication lines. Output can be in any of these forms or in the form of printed reports. The computer I/O module simply follows orders from the arithmetic and control module in "reading" or "writing" the appropriate data on a specified I/O device. In a typical modern computer, the I/O module and its assorted I/O devices can account for 40 to 60% of the total computer cost.

b. The Central Processing Unit

The arithmetic and control module, or central processing unit (CPU) is the "thinking" part of the computer. This module executes the program as instructed. It initiates requests for data, does arithmetic, stores data in the memory, and makes the comparisons to "decide" on further actions. The quotation marks around "thinking" and "decide" are intentional; computers do not actually think or decide, they merely carry out tasks as instructed. The CPU of a computer can account for 20 to 35% of the total computer cost.

c. The Memory Module

The memory module of a computer is a device capable of storing sizable volumes of data. The CPU can put data in the memory module for later referral. Such data can be recovered from the memory module after a long time, after several hours, or after only a microsecond or less. In a modern computer, the memory module can account for 15 to 35% of the total computer cost.

2. The Development of the Computer

Computer technology has undoubtedly advanced more rapidly than any prior technology. The first two electronic computers were built in the mid-1940's; by the late 1940's and early 1950's, such computers had emerged from the research laboratories into industrial use.

It is convenient though not purely correct to trace the "physical" development of the computer by reference to several "generations" of computers. In reality, progress has been continuous with significant breakthroughs in the design of the major modules overlapping in time. A full three "generations" of computer technology have emerged in the past 20 years, with the most profound effects on their power and cost. Now, in the latter 1960's, "fourth-generation" computers are being designed, with initial operations scheduled for before 1970. (Typical operating characteristics of the various generation computers are given in Table 5; various data storage devices and their typical operating characteristics are compared in Table 6.)

Table 5

COMPUTER CHARACTERISTICS BY GENERATION

	First Generation	Second Generation	Third Generation
Control Module	Tubes	Transistors	Integrated Circuits
Memory Module	Drums	Cores, Tapes	Cores, Drums, Disks, Tapes
I/O Module	Cards, Printer	Cards, Printers, Typewriters, Tapes	Cards, Printer, Typewriters, Tapes, CRT's, Remote Terminals
Processor Speed	100 μs/char.	10 μs/char.	1 μs/char.
Primary Memory Size	10,000 char.	16,000 char.	128,000 char.

Table 6

COMPUTER STORAGE DEVICES

	Size (M char.)	Transfer Rate (μs/char.)	Random Access to First Character
Magnetic Drums	1-4	1.2- 5.0	4-20μs
Magnetic Tapes	10-1000	8.0-24.0	3 min.
Magnetic Cores	.032-.128	0.2- 2.0	0
Magnetic Disks			
Single	2-8	2.0- 8.0	20-100μs
Stack	16-40	2.0- 8.0	20-100μs

As computer technology has grown, major changes have been made in the mechanical, electronic, and chemical make-up of the equipment used, and in the physical arrangement of the computer modules. Processor speeds (the time required to retrieve a single letter or numeric digit from the computer memory and make it available in the control module for processing) have increased from about 100 microseconds per character in a typical first-generation computer to less than 1 micro-second per character in the third generation, a hundredfold increase. Primary memories have grown from 10,000 characters to 128,000 characters, a twelvefold increase. (Memories of up to one million characters are not uncommon.) These advances have had much to do with the expanding list of economic computer applications; with every increase in capacity and decrease in cost, new computer applications became economically feasible.

a. First-Generation Computers

The control module of the first generation of industrial computers used vaccuum tubes; input and output of data was accomplished by means of punched cards and printed forms; and the storage module was a revolving metal *drum* on which data was stored in the form of magnetized spots. The absence or presence of these magnetized spots formed a coded image of the data to be stored. By current standards, first-generation computers were slow in executing their commands or program. Yet, input and output of data was at least another order of magnitude slower than computation; and, as applications grew, emphasis was placed on improved I/O devices, because punched cards and printed reports were bulky and slow to process. Also, large-volume, low-cost computer memory devices were a necessity. Drum memories proved too expensive.

The development of *magnetic tapes*, on which information was encoded by magnetizing selected spots on the tape, alleviated these problems. The surface of the rotating metal drum was simulated by a metallic oxide coating on a plastic tape. A much greater volume of data could be stored on these tapes. The first magnetic tape units became operational with the last of the first-generation computers, but they were not used extensively until the second-generation computers appeared in the late 1950's.

b. Second-Generation Computers

In second-generation computers, the control module was constructed with transistors rather than vacuum tubes, and the data storage module used magnetic tapes and banks of magnetic cores instead of magnetic drums. Although magnetic drums had served their purpose well, about one-half of a drum revolution was lost in the search and retrieval of a data point which was randomly stored on the surface of the drum, since the data point had to be located by a serial search of the drum or, at least, of the bands on the drum. Banks of core memories made random access possible—every data point stored in the computer memory could be addressed and retrieved within an equal amount of time, since its access did not depend on drum position.

The second-generation computers also operated at much higher speeds than the first generation machines, because transistors were used instead of vacuum tubes in the control module and *magnetic core banks* were used in the memory module. With the increase in speed, the divergence in operating characteristics between the computer control module and the memory module on the one hand and the I/O module on the other became greater. Frequently, the I/O unit would be 10 to 100 times slower than the control and memory modules, and much potential computation time was wasted while the control module was waiting for I/O actions to be completed. To avoid loss of computation time, *simultaneous processing* was introduced, especially in the larger computers; input and output actions were started, and during their execution, the computer continued to operate in the computer mode on other jobs, returning to the I/O operation after the I/O action was completed. In simultaneous operation, known as *overlapping* or *buffering*, the simultaneous actions can take place on various I/O channels.

Another feature which emerged during the second generation was the use of *magnetic disks* for data storage. The disks operate like a stack of Gramophone records; a movable pick-up arm slides between two disks and reads or writes the data as magnetic spots on the faces of the disks as they rotate. Some units have a single arm which travels up and down along the side of the stack and then move inward and outward to find the proper track on a disk; most have one read/write head between every two disks; and some have even a single disk and a read/write head for every track on the disk. The latter units have operating characteristics similar to those of the original drum storage units and compete with drums in their traditional operating areas.

c. Third-Generation Computers

Besides large magnetic core memories, the third-generation computers are noted for still higher operating speeds and their wide use of monolithic *integrated circuitry* (the new "chips," which perform the functions of several transistors, resistors, and capacitors). Third-generation computers not only carry out I/O operations and computations simultaneously, they also carry out several programs or several sets of instructions simultaneously for separate users. This operation is called time sharing, or multi-programming, the total time available on the computer being "shared" by several users. The initial experiments with time sharing were carried out with second-generation equipment, but this mode of operation is only coming of age with the third-generation equipment.

d. Fourth-Generation Computers

The first- and second-generation computers had a life span of about five years each. With each new generation, the typical performance has improved about tenfold. At the same time, purchase cost or monthly rental of equipment has remained about level, thus giving a 100 to 1 improvement in price/performance ratio in only 10 years. The growth in performance is bound to slacken off in the future because physical and operational constraints are being approached, but growth of applications is still increasing rapidly, and the price/performance ratio may increase by another factor of 10.

One of the physical limitations being approached is the speed of light or of electric current—186,000 miles per second, which is equivalent to approximately 1000 feet per microsecond. The control units of some of the largest third-generation computers operate with switching speeds of 0.1 microsecond, and, of necessity, the circuitry involved in such an operation must be less than 100 feet equivalent, because a circuit which was too long would delay the result of one action beyond the starting time of the next action.

Fourth-generation computers are being designed, and they probably will operate at still higher speeds, employ more efficient memories (e.g., plated-wire or laser memories), make more use of time sharing and remote processing, and proceed further along the path of operational control. However, their operating speed cannot exceed the limits set by the speed of electric current.

e. Modern Input/Output Devices

A major aspect of the new generation of electronic computers is the ability to communicate with the machines in many ways. Originally, all data I/O was limited to punch cards and printed reports; next came magnetic tapes, which were used for temporary bulk storage; and, now, removable disks are also used. One of the main impacts of the third-generation computer technology is the great variety of communication channels and the many methods which have become available.

Input Devices. New input capabilities include optical readers, which can read sales slips and even printed pages, and remote typewriters, which are used primarily in real-time systems. Some difficulties still exist with universal optical reading devices, because of the different type fonts used in general correspondence. The more successful optical character readers have been those which are limited to a single type font.

A third input device is the cathode ray tube (CRT), or television tube, equipped with a light pen. Using this device, a designer can effectively draw on the face of the television tube; the computer recognizes the drawing, stores it away, and manipulates it with further instructions from the originator. One of the first successful applications of the cathode ray tube display and light pen technique was in the military radar systems, in which a human controller was asked to identify certain blips on the radar screen as friend or foe. The communication speed available with a CRT is essentially instantaneous; therefore, the device is extremely useful when quick response is required. In the future CRT devices with a light pen may be used in text editing; the raw text can be read by optical scanning and displayed on a CRT for editing purposes prior to going to automatic typesetting. Such applications use the interaction between computer and editor in a most efficient manner. CRT's also may be used in operator intercepts on automatically routed telegraphic messages. For example, in the telephone industry, when a number is dialed erroneously, it is serviced by an intercept operator. A similar operation could materialize with the automatic telegraphic message routing systems that are becoming operational. In this case, the great bulk of the messages would be analyzed and routed automatically—only those that defied computer analysis would be displayed on a CRT for routing code assignment by an intercept operator.

Output Devices. If a need arises, the technology now exists to develop the special device to record and translate the output from the computer, as well as the input to the computer. Of the output techniques available, the printed report will, of course, remain the most important. Beyond that, however, outputs in the form of voice replies or graphical displays are being implemented. It should be expected that such special-purpose outputs and media will be primarily for specific applications, such as computer-originated voice control guidance of airplanes on a landing path. Similarly, when computers are used for credit reference checking, either voiced replies or replies shown on CRT devices should prove useful.

3. FURTHER TRADITIONAL DISTINCTIONS BETWEEN COMPUTERS

a. Commercial Versus Scientific Computers

Initially, commercial applications used large volumes of input and output, but required a minimum of manipulation. In some computing centers, the most sophisticated mathematical operation used was developing percentages. Obviously, such centers use the I/O capabilities of the computer much more than the arithmetic capabilities. Scientific calculations, on the other hand, have been typified by small I/O volumes and extensive intricate mathematical calculations. As all applications grew in size, the scientific applications started requiring larger volumes of raw data and, simultaneously, the commercial applications started using more sophisticated computational optimization and even simulation techniques. The distinction between commercial and scientific applications has, therefore, been greatly reduced; some argue that essentially it has been eliminated. All third-generation computers are aimed at the total information technology market, although an individual installation can be tailored to particular applications and mixes of applications by its "configuration" (i.e., its balance among processor memory, input, and output units).

b. Digital Versus Analog Computers

The applications considered above relate primarily to the use of general-purpose digital computers. Analog computers are finding important applications, although these are limited to specialized fields. Analog computers are useful primarily for simulating physical processes; their primary advantage is that they can simulate any process almost instantaneously. Digital machines usually require a great deal of computer time to simulate a physical process; an analog machine simulates a process as soon as its currents and voltages have steadied out.

Analog computers are becoming quite large and difficult to control; in the future, their operations may be controlled by digital devices. In these "hybrid computers" the logical actions are controlled by the digital computer, while the process simulation is executed by the analog device.

C. Computer "Software"

1. PROGRAMMING AND COMPUTER LANGUAGE

Computer programming is essentially the task of translating a set of requirements and commands into a language acceptable to the computer. We have described computers as machines which can perform a task. However, the machines must be taught their task; they must be programmed.

a. Machine Language

With the simple machines of the first generation, programming was a relatively easy, but tedious, task. Because the computers were relatively uncomplicated devices the languages were quite simple. Programs were initially written in machine language; and individual instructions were provided for each act performed by the computer. That this procedure was exacting, tedious, and complex is underscored by the following example, which gives a typical machine language instruction for performing the operation $P = A \times (B + C)$.

	Program		
Instruction	Address Modification	Storage Address*	Comments**
+0500	000	047632	C is stored in 20378
+0400	000	047631	B is stored in 20377
+0131	000	000000	
+0200	000	047630	A is stored in 20376
+0601	000	047527	Results are stored in 20375

* Octal, or base 8, notation is used by computer.
** Storage locations expressed in decimal.

As computers became more sophisticated in the second and third generation and began to employ multiple I/O channels, simultaneous operating modes, etc., programming became considerably more difficult. The question was raised, "If computers are so fast and so accurate in handling information, would it be possible to have the computer aid itself in the programming task?" And, of course, it is possible. The computer routines that aid in program development are generally classified as either program assembly routines or program compilers.

b. Assembly Language Routines

Assembly language greatly eases the burden of the professional programmer in two ways: (1) by allowing him to write his commands or program steps in a more descriptive form (higher language) than the very cryptic internal computer machine language; and (2) by providing concise statements for frequently repeated series of commands. In addition, an assembly routine keeps track of memory assignment, and it checks for program consistency. In assembly language, data items can be given descriptive names (mnemonics); when the program is assembled, these data are assigned to specific memory locations (addresses), and the assembly routine assures that these memory locations remain reserved for the specific data. Furthermore, during assembly, comments are provided by the assembly program concerning consistency and adequacy of the user program. For example, the mathematical formula from our previous example, $P = A \times (B + C)$, can be written in assembly language as:

Program		Comments
CLA	C	Clear and add C into accumulator
ADD	B	Add B into accumulator
XCA		Exchange contents of registers
MPY	A	Multiply by A
STO	P	Store results into P

The advantages of the simplicity and brevity of assembly language are readily apparent.

c. Procedure-Oriented (Compiler) Languages

The first assembly-type languages originated in the late 1950's. Very soon, however, it became clear that as the complexity of the computers increased and as more sophisticated tasks were programmed for computer solution, improved programming languages would be needed. This need prompted the development of higher-level languages and special computer programs to translate (compile) statements made in the higher-level language into machine language. When using a procedure-oriented language, the programmer writes quite detailed statements; these statements are translated by the compiler program into a series of computer program steps in machine language which perform the desired commands.

FORTRAN (Formula Translation), the first and most frequently used procedure-oriented language, was developed jointly by IBM and several industrial computer users in the late 1950's primarily for scientific work. (The European counterpart of FORTRAN is ALGOL, Algebraic Compiler Language.) Since its initial development, FORTRAN has undergone several extensions and modifications, but its basic format has remained unaltered. Using the example given above, $P = A \times (B + C)$, a single FORTRAN statement of the form, $P = A^* (B + C)$ suffices. The actions taken by the computer after compilation are identical to those shown in the assembly language format above.

COBOL (Common Business Oriented Language), the second major compiler language, was developed partially upon the insistence of the Department of Defense. Its primary use is for commercial data-processing operations. FORTRAN is particularly useful for programming complex statistical and mathematical problems; however, it is not as good in applications requiring much data organizing, aggregation, and cross tabulating. Moreover, it is not easy to specify complex data I/O formats with FORTRAN. COBOL was developed for use in applications for which FORTRAN was not suitable.

PL/1 (Programming Language/1), a new compiler language, was developed by IBM. Hopefully, this language combines the best elements of both FORTRAN and COBOL.

Programming in any one of these compiler languages is less tedious than programming with assembly language. Developing programs in machine language or assembly language also becomes more difficult as the computer techniques used become more sophisticated. Since the last of the second-generation computers and all the third-generation computers employ simultaneous I/O modes and some even employ time-sharing features, most programmers have turned to compilers and compiler language to aid them in the program development.

The early procedure-oriented programs, and even the current ones, that operate on small computers, can be inefficient, because the small computers frequently cannot accommodate a program of the size and complexity of an elaborate compiler. And yet, compilers are demanded by the user. The way out of such an impasse is to construct compilers which have neither the full range of capabilities nor the facility to produce highly efficient object programs. On larger third-generation machines, however, good compilers exist and these compilers should be able to produce operational programs which are 90 to 95% as efficient as the most cleverly designed and hand-coded programs in assembly language.

A second major advantage of procedure-oriented languages is that programs written in such languages as FORTRAN or COBOL assume a measure of computer independence. For example, programs written in the FORTRAN IV language can be operated almost without any modification on at least 40 different computer models. In a rapidly growing technology, this adaptability is advantageous, for as newer and better computers become available, applications can be switched to the newer machines without major reprogramming efforts.

Despite the development of more sophisticated compilation techniques, program development costs have risen sharply in recent years. In many installations, programming and program maintenance costs now exceed monthly rental costs for the actual hardware. Computer programming is an expensive task, and all assistance which can be provided by the computer itself in the form of compiler languages is welcome.

d. Technique- or Problem-Oriented Languages

The development of successively higher-order languages is a response to the real value of closing the communications gap between the ultimate user (the operating executive not the programmer) and the computer. This motivation has resulted in technique- or problem-oriented languages, conversational languages (to be discussed next), and ultimately the applications packages (see below). Problem- or technique-oriented languages relate to specific problems. The vocabulary and syntax used is that of the problem-solving technique itself. These languages refer to the common *vocabulary* of a problem whose solution may require a number of techniques. FINANAL has a special vocabulary close to that used for the analysis of financial statements for purposes of security appraisal.

e. Conversational Languages

Recently languages such as JOVIAL, BASIC, JOSS, CAL, and QUIKTRAN have been developed which enable the user to communicate (interact) directly with the computer. Several of these languages are interpretive in the sense that each instruction is executed as it is typed in by the user. This method allows for the immediate feedback of errors, but does reduce the flexibility of the language. At the present time, these languages do not simulate English well enough to be useful to a potential user without programming experience, although they are a step in the direction of moving decision-makers closer to the computer.

f. Compilers, Utility Programs, and Loaders

Instructions to the computer in higher-level languages must ultimately, of course, be translated (compiled) into machine language. Compilers are programs which accept as input a program in a higher language and produce as output that same program in machine language. It is possible, therefore, by the use of individual compilers to be able to execute a single program written in higher-order language on any of several machines. In addition to the translation function, compilers generally perform another important task—error checking. As a program is compiled, the compiler will stop if it reaches a programming error, issue a diagnosis of the error, and then continue. This twofold task gives rise to the fact that some compilers are relatively efficient at one or the other task.

Utility programs have been developed to aid the programmer. The simplest of these provides a list of the original program (with error diagnostics if any) and a map of the location of program instructions in the computer. If a program fails to execute, either properly or at all, a "core dump" may be requested which prints out the information in all locations at the moment the error occurred which caused the problem.

After compilation (translation), the program instructions and data must be loaded into the memory core of the computer where each element of information (instruction or data) is given a location and an address. As it is the loader which binds all parts of the program together, its design is crucial to the flexibility and speed of any program language. Loaders differ principally according to the time at which information and linkages are bound. The absolute loader is the least flexible. It establishes locations (addresses) at compile time. The dynamic loader, which establishes locations only when execution requiring a bit of information or data is required, is the most flexible though the most complex.

g. Emulation and Simulation

Because of the rapid increase in the total effort (costs) of software development and modification relative to computer hardware, it is not economical to instantaneously and continually adapt existing software to changing hardware. The costs of attempting to do so are enormous. To avoid these costs, emulation and simulation programs have been developed. Under the guidance of such a program a computer behaves (indeed "thinks" it is) as an older or smaller version of itself—another machine entirely. The result obviously is a significant loss in efficiency in the use of the machine utilized. While it is theoretically possible that a larger or newer machine may operate more efficiently (specifically faster) than the one it is emulating, emulation techniques have generally resulted in less efficient execution even relative to the machine emulated. But emulation is greatly useful in a computer transition when programming talent is not immediately available to reprogram existing machines.

2. APPLICATIONS PACKAGES

Yet another dimension of high-order software is the design of business and scientific applications packages. Many business functions are so alike from company to company that a package of programs can be designed for general use—thus saving on what would otherwise be repetitive program development costs. Examples of such business applications packages are those developed for payroll accounting, billing, inventory control, bank demand deposit management, etc. Similarly, there exist many scientific applications which have been packaged including statistical routines for time-series analysis, multiple-correlation, and various kinds of mathematical programming. The stock (library) of packages is already prodigious and seems capable of growing almost without limit.

3. EXECUTIVE ROUTINES, OPERATING MODE, AND DEVELOPMENT SOFTWARE

In addition to emulation and simulation there has been developed a class of executive routines which, as the name implies, coordinates the use of other programs. This hierarchy of programs (as opposed to languages) represents the preponderance of the real systems capabilities of computers. By and large these programs control the way the computer operates on a job as distinct from the way a particular job is done itself which is determined by the program written expressly for it. For example, executive programs determine the sequence with which the system will execute individual jobs (according to priority, length, and communality of machines and subroutines required). Other executive programs search out and relay the source and cause of failures in the hardware and/or software system to the operator.

A second category of routines, which cause the computer to "reflect" on its own operations at a higher level, have been developed to aid in computer systems development and program design. The computer is obviously an important tool in the design and testing of bigger and better computers. Techniques have been programmed in which simulation and network theory are brought to bear to facilitate the generation and introduction of new machines.

D. Computer Systems

Computer systems represent a goal-oriented collection of machines, programs, and skilled personnel. A major problem in the discussion of computer "hardware" or "software" individually, is presented by the possibility of substitution between software and hardware in the design of computer systems. It may be conceptually useful to regard "hardware" as merely solidified or "concretized" software. After all, specialized computers are really "physical" representatives of a set of instructions to perform a special task. The more flexible or general the computer, the more it relies on software to execute a particular task. In these terms the evolution of the terminology—"hardware" and "software"—take on an important meaning. Thus there exist a strong interdependence or "systems" relationship between the two—particularly at the design stage.

The development of computer operating systems is characterized by three important functions: computation, communication, and information storage and retrieval. All three functions are present in any computer system and we categorize systems merely by which function is emphasized.

1. COMPUTATION

a. Types of Computation

Probably more than 60% of the computer systems installed in the United States to date have been used to automate and accelerate clerical procedures, including such standard accounting functions as payroll, accounts receivable, and cash reconciliation. In these applications, the computer is used primarily as a reporting system which makes detailed accurate information on operating conditions available to managers and operating personnel.

1) MATHEMATICAL BUSINESS MODELS

The managers can use data generated by such accounting applications in making decisions; however, such reports contain primarily historical operating data, and the task of the decision-maker involves the forecasting of future operations. His task would be lightened considerably if he could simulate future operations. It has been shown in a number of cases that mathematical models of operations can be developed in such a way that the decision-maker can use the mathematical expression of his future operations to explore the results of various decisions. By simulating the future under hypothetical conditions, the decision-maker can gain insight into the important aspects of his operation and, therefore, can make better decisions. Fortunately, the fields of systems analysis and operations research have matured concurrently with computer technology, since these techniques complement each other in aiding the manager in making better decisions.

Mathematical modeling already has become well established in the petroleum and steel industries where much use is made of such mathematical modeling techniques as linear programming and automated inventory control. Until recently, mathematical models of operations were frequently limited to segments of a total corporate activity. In the petroleum industry, for example, there are mathematical models of petroleum refining operations, models of pipeline operations, and models of marketing operations. Recent emphasis, however, has been in the development of models which describe the operation of a company in its totality. These models are known as simulation models, business models, or corporate models.

Building mathematical models of operations, although difficult, appear to be the aspect of the total information technology which will grow faster than all other segments because such models help management make better operating decisions for the medium and long term.

2) PROCESS CONTROL

Computer control of processes is an entirely different branch of computer technology. As noted, most industrial organizations use computers initially to speed up routine paper work. Beyond that, computer applications tend to branch in different directions. Some companies use the computer to aid in planning or decision making, especially intermediate- and long-range planning. Other companies put computers in direct closed-loop control of intricate processes, such as crude oil refining, glass making, and steel making. The main justification for using computers—which are costly—rather than human operators in these processes is their tremendous speed, which permits them to react more swiftly to changes in environment and, hence, to control processes closer to their desired limits, providing improved product quality and operating reliability.

Some of the second-generation computers were capable of automatic control of processes. Such installations were largely experimental, and the true impetus for computer control is not expected until the third-generation computers come of age. The real impact of computer control of processes, however, will materialize with fourth-generation computers which are being designed specifically for the task.

b. Processing Mode

The processing mode under which a computer operates is determined by the relationship of the timing of its functioning (its internal clock) with the real world. If jobs are done sequentially from a queue (batch processing), or executed upon command with answers required continuously or randomly at command (real-time processing), or many jobs executed "simultaneously" for many users (time-sharing), basically different computer systems are involved.

1) BATCH PROCESSING

Originally, all computer applications were of the batch-processing variety. As in a job-shop, individual, self-contained jobs were completed sequentially. This operating mode has declined in relative though not absolute importance in relation to more continuous and simultaneous operating modes. As in the scientific management of a job-shop operation, higher-order programs were developed so that more than one job might be run simultaneously on the same machine (multi-programming) and/or parts of a given job might be run simultaneously on several machines (multi-processing). Additionally, *"executive" or control routines* were developed which schedule the jobs to be done according to their size and priority and the combination of hardware and software required by each.

2) REAL-TIME SYSTEMS

Some second- and all third-generation computer systems can perform tasks in real time. In real-time computations, the interaction of an individual or a process and a computer is conducted in a conversational mode; when the originator poses a question, the reply returns from the computer in 5 to 30 seconds. Well-known examples of real-time processing are the information and reservation systems of the airlines. Files detailing reservation status for flights are kept at a central utility. Airline agents throughout the nation can query the files and update and change them in a conversational mode. Essentially, the airlines' problem is an inventory control system with the specific aspect that the inventory—seats on future flights—has a high obsolescence cost. At flight time, any unused seat is essentially worthless; hence, in inventory control terms, its obsolescence cost is high, justifying a real-time computational system.

3) TIME-SHARING SYSTEMS

The synthesis of a high degree of "management" over batch-type operations made possible by higher-order software, with real-time capabilities, and with improved methods of data communications (discussed next) make possible the "simultaneous" use of one computer installation by several remote users *(time-sharing)*. Within such a system, several users enter, use, and modify their own programs into a central computer from a remote computer console. The central computer, under the guidance of higher-order software, sequentially polls the various consoles that are currently activated and devotes a small variable portion of computer time to each. The process is conducted so rapidly that it is as if each user has sole, continuous command of the central computer when in reality he is waiting in line most of the time.

2. DATA COMMUNICATION SYSTEMS

Real-time and time-sharing systems operate best on large computers, because these machines can operate as computer utilities with access from multiple remote stations. With the advent of such large systems, data communications systems have become important to the pattern, and perhaps the volume, of future computer use. At present, ordinary voice-grade telephone lines are adequate for data communications at typewriter speeds. However, communication demands are increasing so rapidly that higher capacity communication circuits which can send large volumes of data very quickly will soon be needed in large numbers. Such high-speed communication systems are similar to those used by the television networks.

An ordinary telephone circuit is capable of transmitting only the data contained in about 150 punched cards every minute. Several major U.S. industrial concerns are considering setting up their own computer utilities. Large volumes of data will move between their branch offices and the computer; transmission speeds equivalent to 150 cards per minute will be totally inadequate, particularly if the computer utility is used not only for scientific calculations, where the I/O demands are relatively small, but also for commercial data-processing operations which involve such applications as voluminous sales reports, accounts reconciliations, and payrolls. It is expected that the addition of digital encoding techniques will revolutionize the capacity of the telephone network, so as to allow, for example, the transmission of a TV channel over a single one of today's telephone lines.

Intracompany communication systems are already operational and have been successful, and some intercompany communication systems have become operational recently. For example, some systems in the food distribution industry connect the computer system of the retailer directly to the computer of the wholesaler. Still missing is the tie-in with a transportation company computer. Intercompany communication systems are also operational between some industrial concerns and remotely installed computers at service bureaus. As yet, such circuits are set up as individual endeavors, but intercompany computer communication systems will become commonplace once signals, terminals and methods have been standardized.

3. DATA STORAGE AND RETRIEVAL

Second-generation computers were oriented primarily toward magnetic tapes. Retrieval of randomly stored data was usually prohibitively time-consuming with these machines. Instead of inaugurating a retrieval sequence for each request, it was generally more economical to batch a number of requests and to carry out a request-response run when a batch was filled. With the third-generation equipment, the retrieval of randomly stored data on magnetic disks or drums became much less expensive. More recently, because of the time-sharing capabilities of third-generation equipment, retrieval of data from a magnetic tape file, while at the same time processing other jobs on the computer, has become feasible. In this case, the retrieval process is charged only with the actual time spent in retrieval and not the total time required to search through a magnetic tape. Thus, retrieval of randomly stored data is becoming considerably less expensive because of improvements in hardware as well as in software.

An additional advantage to modern retrieval methods is that graphic displays on CRT's are entirely feasible. Display of retrieved data is quicker and more legible with these devices.

4. TOTAL CORPORATE SYSTEMS

A number of industrial concerns have started to develop corporate data banks, or computer systems in which all the relevant operating data of the firm is stored in the computer in retrievable form for use with real-time and time-sharing systems. Although they have many potential advantages, development of such total system has been slow, primarily because data collection and systems design problems are great; furthermore the true economic value of total system data banks is quite difficult to measure.

As computer systems and software capabilities improve and systems analysts' experience matures, total systems development will progress. The necessary computer hardware is available, and computer software is becoming available. The major problem now is the availability of trained and experienced personnel; this problem should ease as time goes on.

CHAPTER 14

Research and Future Information Technology

*The Machine / The Man-Machine Interface /
Information Systems and Business Performance / The
Organization of Research and Development Effort*

RESEARCH ON MANAGEMENT INFORMATION SYSTEMS and on information technology is proceeding on a variety of fronts, and the pace of progress in many areas suggests that information systems of the future will be strikingly different from those now in use. We will look briefly at developments now in process and at the research which we see as necessary for the full development of future information systems. We view information systems and information technology as goal-oriented man/machine systems. We will discuss developments involving the machines, then explore developments involving the man/machine interface, and finally discuss the need for research and development in the role of information systems in larger organizational and social contexts. The organization and support of research and development work is discussed at the end of the chapter.

A. *The Machine*

We have stressed that computers are too frequently regarded as computing devices without due regard for their other two principal capacities—information storage and retrieval and data communications. In some respects, this limited vision has been a characteristic of the computer industry itself. Developments in the latter two areas have been secondary to the concern for more rapid computing capacity; bottlenecks in these two areas have had to be overcome in order to increase computer capacity.

In the future, major gains in computation capacity will come as a result of the extension of the time-sharing concept. Because present computers can process more jobs simultaneously, capacity can be increased greatly, without any further increases in actual computer speed, merely by filling in the myriad of tiny gaps in time attendant to any individual job. The need for changes in the physical makeup of the computer has thus been decreased, at least for the present, and greater emphasis is being placed on the development of better information storage and retrieval techniques and improved data communications.

1. INFORMATION STORAGE AND RETRIEVAL

In recent years, information storage and retrieval has become an independent technology. The idea of the computer as a high-speed automatic special- or general-purpose library has received considerable public attention. Technologically differentiating this field from computation is the medium which it manipulates—words, ideas, and meaning rather than numbers. The problems in this medium are complex, since higher-order blocks of information must be manipulated as units and all of the philosophical problems of meaning must be dealt with. Two recent developments indicate that much of the computer's potential in this area may be realized.

The first major advance copes with the indexing problem. The steps in the information storage and retrieval cycle are: gathering, summarizing and indexing, input, storage, searching, and display. Aside from the collection of the initial information, the costs of which vary widely, the summarizing and indexing activity has been the most costly per unit, largely because it has had to be performed by humans. Techniques have been developed which employ the computer to scan materials and code them automatically, by word frequency and association.

The second major advance is the development of associative memory search techniques. Formerly, computers were instructed by their programs (software) to scan the memory bank for locations containing information on a request. Every location was compared with the request, and the computer moved on if the information in the particular location was not relevant or printed out the relevant information at that location and then moved on. This process used a great deal of expensive computer time. The new techniques are content-oriented rather than location-oriented, and the information storage configuration is a hardware function rather than a software function; thus, considerable time and money are saved.

2. DATA COMMUNICATIONS

The development of time-sharing systems may cause a complete change in the spatial allocation of computer power. The idea of continuous instantaneous availability of computer power, as opposed to sporadic batch loading, may lead to the development of large central computers, perhaps surrounded with planetary smaller computers, which, in turn, would be surrounded by many satellite terminals.

A major limitation on the development of this type of computer network is the need for more powerful data communication facilities. The limited capacity and speed of input/output terminals is currently a major restriction on the performance of time-sharing systems. (This limitation explains, in part, why present applications of such systems generally are scientific rather than commercial, the ratio of internal operations to input-output information being higher in scientific applications.) In the future, advances in data communications will lead to more sophisticated time-sharing networks.

B. The Man/Machine Interface

As management information systems become larger and are used by more people, the interfaces between people and information system become increasingly important. The interfaces for individual users are represented in the programming languages, the user-computer dialogue being developed for some applications, the data requirements for input, and the display and information content characteristics of output.

1. PROGRAMMING LANGUAGES

Programming languages are becoming closer to human languages in structure and syntax. Developments in this area are aimed at fostering direct contact between users and the computer, drastically reducing the need for intermediaries. Unfortunately, there is a severe limitation on achievements in this area. The multiple goals of a computer language are not compatible; the ideal computer language would (1) be easy to learn and use, often closely resembling the user's spoken and written language, (2) be general in its application to scientific and commercial problems and to hardware systems, and (3) be very concise. These three goals are conflicting.

Although we are confident that great strides will be made in this area, we believe that programming will always exist in the corporation as a specialty, though possibly even in a more consultative and project-oriented role than is presently the case. Users will never avoid the necessity of becoming directly involved in the development and operation of the management information system on which they depend and will usually be required to learn some specialized language(s) for communication with the information system.

2. MAN/MACHINE DIALOGUE

Research and theory point to the great potential gains to be derived from two-way, as opposed to one-way, dialogue between users and computers. Current information systems are one-way interrogation systems in which the computer plays a passive role, responding to inquiries. Project Doctor at Massachusetts Institute of Technology is concerned with the ability of the computer to adopt both inquirer and respondent roles. Computer-assisted instruction also requires a two-way flow of information and inquiries between student and computer.

Some research in communication has shown that it is frequently a more efficient means of communication to have a receiver guess at the information being sent and for the sender to merely advise whether he is "hot or cold." This process is particularly efficient where there is a possible loss of meaning in encoding concepts into signals to be sent and/or received in transmission. It is also true, in these systems, that no matter how frequently the receiver indicates that he understands ideas that have been transmitted, the sender has no guarantee that this is indeed so until the receiver demonstrates his understanding through elaboration, incisive questioning, or the taking of compatible action. Programs for computer-assisted instruction may be based upon this principle. The management information systems of the future probably will incorporate both the mode of response-to-an-inquiry and the mode of generate-an-inquiry in their capabilities.

3. DATA REQUIREMENTS FOR INPUT

Present systems, particularly those utilizing computers, sometimes have been conceived as having input in machine-readable form. This conception has led designers into overlooking the requirements surrounding data observation and capture. Increasing capacities and sophistication of information systems have increased the demand for input, sometimes requiring data capture which is abstract, illusive, or difficult to describe. Systems design often has allowed the apparent "system-imposed" input requirements to be transferred to the data supplier with the result that data quality has suffered and supplier cooperation has degenerated. These problems are more generally recognized today than they were a decade ago.

The research needed to develop input codes and data-capture methods still is seldom found as a part of a system development project or as part of a system maintenance effort. It is our judgment that this will receive increasing attention as the amount and complexity of information input continues to rise.

The design of consoles and work spaces for operators and users, including managers, utilizing cathode ray tube display devices (or other displays) and keyboard input devices (or other inputs) will also need research attention. Some of these problems have been studied in military and defense environments, but have received scant attention in the environments of management information systems for business or government.

4. CONTENT AND DISPLAY FOR OUTPUT

What information to display as output from a management information system, and how to display it, represent concerns which have already received a little research attention. For example, the comprehension of numerical facts seems deceptively simple. In fact, numerical facts are seldom single-valued. Numbers represented in the output of the information system contain all the shortcomings of input errors, time delays in assembling and displaying the information, and errors of classification and aggregation introduced in the processing. At best, they often represent best estimates of a varying and dynamic situation at one point or period of time. This truth about numerical facts can be illuminated by adding a number which conveys the degree of uncertainty about a numerical fact, or by displaying simultaneously other facts which pertain to it such as the past history of that particular fact, or by presenting the fact in a graph or other picture, or by manipulating the fact in a mathematical model to show how sensitive it is to changes in other conditions.

While there has been research which treats the questions about how information content and configurations of various kinds affects the conclusions, decisions, or behavior of the user, the research has not focused upon uses of information in the management of business enterprise. Not even reviews of research have attempted to focus research findings upon the design of reports for varieties of users in business and industry. We feel certain that this represents an important need and that it will receive increasing attention in the decade ahead.

C. Information Systems and Business Performance

1. Business Goals and Information System Effects

In business today, information about the business usually is shared among members of management and sometimes is shared among employees, stockholders, customers, government agencies, and the public. Decisions by management frequently are the result of consultative processes rather than the choice of a single individual. While the effect of information of a particular kind upon the decision, behavior, and action of an individual needs to be understood, the effect of the *distribution of information upon business and organizational performance* also needs to be understood. One purpose of profit-and-loss statements is to allow management to detect an out-of-normal condition and take appropriate diagnostic and corrective action. In spite of the presence of such statements in most businesses, some businesses get into difficulty which the information system seems not to have detected or not to have forecast in sufficient time or force for appropriate and effective action to be taken. What kind of information systems lead to organizational "success" in those aspects of performance which the business or organization has chosen as important?

It seems likely that the variety of reports, report content and information display, report frequency, use of comparative data (such as from the prior month or year), the number and kinds of persons receiving the reports, the settings for discussion of reports, the diagnostic information systems which can be used, and yet other considerations can affect management's responsiveness to changing business conditions. Systematic study disclosing the effects of content, timing, and information distribution on organization behavior seems to us to be essential for the continued development of management information systems during the next decade. The studies probably will be done using both observational and experimental methods where the decisions and outcomes are of modest importance and mistakes are correctable. Studies will use primarily observational methods where the strategic decisions of a business are being examined for the contributions of the management information system to management decisions and subsequent business performance. While understanding the role of management information systems in affecting business performance is admittedly a complex task, it is likely that today's technologies in the behavioral and statistical sciences are equal to the challenge. It is equally likely that the development of future management information systems will profit from the guidance provided by this research.

2. Implementation of Systems Change

We have discussed the considerations affecting changes in management information systems. Our comments are based upon current knowledge of the processes of change in business organizations and upon practical experience in making changes in management information systems. Yet research-based knowledge is incomplete, and we feel that research on the process of introducing changes in management information systems can lead to greater satisfaction with developed systems, lower development and implementation costs, quicker changes, and greater success with continued change and adaptation. It is likely that this research will be done in situations in which actual systems changes are occurring, either by monitoring events during the change, making observations before and after the change, or examining the change in retrospect.

D. The Organization of Research and Development Effort

Generally a change in management information systems is viewed as a small matter, or is viewed as an important but infrequent event. In either view, the use of resources to support research in information systems may seem unwarranted. Even when some effort can be channeled to research, the number of unanswered questions seems large and the choice of the research objectives difficult.

The research task itself probably requires that experience from a variety of circumstances and uses of management information be accumulated before generalizations of far-reaching practical value can be developed. Few business organizations are large enough to have within their own organization the widely varying management information practices and problems required by the research.

It seems to us that the combined requirements of (1) large resources and (2) a broad spectrum of use and experience with management information systems indicate that *the needed research in management information systems will be conducted through the cooperation of several—even many—sponsors and users.* There are important exceptions. Programming languages probably will continue to be products of the computer manufacturers, although the last decade has shown associations of users to have an important role here. Consoles, display devices, and software will be developed and tested by the manufacturers of computing hardware, although some special-purpose software will be developed under user sponsorship.

Research that examines information system effects, costs, and methods of change and implementation, probably the most complex and the most meaningful of the several research tasks, is not likely to be done by the computer manufacturers. The questions raised in these tasks are clearly of interest to the computer users, and much less clearly of interest to computer manufacturers. While computer manufacturers have been very supportive of users in matters like the training of computer programmers and the development of some of the basic programming languages, these things are essential for any computer use to occur at all. Effective use of management information systems, and of computers in management information systems, may be born of a different set of considerations than the "use-versus-non-use" decisions to which computer programmer training, computer programming language development, and even increased computing capacity with lowered computing costs are fundamentally addressed. The cost-effectiveness and adaptability questions about management information systems come out of concern for organizational goals and objectives and organizational survival and seem to be extensions of the concern for operating economies and timeliness and responsiveness of operations.

If some of the research and development work of the future in management information systems is to be done under the sponsorship of computer users, as we guess, then the organizational means for accomplishing this work needs to be identified. Associations of users form one vehicle for coordinated effort. Financial support to these associations, and management skill in the associations, can be used to sponsor and coordinate the work as well as share the results. The research seems most likely to be conducted by staffs in research and development organizations, either university-sponsored or separately organized. Since the "laboratory" for study of management information systems will be business and industry itself, the research will be done with the consent and cooperation of the sponsors, and more probably with their active participation.

The corporate leader and business manager may want to look for the situations in which his firm, and his people, can support and participate in some of the research and development work essential to improved management information systems.

E. Conclusions

CHAPTER 15

A Continuing Learning Experience

Coda / The Questioning Approach /
Your Personal Education / Conclusion

A. CODA

1. AS STATED in Chapter One, the purpose of this book has been to present the issue of the computer, its history, its opportunities, its problems and its future. The information presented in the text gives the manager of any business a good base upon which to build. The various middle-chapters have given examples of case histories, and these histories abound in every field whether oriented towards the financial manager, production executive or strategic planner. National magazines and national conferences constantly keep the reader updated, some in non-technical terms, so that with today's communications media, there is little reason for the executive who wishes to be informed to be denied knowledge in his field.

2. As stated in the introduction, within the next few years the computer will be in common use. Therefore a manager can either master its concepts, or ignore them and depend completely on trained subordinates for information concerning its function and application. Judgment of even the most capable subordinate, as well as the salesmen for the vendors who are selling a system, is not adequate for the manager who wishes to control his job and plan for the future. Within the next few years many corporations will be led by men whose knowledge of computers is thorough enough to permit their personal use of them in strategic planning. Therefore, from both a technical and political standpoint, the middle and top managers must be able to match that knowledge.

Perhaps one of the most important statements in Chapter One is the definition of the word "computer" as defined from the management point of view. When any manager thinks of the computer, and attempts to operate his daily job and make his long range plans based on it, he should remember that the computer is not in this sense a piece of metallic hardware. In every decision he makes, he should remember that the "computer" is a powerful management tool combining people, procedures, maintenance and machines. To think strictly in terms of hardware becomes a tunnel approach to possible failure.

B. *The Questioning Approach*

AS THE manager of today's and tomorrow's business starts to use the computer, many non-technical somewhat esoteric questions present themselves. They will find as they implement their first computer project, that not all of the problems concern technical matters. For example, one of the greatest causes of system failure is the failure of the architect to design a system for the people who will use it. A great deal of care must be taken, sometimes to the point of bringing in human factors experts early in the design stage, to assure that the system and the people will work compatibly together.

1. One such example of success in that field is illustrated by the Centralized Business Record Office implemented by the Bell System in surburban Philadelphia. Basically, the system replaced approximately 250,000 paper records by computerized files accessed through display terminals. From a work standpoint, Service Representatives under the old system would answer a customer's call, then excuse themselves while they search through the files for the proper paper record to use in answering the subscriber's question. Under the new system, no files exist and the girl interrogates a display terminal using a keyboard. In effect, each girl has a miniature television set with keyboard on her desk and has access to all records in the office.

Early in the development, the Bell System recognized the need for making these young ladies feel as if they were a part of this new computer application. Service Representatives were flown to a design laboratory where they helped to choose the proper screen format to be used on the Display Terminals. While spending three days at the laboratory, they participated in tests that led to the ultimate design of a new type desk, and to a redesign of a vendor's keyboard.

Then, throughout the twelve-month-design phase of the trial, the project team met at bi-monthly intervals with the Service Representatives to describe exactly what they were doing. At these meetings, held after hours and including cocktails and dinner, the members demonstrated selected pieces of hardware, and discussed system design in non-technical terms.

When the system was implemented, there were many initial programming errors which caused a great deal of pressure and uncertainty on the part of the Service Representatives when they performed their work. It took approximately 15 weeks to debug the 300,000 instructions to the point where the system was working adequately, and during this time interviews conducted professionally by representatives of a leading university, showed that the pre-conditioning was so good that the girls' opinion of the system remained constantly high through the first difficult weeks until it was finally justified by corrected design.

2. Once the computer concept takes hold, the manager will find himself in a position of holding back on many applications rather than implementing them. And well he may! As stated in Chapter Five, a manager must take the same interest in the return on investment for a computer system as he would for any other type of business investment. There are many cases when individual departments will actively seek for computer help when, frankly, the application is such that it could be performed manually at less cost and with no deleterious effect in other ways. This is not to say that every computer application, when cost of equipment, etc. are pro-rated, must pay for itself; there are some cases where computer accuracy or the ability to build future systems on a certain application base, may dictate that the application be installed even though the initial breakeven point is not financially successful.

3. Concerning applications, the manager will find himself in a position where a project lends itself to the production of reams of reports. As soon as a great deal of base information enters a system, everyone seems to find a use for having it displayed in a different format. A typical example could include a computerized application of a production run, where the engineers wish a great deal of information in a specialized form while the sales people wish information on the same item in a marketing format and the production manager wishes a third series of reports using the same data but displayed for operations personnel. Before the report portion of that application is finished, people will be carting paper printouts home by the carloads

from the computer center. In many cases, only key data is really needed, and the manager must guard against the printed output being so voluminous that it is impossible for anyone in the requesting department to digest it.

This problem can become one of diplomacy rather than one of technical capability. To tell a person that he can't have information the person feels he really needs, takes a great deal of understanding wisdom and persuasion on the part of the manager in charge of the computer application. Yet such negative decisions are absolutely necessary, and a visit to any one of a number of major corporations' computer centers will point up the fact that printed output can be a great problem.

4. Continuing to speak in the vein of Computer Dictator, the manager will also find that many people will want to experiment with new hardware devices. In the case of the Bell System implementation of the Centralized Records Business Office, a great deal of pressure was exerted to place display terminals on the desk of managers up the lines of organization who had no real need to see the information that was displayed on those screens. At a monthly cost of approximately $150 for the display terminal and an additional $100 for the control unit and associated lines, a great deal of diplomatic persuasion had to be done early in the design phase to convince some executives that it would not be desirable to grant them a display terminal.

5. One of the great questions that a computer application brings forth is that of personal faith. For one thing, a decision is coldly logical when the computer makes it. If the designer does not put all the factors into the system, the computer will base its decision on the information in its file.

This type of example was brought home by a large corporation which initiated its first major computerized billing application. Prior to implementation, bills were sent out and after a period of time became delinquent if not paid. A special group of employees would then write first, and finally telephone the delinquent account to bring in the money. There were many people who were never bothered. Important executives, stockholders with large holdings, political officials in cities or towns were rarely called until the amount on the bill became outrageously out-of-hand, and then the call was handled by a middle-manager.

The designers forgot to put many of these exceptions into their computerized system. Needless to say when the computer produced its first set of delinquent notices, these privileged subscribers were outraged, since many who had been spasmatically paying their bills for years had never received any type of notice for delinquent payments. The system was almost postponed for political reasons before the changes could be programmed so the computer would stay away from these VIP's.

Closely associated with this coldness of decision is the need for personal faith once the system is designed. Many computer answers, especially in the scientific field, are based on complicated Operations Research formulae, selected sampling principles and mathematical validity checks. There is little reason and probably no conceivable way in which a business-oriented manager could be trained to completely understand these types of formulae. This is a case where he must be sure that he has capable subordinates and then believes in what they do.

Many decisions based on Operations Research formulae cannot be checked in the near-term and, in some of them which involve marketing strategy, can probably never be completely validated. When properly designed, the computer can perform these functions much better than the current "seat of the pants" decision-making process, and the untrained manager is going to have to accept this on faith.

6. The question of personal privacy always arises in the design of a computer system where input includes personal statistics or corporate financial information. There are ways of placing various checks and codes to keep unauthorized people from gaining access to the computer files. The question of personal privacy or, to state it another way, the misuse of accurate information, is more of a diplomatic question to be handled by the manager.

In most cases, when the particular concern is summarized and stated in basic terms, it appears that the same violation of privacy can take place today with a paper record system and the situation becomes no different, and probably more controllable, when information is placed in the computer file. It is, however, the job of the manager to explain this to people at all levels of the organization who become concerned.

Often one of the basic points made by those who fear invasion of privacy, is that under the paper system, information exists in widely scattered points. Since one of the basic design principles of computers is to bring all information together and to form a single file, opponents sometimes point to this as providing ease of access to personal information that would have been difficult to secure under the paper file circumstances.

7. With the computer age upon us, there is the need for making rapid decisions. The manager is going to find that his statements must be machine-paced, not people- or paper-paced. If computer design is done well, we will experience a paperwork implosion where printed reports will become less and vital information will replace it and arrive faster. The manager can no longer delegate a task force to spend a week or two preparing a report, and use that time as "think" time or "hope something happens to help me make this decision" time. The computer will be there with the answer, and the manager will be expected to produce an accurate, rapid decision.

These, then, are some of the problems that the manager will face which are above and beyond the technical design of a computer system. To make these decisions, however, the manager must train himself to understand what is going on in the mechanized process. This text is a start; a base upon which the reader can build. It seems fitting, therefore, to conclude the book with a discussion concerning how a manager may make the best use of the time he can allocate to train himself.

C. Your Personal Education

The modern history of curriculum development at major graduate schools of business administration indicates that management and decision-making is based on fundamental knowledge gleaned in systematic and quantitative ways and that the computer plays a continually growing means of putting this knowledge into effect. As discussed before, the manager cannot, therefore, rely completely on subordinates or experts outside his business. He must be an active, informed party, and at least to some extent participate in the design of information systems affecting his area of responsibility. He must be confident enough to judge and monitor the performance of these systems as they affect his overall job.

One example of this, although the problem is fast getting resolved, is the proper use of a programming language. A manager implementing a computer project into his sphere of responsibility may find that there is a major discussion raging on whether the programs should be written in basic assembly language or in a higher level language such as COBOL. It is not necessary for this manager to be a coding expert in both, but it is necessary for him to realize the impact that this might have on the project.

On one hand, the use of basic assembly language might require a longer period of time and more highly technical people. COBOL might take less time (and this can be expressed in terms of dollars) and be able to use untrained programmers. On the other hand, various instructions might be carried out more economically using basic assembly language; and as a result, it is possible that a smaller computer or less time on the same size computer may be taken to do a similar job (this can also be expressed in dollars). Therefore the manager must know enough about computer systems to be able to ask the correct questions so that he may get answers on which to base his decision.

1. A manager may learn more about the computer profession through subscriptions to certain journals. It is not the purpose of this text to produce a literary critique on the publications, but we do suggest that they range from very basic to highly technical. The manager should go into his local computer center or to a library (corporate or public) and scan just a few copies of the publications. He will soon find those he can understand and those that he cannot. It is best if he starts with the basic publications, and as he grows in knowledge, he can expand to the more technical journals. He will have to take the same course of action with books, although the bibliographies given in this text should provide an excellent start.

2. To sit down and read a technical journal without adequate background can be deadly, discouraging and lead to a discontinuance of this form of education. One of the most pleasant ways, therefore, to gain a background is to attend some of the many conferences available on the subject. There are many sophisticated sessions given by computer organizations, and some software houses in particular find this is an excellent way of advertising their wares. Usually, these technical sessions give a great deal of information and are well worth attending.

3. When making a decision on which course to take, there are five

fields growing rapidly, and which will be of vital interest to the manager of the Seventies. First of these is in the field of real-time systems. With the popularity of third-generation computers, the ability to get information on the spot is becoming more and more important to the operations of some businesses. The ability to know when this is necessary, as well as when to save considerable money by staying away from real-time, is equally important from a financial point of view. A good course in real-time systems will point out the differences, and then develop some of the ways to best use a real-time concept. Next in a list of importance is the concept of time-sharing. Particularly if a business is medium-sized or small, it might be uneconomical to own a computer. Even if a company has a large hardware installation, some applications might more readily lend themselves to time-sharing with a central computer run by a professional staff rather than adding equipment in one's own organization. A good time-sharing course will be well worth the effort when looking ahead to the Seventies.

In terms of decision making and strategic planning, simulation and computer modeling are becoming extremely important. More and more simulation programs are available through standard vendors as well as specific simulation corporations, and it is important for the manager to learn what these do and how they can be used in the planning process. A fourth category to investigate is that of hardware selection. Knowledge of a vendor's hardware can be gleaned by attending one of his schools (sometimes held as a three- or four-day conference) but it would be necessary for the manager to attend the schools of perhaps four or five vendors before he could make an intelligent decision. There are many conferences given by independent corporations speaking to this point and one of these is well worth attending. Finally, it seems that the terminal of the future will be a display device. Although it is placed fifth on the list from a standpoint of learning priority, when a manager can find the time he should delve into information display and learn how some of these television sets with keyboards could be used in his business.

4. Local computer organizations are of great value in learning of developments in the field. Anyone living in or near a major city should be close to a Data Processing Managers Association (DPMA Chapter). The group here tend to be managers of systems rather than designers. As a result their interest is usually more non-technical and talk is directed toward applications and implementation. A DPMA Chapter is an excellent place for a manager to go to start to increase

his knowledge of what the computer is doing for organizations throughout his area. Once he has the technical background, the meetings of the local Association for Computing Machinery (ACM) Chapter will get him much more deeply into the detail of system design, programming and hardware selection.

Various suggestions given above are far from theoretical. One case history showing how these steps were accomplished concerns a 35-year-old manager who had 13 years' experience in the line organization of his business, except for brief periods on the technical and then the marketing staff. He directed people performing work operations. He was promoted into a position where he directed a number of computer projects which needed to be implemented. He had a group of people who did the systems design work, then directed the programming which was done in another section of the organization. In effect, this group managed a project from start to finish.

Upon entering this new job, and with no prior knowledge of computers, our manager first went to a vendor's basic computer course. Then he attended one of the basic EDP courses given by the American Management Association. He started to read various periodicals, and attended one or two meetings of the DPMA. This took place in a period of a year, along with handling all the responsibilities of a new job. He was transferred to direct the development of an overall management information system for his company. He then became more interested in the details of the operation, subscribed to a program instruction course in FORTRAN, and joined the local chapter of the ACM. He estimates that, by this time, his out-of-office devotion to self-knowledge in the computer field was reaching approximately five hours a week.

He then was placed in charge of a new, computerized experiment for his company and successfully implemented the project a year later. A combination of the job and an intense self-study program in his new field, were responsible for these accomplishments.

To survive in the Seventies a manager must be able to assess the successes or failures of applications involving the computer in his own business, as well as in a competitor's business. Finally, he must translate this data into improvements for his own system. The ability to do this can only be based on a growing degree of formal knowledge.

D. Conclusion

In summary, we stress that the study of computer technology is only one of three areas within which the executive should seek continued learning. The second and most important, of course, is the formal study of his own discipline associated with his corporate sphere of responsibility. The third, combining the information learned in the study of computers and his own discipline, is the study of organizational behavior and methods of implementing change. The executive must be able, first, to know what he wants to do to improve his own technical end of the business; second, whether computer technology will help him to do it; and third, assuming that it will, the manager must know how to put these two goals together and carry them out through people.

Challenge is the core and the mainspring of human activity. It exists daily in the world of business. Nowhere will the manager of today find more of a challenge than adapting computer technology to his own job. He should remember, therefore, that in business as well as in life, the greatest joys are for the venturers, for what they gain is more than victory; it's a taste of life itself.

CHAPTER 16

Computers and the Future

THERE IS LITTLE DOUBT that computers are profoundly affecting businesses and our way of life. Many clerical operations have been partially if not totally displaced by electronic computers. Checks are sorted and cleared by computers. Credit card slips are processed and billed by computers. Sales orders are screened and shipping papers produced by computers. Airline tickets, rail tickets, theater tickets are issued and controlled by computers. And on and on.

It is important to realize that these changes have all taken place since only the early fifties. It was then that the first commercially available internally programmed electronic computer became a reality. Those machines had modest capabilities compared to today's giants and the super giants of tomorrow, but they paved the way for automated payrolls, inventory control, and accounting systems, to name a few.

In this short span of time the speed of computers has increased by factors of thousands and even tens of thousands over that of the early models. Their voraciousness for data and their ability to handle it and reproduce it in a myriad of combinations has correspondingly increased. All of this is having its consequences; it is bringing about a variety of changes in people, in business, and in society. What are these changes and, more important, where are we headed?

We must recognize that we are now in the very midst of this change. While it is easy to perceive changes once they have taken place, and we can look back with a certain degree of perspective over the past, it is much more difficult when one is in the midst of these changes. Even more difficult to grasp are the secondary consequences of technological innovation and change. Henry Boettinger, American Telephone and Telegraph Assistant Comptroller for Management Sciences, relates an anecdote which illustrates this point:

"Let me tell you this little story to point up the significance of the secondary consequences of our acts. It shows you really can't predict what's going to happen from the impact of inventions and technological change.

"We can make a lot of predictions about what is going to happen, but those are all primary consequences. You can't put in a staff study of the real wingdinger stuff, which is the secondary effect of things.

"I'll give you one illustration of secondary effects. A friend of mine —a sort of non-violent James Bond correspondent in the Middle East —wanders into Third Avenue bars every now and then. And one day he was there when one of the boys asked him, 'What's all this with the Arabs? They're kicking up all this fuss in the Middle East. For a thousand years they've been asleep, and now we got all this uproar. What's causing it?'

"Well, after three martinis my friend answers, 'Japanese transistor radios.' Even in that atmosphere an answer like that calls for some explanation, so he goes on to explain that Radio Cairo is the largest broadcasting complex in the world. They broadcast 24 hours a day in 26 dialects and they push fairly hard stuff, not just rock and roll— and the illiteracy rate is very high. But everybody has a transistor radio. A poor soul is dying of starvation in the gutter and he's clutching a transistor radio to his ear. All these people all over the Arab world are listening to these unity messages from Cairo.

"So let's go back to Bell Telephone Laboratories and walk through one day. You have to pick the day carefully. You see three guys in shirtsleeves and ask them: 'Fellows, what are you working on?' The guys say, 'Well, you're in luck. Today we just invented the transistor.'

"Now, if you're really good at predicting the future, you're supposed to say, 'That's wonderful, and that'll be a fantastic force for unity in the Arab world.'

"Now, if you say this, they'll throw you out, but if you don't say it, you're not very good at looking ahead. This sort of thing happens all the time."*

---

* "A Monologue on Secondary Consequences: Or, How the Transistor Affects Arab Unity," *Bell Telephone Magazine*, July/August, 1968.

One significant trend is the increased interest in the development of large and highly integrated operating systems, that is, computer systems that involve and link together more than one business application. In most firms, the computer has been handling applications such as sales order entry, inventory control, and shop scheduling as separate applications. Sales orders, for example, are collected for a time, say a day or week, and then processed in one batch on the computer. In a similar way, periodic inventory control runs are made, inventory levels calculated, and orders for replenishment then issued by the computer. Sometimes the output from one application run is used as input for another, but more often than not the computer runs are fairly independent.

With the increasing acceptance of random access files, real-time on-line and remote terminals linked via communications to a central processor, the trend is toward integrating a number of business operations. In our example, the sales order would be accepted by a remote entry keyboard from the salesman in the field, the computer would automatically check the customer's credit, issue shipping orders to the appropriate warehouse if it is a stock item (or release a shop order otherwise), update the inventory records, request replenishment from the factory if the order point has been reached, update all the files containing the management reports, and confirm to the salesman at the remote terminal, all in a matter of seconds.

The importance of such systems lies not in their size or sophistication but in the competitive advantage they may provide those corporations which develop them and use them wisely. Any corporation that spends the time and resources to develop and implement one of these highly integrated operating systems has had to carefully analyze and streamline its own operations. This in itself is very often a concealed advantage in new systems development. But beyond that, it has placed itself in a better position to react to the changing market place. Its information will be more timely and more accurate, and, presumably, it will be able to make better and wiser decisions.

Another very important trend is in the development of models and simulations of the business firm of some of its major functional areas. Admittedly, the conceptualization of a business model, and its translation into the mathematical language, which can be manipulated by computers, is difficult and in its infancy. It is also fraught with the danger of putting too much reliance on what is at best an approximation of the real world. But progress is steadily being made, the models are becoming more complex as they attempt to portray more realistically the business operations. Speed and power of computers have kept pace with this increased complexity so that it is possible to simulate years of actual operations in a matter of hours or even minutes.

In the future, therefore, managers will be able to study the consequences of various alternative actions. Surely the initial attempts will be sketchy and incomplete, but as analysts gain experience, and as managers learn to work with the analysts (and vice versa) improvements will be made. This will eventually prove to be one of the most significant and rewarding trends in the computer field.

Consider finally the startling increase in the computational speed and flexibility of today's computers as compared to those in the early beginnings. We said factors of a thousand or even tens of thousands are commonplace. The super giants of the coming decade will be marvels of technology, operate on real time, sharing many jobs and demands on them, satisfying many users simultaneously, and manage to continue operating, although perhaps at a slower pace, even though parts may malfunction. And consider also that during this short span of less than two decades some $18 billion in computers has been installed, and this figure will reach 30 billion by the end of 1973.

It is increasingly obvious that one trend is for the almost total disappearance of simple business clerical tasks as we now know them— all the way from routine preparation of payrolls to the compilation of special reports—and their replacement by computer systems. This will be true in small businesses as well as in the giant enterprises. The computers they use will range likewise from today's mini-computers through tomorrow's very large multi-processors. Perhaps more and more businesses, especially the smaller ones, will turn to the services of the emerging computer utilities.

This will have some important effects on the relative proportion of various levels of the working force. In effect, the proportion of the most unskilled clerical force will decrease, relative to that which can intelligently use the output from the computers for some kind of decision making. This does not mean that relatively unskilled support will not be required to prepare and provide the data to the computer, but their proportion will be small relative to that proportion concerned with programming the computer, keeping it running, and understanding and using its output for decision making.

Mr. Terrance Hanold, President of the Pillsbury Company, described it this way:

"To date, then, we have succeeded in our aim of diminishing to a limited degree the primary levels of salaried employees within the corporation, and we succeeded in our objective of severely curtailing the administrative side of middle management. And we have been vastly successful, without at all intending it, in expanding both the analytical and executive functions and the absolute numbers of middle management. This latter fact has not been sufficiently described, and no attempt has been made to measure the rate at which this trend is continuing. Certainly, there has been no speculation respecting the future effect of this phenomenon upon the business corporation and its management.

"The rate of advance of middle management people in our firm has been marked. Since 1960 their proportion of salaried personnel has increased from about 22.5% to about 30.5%. Just as radical has been their change in function. Their activity has totally shifted from the supervision of other employees to the management of the business."*

And what demands will this place on the management of the enterprise? In some ways their jobs will be easier—data will be available faster, it will be more timely and more accurate. And it will be presented in better formats, perhaps already analyzed under a variety of assumptions and based on several models, even displayed on demand on a Cathode Ray Tube.

It is precisely this increased sophistication in analysis and promptness in reporting that will tax tomorrow's manager in ways we can only dimly perceive today. He will no longer be able to put off taking corrective action to a degenerating trend. He will know that his competition's information system is equally responsive and that its management may well make the better decisions in the long run.

---

* Terrance Hanold, "A President's View of MIS," *Datamation*, November, 1968.

Appendices

The Nature of Decisions: Classical Versus Modern View

The Classical Approach

PREDICTION

THE CLASSICAL APPROACH to decision making views the decision problem as a set of alternatives[1] and requires the selection of the best course of action on the basis of accomplishing some designated purpose. To make a decision, the possible outcome of each of the alternative courses of action must be forecast.

VALUES

To select from the alternatives, we must be able to rank possible outcomes according to their desirability. Classical decision theory generally avoids the problem of multiple goals and, hence, multiple dimensions along which the decision-maker must measure the desirability of outcomes. When all the values in a problem cannot be reduced to a single dimension (e.g., dollars), as is the case in most decision problems, the assignment of net total desirability to an outcome is difficult to determine and generally depends on all other possible outcomes.

The problem of multiple value systems has received a great deal of attention, but results have been sufficiently meager to warrant the

---

[1] While only one line of action can be taken, this approach presents no conceptual difficulties in that a single action may be comprised of a subset of actions and, hence, merely involves the rearrangement of the list of alternatives.

conclusion that "executive judgment" must continue to function as the synthesizer. The process of assigning values and the reconciliation of multiple goals is carried out by the "Value System" (Figure 1).

CRITERIA

The "Decision Rule," or "Criterion," (Figure 1) in the classical approach is very simple: Choose the action which leads to the outcome(s) having the highest desirability.

Modern Decision Theory

PREDICTION

Modern, or statistical, decision theory considers multiple outcomes for each alternative course of action. It begins with the admission that predictions are fallible and abandons "all or none" types of predictions. For example, a prediction that a new product can achieve sales of 1000 units in two years has an infinitely small chance of being accurate. Rather, such a prediction is interpreted by its makers and users as the average of the probabilities of the event. Statistical decision theory requires that the decision maker estimate and state the relevant probabilities explicitly. Although these estimates generally are based on past experience, they always contain a subjective component.

The use of statistical forecasting techniques is compatible with this decision theory because they generate measures of the uncertainty of forecasts as a by-product of the forecasting process. Under statistical decision theory then, the "Predicting System" becomes a "Probability Predicting System."

VALUES

The application of statistical decision theory does not fundamentally affect the "Value System." However, it does place a greater emphasis on the need for reconciling multiple goals and values. To carry out the mathematical steps required, a homogeneous measure of desirability is essential.[2] It is not fruitful to apply anything but the structure

---

[2] In this respect, statistical decision theory suffers from the same frustrations as game theory, its closest relative.

of modern statistical decision theory, as distinct from its mathematics, to problems with weakly defined value systems.

THE CONCEPT OF UTILITY

Formal decision techniques break down where the relationship between the degree of desirability of an outcome and changes in the outcome are not strictly proportional, or linearly related as in Figure 14a. Unfortunately, this condition is common. For instance, the one million and first dollar that hinges upon a particular decision is not as important as the one hundred and first dollar. We know that over wide ranges of uncertain outcome, the desirability ("utility") or value, of an extra dollar is not constant. To ensure that payoffs are measured in a linear scale, therefore, prospective payoffs in any dimension (dollars, barrels, etc.) are frequently converted to a common linear measure "utility." The "scale of utility" is developed by placing the decision maker in a gambling situation, where he is required to make a series of choices involving fair bets at various stakes. Since the resulting utility measure combines the value of outcomes in their original measure (e.g., dollars) and the decision makers attitude toward risk, this measure is only appropriate in situations involving risk; therefore, it is properly a subject only of statistical decision making.

CRITERIA

Classical theory is limited to one decision criterion; statistical decision theory recognizes several criteria, one or more of which can be appropriate for the selection of the optimum course of action. These multiple criteria are easily described by an illustration of a payoff matrix.[3]

A payoff matrix (Figure 15) is a two-dimensional array of numbers, which is used as a simple medium for representing a decision problem. The rows represent the alternative strategies developed for the problem; the columns represent the possible future states of the world. The entries at the intersection of the rows and columns are the predicted outcomes, generated by the Predicting Systems, of each alternative for each state. Numbers by the Value System indicate the desirability of each outcome (in this case desirability is measured in dollars and cents). For each future state of the world, we have the probability of its occurrence (P) as directly or subjectively forecast

---

[3] We have adopted and extended the example used by D. W. Miller and M. K. Starr, *Executive Decisions and Operations Research*, Prentice-Hall, Englewood Cliffs, N. J., 1960, Chapter 5.

Figure 14

A.

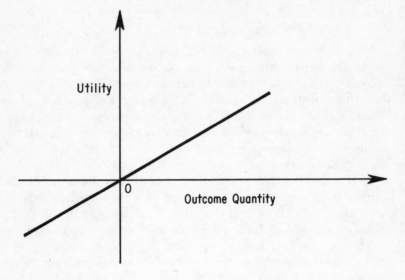

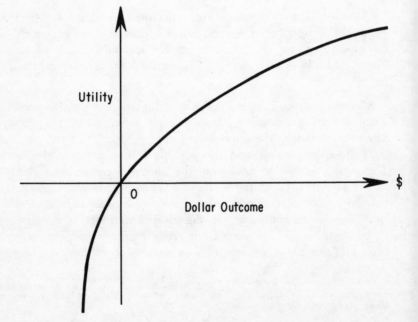
B.

Figure 15

PAYOFF MATRIX

| | Possible Outcomes | | | |
| Alternative Strategies | Peace | War | Depression | Probabilities |
	P1	P2	P3	
1 Stocks	20	1	−6	Possible Payoff Values (V)
2 Corporate Bonds	9	8	0	
3 Government Bonds	4	4	4	

by the decision-maker(s). The nature of these probability statements can be used to characterize three types of decisions, each of which is discussed below

- *Decisions Under Certainty:* One of the probabilities is 1, and the others are 0. The payoff matrix is reduced to a single-column list.
- *Decisions Under Uncertainty:* All of the probabilities are non-zero and equal to the reciprocal of the number of states of nature considered. The equality arises from the fact that there is insufficient information to assume them unequal.
- *Decisions Under Risk:* All of the probabilities are non-zero, and at least two of them are not equal. They must, of course, sum to 1.

DECISION CRITERIA UNDER UNCERTAINTY

We will discuss each of the several decision criteria that have been developed for this class of decisions, labeling them according to the nature of the selection of alternatives made, the nature of the decision-maker implied, the name of the statistician who first formally investigated the criterion, and its statistical name.

(1) *Criterion of Pessimism—Cautious (Wald-maximin):* The decision maker behaves pessimistically, acting as if nature were completely malevolent. Under this condition, the decision-maker selects that action which maximizes the minimum payoff (Figure 15, A3).

(2) *Criterion of Optimism—Adventurous (Hurwicz-maximax):* The decision-maker behaves optimistically, acting as if Nature were completely benevolent. In this situation, he selects that action with the

maximum payoff (Figure 15, A1).[4]

(3) *Criterion of Regret—Bad Loser (Savage-maximax):* After a (selection of an action) has been made and a state of nature has occurred, the decision-maker may wish that he had selected some other action. The decision-maker may wish to select that action which will minimize his maximum potential regret. Regret may be measured as the difference between the payoff actually received and that which he could have received had he known with certainty the state of nature that would occur. To analyze this condition, we transform the payoff matrix of Figure 15 to a regret matrix (Figure 16). For example, if

Figure 16

REGRET MATRIX FOR FIGURE 15

Alternative Strategies	Possible Outcomes			
	Peace	War	Depression	
	P1	P2	P3	Probabilities
Stocks	0	7	10	
Corporate Bonds	11	0	4	Possible Regrets
Government Bonds	16	4	0	

war actually occurred, the measure of regret for each action, in case of peace, would be R1 = 20 − 20 = 0, R2 = 20 − 9 = 11, and R3 = 20 − 4 = 16. The other states of the economy can be transformed similarly. The decision-maker selects from the regret matrix that action which minimizes the maximum possible regret (A1).

(4) *Criterion of Rationality—Rational (LaPlace):* The LaPlace criterion may be considered rational in that the decision-maker is required to act as if he did not know the relevant probabilities if he indeed does not know them (decision making under risk). It is generally agreed that if a decision-maker makes a selection by other than the LaPlace criterion, it is a reflection that:

(a) The Value System is sufficiently weak that the entries in the payoff matrix are not an adequate representation of how the decision-maker feels about the relative desir-

---

[4] The development and use of this criterion is less simple than it appears; however, further discussion of it is beyond the scope of our introductory survey, and the reader is referred to Miller and Starr (pp. 87-88).

abilities of the various action/outcome possibilities; or
(b) The decision-maker favors the probability that one or more future states of the world will eventuate (decision making under risk).

The LaPlace criterion makes explicit use of the lack of information concerning the probabilities of the possible future states of the world. Following Bayes' Principle of Insufficient Reason, probabilities are assigned on the assumption that all of possible future states of the world are equally probable. This assumption, combined with the restriction that the sum of the probabilities must be 1, implies that each probability is equal to 1/n, where there are n states of nature. The expected payoff of each action is then calculated as the sum of the possible values subsequent to the action, each multiplied by the probability of its occurrence. In our example,

$$E(A) = p_1V_1 + p_2V_2 + .p_3V_3$$

where

$$p_1 = p_2 = p_3 = \tfrac{1}{3}$$

Thus,

$$E(A) = \tfrac{1}{3}(V_1 + V_2 + V_3)$$
$$E(A1) = \tfrac{1}{3}(20 + 1 + (-6)) = 5$$
$$E(A2) = \tfrac{1}{3}(9 + 8 + 0) = 5.67$$
$$E(A3) = \tfrac{1}{3}(4 + 4 + 4) = 4$$

The LaPlace criterion counsels the decision-maker to select that strategy with the largest expected payoff (Figure 15, A2).

DECISION CRITERIA UNDER RISK

When the decision-maker can estimate the probability of the occurrence of relevant future states of the world, decisions are considered to be made under conditions of risk. This class of decisions may be considered an extension of the Bayes/LaPlace scheme, and represents the common case. Seldom is a manager completely unable to estimate the relative probabilities of future events, if only on a most intuitive, or subjective, basis. This ability is what executive experience and judgment consists of. If an executive has absolutely no feelings about the relative probabilities, it is at least a tacit argument that he lacks experience and/or judgment about the problem at hand and, consequently, that the decision is inappropriately lodged within the organization.

In our example, we assume that the decision-maker holds the following expectations: P (Peace) = .5, P (War) = .1, and P_3 (Depression) = .4. We use these probabilities to transpose the Payoff Matrix (Figure 15) into an Expected Payoff Matrix (Figure 17). The

Figure 17

EXPECTED PAYOFF MATRIX OF FIGURE 15

Alternative Strategies	Possible Outcomes			
	Peace P_1 2.5	*War* P_2 2.1	*Depression* P_3 2.4	*Probabilities*
A1 Stocks	10	0.1	− 2.4	7.7
A2 Corporate Bonds	4.5	0.8	0	6.3
A3 Government Bonds	2	↱ 0.4	1.6	4

Expected Payoff of Alternatives

└── Expected Payoffs (pV)

appropriate decision criterion under risk is the LaPlace/Bayes criterion: select the strategy which yields the largest expected payoff. Following the previous example, we have:

$$E(A) = p_1V_1 + p_2V_2 + p_3V_3$$

where

$p_1 - .1, p_2 = .5,$ and $p_3 = .4$

Thus,

$$E(A1) = .5 (20) + .1 (1) + .4(-6) = 7.7$$
$$E(A2) = .5 (9) + .1 (8) + .4(0) = 5.3$$
$$E(A3) = .5 (4) + .1 (4) + .4(4) = 0.4$$

The results counsel the decision-maker to select (A1).

One interesting and fruitful approach to decision problems under conditions of risk, which is frequently employed in operations research, is to arrive at a decision of this type by "coming in the back door." This technique involves continuously modifying the probability estimates (and/or the payoff values) of the problem until an alternative other than A1 is selected by the LaPlace/Bayes criterion. At this point, the probability estimates (and/or payoff values) are reviewed. If these quantities are far out of line with the decision-maker's expectations, the original decision can be held with confidence. However, if the alternative selected is quite sensitive to small changes in the underlying probability and value estimates, the original decision must be held with caution, subject to better information.

Thus, modern statistical decision theory represents two important extensions of classical decision theory: (1) It copes explicitly with problems of risk and uncertainty; and (2) it has developed an embarrassment of riches about appropriate decision criteria. In our example, each alternative was selected by one or another criterion. Although the prospect of multiple decision criteria is disturbing to many executives exposed to formal analysis of decisions, a little reflection reveals that it is the necessary consequence of uncertainty. Since attitudes toward gambling and financial circumstances differ from person to person and even for a single individual from time to time and since people's aversion to risk tends to vary with the size of the stakes involved and their own resources, there can be no universally valid decision rule.

Each of the various decision rules described is internally consistent, and each is appropriate given a particular attitude on the part of the decision-maker. However, two aspects of the rationality of the expected value criterion stand out. First, it is the only criterion which utilizes all of the information in the Payoff Matrix. Each of the Wald, Hurwicz, and Savage criteria concentrates only on the extreme values in each row, completely disregarding the values of the other elements. It is always possible to find situations in which the relative magnitudes of these other elements cast doubt on the wisdom of such choices. Only the LaPlace/Bayes criterion fully utilizes all of the available information relevant to the problem. Second, as Miller points out, Savage's Regret Matrix is nothing but the definition of economic opportunity costs. In those cases where dollars and cents are the appropriate value measures, economic logic and business common sense require that a decision criterion should select the same alternative, whether the problem is stated in terms of original dollar payoffs or opportunity costs. The Wald, Hurwicz, and (by implication) Savage criteria fail to meet this test; only the LaPlace/Bayes criterion does. Hence, in the extreme case of linear utility functions the LaPlace/Bayes criterion is the only rational method.

Glossary

A

Access, Memory. See: *Memory.*

Accumulator. (1) Part of the hardware of a computer; the register (similar to that of a desk calculator) in which arithmetic and logical operations are performed. (2) A unit in a digital computer where numbers are totalled, i.e. accumulated.

ALGOL. An acronym for *AL*Gorithmic *O*riented *L*anguage, a procedure oriented *compiler language* (cf. FORTRAN) used widely in Europe.

Analog Computers. See: *Computer, Analog.*

Arithmetic Control Module. The physical part of the computer that performs arithmetic and control functions.

Assembly Language. A programming language unique to a particular computer which is somewhere between *machine language* and *compiler language* in incomprehensibility. A program written in assembly language must be translated by an assembler or *assembly routine* into machine language before execution.

Assembly Routine (or Assembler). A program which translates a program written in *assembly language* into *machine language* instructions. The assembly routine generates one machine language instruction for each assembly language instruction.

Associative Memory Search. A method of retrieving information by identifying each storage location by its contents.

B

Behavioristic Decision Making. Decision making in circumstances where no well-defined set of rules or heuristics is available for studying a decision problem. This type of decision making involves the use of abstractions, sudden insights and serendipity as a means to create, develop, and analyze the decision alternatives.

Bug. An error in a program that causes the computer to stop before completing the job or to produce results that are wrong.

Burroughs. See: *Computer Manufacturers.*

C

Cathode Ray Tube. (1) An electronic vacuum tube containing a screen on which information may be stored by means of a multigrid modulated beam of electronics from the thermionic emitter storage effected by means of charged or uncharged spots. (2) A storage tube. (3) An oscilloscope tube. (4) A picture tube.

Central Processor. See: *Processor.*

Classical-Decision Theory. The theory that an optimal decision consists of the maximization of some objective function subject to certain constraints.

Closed-Loop. Pertaining to a system with feedback type of control, such that the output is used to modify the input.

COBOL. An acronym for Common Business Oriented Language, a business data processing language.

Commercial Computers. See: *Computers, Commercial.*

Compile. The act of translating a *program* written in a *compiler language* into *machine language* instructions. The compiler or translator is itself a program which generates many machine language instructions for one compiler language instruction.

Compiler Languages. Languages much like English in which programs are written and then translated by a compiler into *machine* language. Compiler languages include *ALGOL, FORTRAN, COBOL, P/I,* etc.

Computer. (1) A device capable of solving problems by accepting data, performing prescribed operations on the data, and supplying the results of these operations. Various types of computers are calculator, digital computer, or analog computer. (2) In information processing, usually, an automatic stored program computer.

Computer, Analog. A computer which represents variables by physical analogies. Thus any computer which solves problems by translating physical conditions such as flow, temperature, pressure, angular position, or voltage into related mechanical or electrical quantities and uses mechanical or electrical equivalent circuits as an analog for the physical phenomenon being investigated. In general it is a computer which uses an analog for each variable and produces analogs as output. Thus, an analog computer measures continuously whereas a digital computer counts discretely.

Computer, Commercial. Computers designed and used primarily for business data processing, e.g., accounting.

Computer, Digital. A computer that solves problems by operating on discrete data representing variables by performing arithmetic and logical processes on these data.

Computer Down Time. The period during which a computer is malfunctioning or not operating correctly due to mechanical or electronic failure, as opposed to available time, idle time, or standby time, during which the computer is functional.

Computer Generations. Classes of computers generally defined as follows: first generation—all pre-solid state computers; second generation—solid-state computers; third generation—computers with the features which permit multi-programming.

Computer Hardware. See: *Hardware.*

Computers, Hybrid. Computers which combine *analog* and *digital* components.

Computer Independent Languages. Languages that are the same for different computers. Programs written in computer independent languages can be executed on various computers, even those made by different manufacturers.

Computer Language. Program instructions may be written in one of many possible languages, but a computer can execute instruction in only one language, called its *machine language.* Machine language instructions consist of patterns of numbers and letters. These instructions are practically incomprehensible and are very difficult to write. Consequently, translators were designed to translate languages more like English into machine language. There are two kinds of translators: *compiler* and *assemblers.* *Compiler language* instructions are translated by a compiler into machine language; for one compiler language instruction, there may be many machine language instructions. *Assembler language* instructions are trans-one-to-one into machine language. See: *COBOL, FORTRAN, PL/1, Compiler Assembler, Machine.*

Computer Manufacturers, Primary. Vendors of computing equipment who market a full line of computers and peripheral equipment.

Computer Memory. See: *Memory.*

Computer Models. See: *Mathematical Business Models.*

Computer Mythology. A mistaken set of beliefs that results in overestimating the computer's potential and underestimating its costs.

Computer Output. See: *Output.*

Computer Peripheral Equipment. The auxiliary machines which may be placed under the control of the central computer. Examples are card readers, card punches, magnetic tape feeds and high-speed printers.

Computer Processor. See: *Processor.*

Computer Program. A series of instructions which, when executed, will perform some task, e.g. arithmetic computation, report production, etc. These instructions are all stored in the computer prior to execution and are executed sequentially.

Computers, Scientific. Computers designed and used primarily for scientific data processing, e.g., statistical analysis, simulation.

Computer Simulation. See: *Simulation.*

Computer Software. See: *Software.*

Computer Time Sharing. See: *Time Sharing.*

Control Data Corporation. See: *Computer Manufacturers.*

Controller. The interface between a peripheral device and the central processor.

Conversationalist Mode. A method of giving *input* to the computer in which the computer asks questions or displays alternatives and the user answers in the language of the questions.

Core, Memory. A physical part of the computer into which instructions and data can be entered and from which they can be retrieved at a later time.

Corporate Data Bank. A readily retrievable file containing data related to all aspects of corporate activity and from which summary reports on specific matters are easily prepared to order.

Corporate Systems. See: *Corporate Data Bank.*

Cost-Benefit Analysis. The analysis of the costs and benefits of alternative decisions and an attempt to establish a desirable relationship between them.

Cross-Tabulation. A form of data summary or table by two or more of its characteristics, e.g., a table showing the number of people in the U.S. in each of five age groups and each of six income groups is called a cross-tab of age by income and has thirty separate totals.

Cybernetics. The comparative study of electro-mechanical control systems and the human central nervous system.

D

Data Communication. The transfer of information from one place to another.

Data Manipulation. A catch-all term covering all computer operations with data; arithmetic operation, preparing data for reports, etc.

Data Processing. See: *EDP.*

Data Retrieval. The act of retrieving data from a storage device, e.g., from magnetic tape, disk, drum.

Debugging. The act of checking and altering a program until it operates correctly.

Decision Making, Behavioristic. See: *Behavioristic.*

Density, Core. A measure of the amount of information that can be stored per unit of volume inside computer memory.

Digital Computers. See: *Computer, Digital.*

Display. A presentation of information by the computer in a form such that it can be read by people.

Down Time. See: *Computer Down Time.*

E

EDP (Electronic Data Processing). Data processing largely performed by electronic means.

F

Files, Memory. Information stored on tapes, disks, or drums, or temporarily in the computer itself. It is usually organized in the same way as any physical file.

Flow Chart. A graphic representation of the major steps of work in process. The illustrative symbols may represent documents, machines, or actions taken during the process. The area of concentration is on where or who does what rather than how it is to be done.

Forecasting. An attempt to predict the future.

Extrapolative. A prediction of future values of some entity by a study of its past trends. The procedures used may be statistical or merely graphic, e.g., the extension of a trend line.

Associative. A prediction of future values of some entity by a study not only of its past trends but also of the past behavior of other entities which have been and will probably continue to be related to the entities of interest. Its techniques are, in general, considerably more complex, and their results often more successful, than those of extrapolative forecasting.

FORTRAN. An acronym for *FOR*mula *TRAN*slation, a procedure oriented *compiler language* used for scientific data processing, e.g., a statistical analysis, engineering applications.

FORTRAN IV. A more powerful and flexible set of instructions than FORTRAN, of which FORTRAN is a subset.

G

General Electric Company. See: *Computer Manufacturers.*

GIGO. An acronym for "Garbage-In, Garbage-Out." This catch-phrase, which refers to the hopelessness of processing bad data by electronic computers, was popular a few years ago among those who favored alternative methods of processing their garbage.

Gyorgy Polya. An American mathematician born in Budapest in 1887. He is the author of *How to Solve It,* a basic text in *Heuristic Problem Solving.*

H

Hardware. The physical equipment or devices forming a computer and peripheral equipment. Contrasted with *software.*

Heuristic Problem Solving. An attempt to find a satisfactory "happy" solution to a problem—in contrast to optimizing, which is an attempt to find the best possible solution.

Honeywell. See: *Computer Manufacturers.*

Hurwicz Criterion. One of several criteria that the decision-maker can use as the basis for a strategy in games against Nature when no information is available about Nature. If the matrix of the game is such that the decision maker selects a row and Nature a column, using the Hurwicz criterion the decision maker selects a constant, ∞, between zero and one which reflects his optimism. For each row he then computes. $H = \infty$ (largest element) $+ (1 - \infty)$ (smallest element), and selects the row for which H is maximized. For $\infty = 0$, the Hurwicz criterion is equivalent to the Wald criterion. For $\infty = 1$, the Hurwicz criterion is equivalent to the maximax criterion.

Hybrid Computers. See: *Computer, Hybrid.*

I

IBM. See: *Computer Manufacturers.*

IMPACT. An acronym for *Inventory Management Programs and Control Techniques,* a group of general purpose computer programs for the control of inventories in retail and wholesale trade. Retail and Wholesale Impact are owned and supplied by International Business Machines, Inc.

Indexing, File. A method of storing information so that its storage position is identified by a unique index value.

Information Overload. The inundation of executives with too many reports and figures.

Information System. The network of all communication methods within an organization. Information may be derived from many sources other than a data processing unit, e.g., by telephone, by contact with other people, or by studying an operation.

Information Technology. Technology of the storage, access, and search for information using computers.

Input. Information fed into the computer in the form of punched cards, magnetic tape, disk or drum, etc.

Input/Output Module. A general term for the equipment used to communicate with a computer.

Punched Cards. Cards made of heavy stiff paper of uniform size and shape, on which program instructions and data are recorded in the form of punched holes in the card. These cards are then fed into the computer, where wire brushes sense electrically the pattern of punched holes and translate the patterns into a letter or number.

Drum, Magnetic. A cylinder having a surface coating of magnetic material, which stores binary information by the orientation of magnetic dipoles near or on its surface. Since the drum is rotated at a uniform rate, the information stored is available periodically as a given portion of the surface moves past one or more flux detecting devices called heads located near the surface of the drum.

Disk, Magnetic. A storage device on which information is recorded on the magnetizable surface of a rotating disk. A magnetic disk storage system is an array of such devices, with associated reading and writing heads which are mounted on movable arms.

Punched Paper Tape. Tape on which instructions and data are recorded in the form of punched holes in the tape; an alternative to punched cards used primarily for *remote* consoles.

Printed Reports. Output from a computer program produced by the printer attached to the computer.

CRT. See: *CRT.*

Tape, Magnetic. A tape or ribbon of any material impregnated or coated with magnetic or other material on which information may be placed in the form of magnetically polarized spots.

Bulk Storage. Supplementary computer storage with slower access time than main storage.

Integrated Circuits. Circuits combining several logical elements into one physical device.

Integrated System. A system that treats as a whole all data processing requirements to accomplish a sequence of data processing steps, and which strives to reduce or eliminate duplicating data entry or processing steps.

Intracompany Computer Communications System. A system within a company where there are many remote terminals, all of which collect and disperse information to various parts of the company.

K

Keypunch. A machine used to prepare data (figures, letters, etc.) in machine-read form. An operator seated at a typewriter-style keyboard reading the original document types the information which she reads and thus transfers the data into a pattern of punched holes in a card. The size of the card as well as the code by which figures and letters become holes in a card varies from one computer manufacturer to another. The keypunch machine is the most frequently used device to create machine-readable records.

L

LaPlace Criterion. One of several criteria that the decision-maker can use as the basis for a strategy in games against Nature when no information is available about Nature. If the matrix of the game is such that the decision-maker selects a row and Nature a column, using the LaPlace criterion, he assumes that all of the states of Nature are equally probable and selects the row which maximizes the expected value of his gain.

Laser Memory. A new experimental storage device using laser techniques that will pack about 10 times more in a given space than state-of-the-art practice will allow.

Linear Programming. A technique for achieving the best allocation of scarce resources, each of which may involve different costs and have different degrees of productivity. A characteristic of the technique is a formulation of an "objective function," the weighted sum of some measure of each resource, which is to be minimized (if, for example, the measure is cost) or maximized (if, for example, the measure is productivity.) The technique has proved extremely flexible and applicable to an astonishing diversity of practical problems.

Logistics. Until recently a military term referring to the art of obtaining, maintaining, and transporting troops and material. In recent years the term has acquired a broader meaning: "the art of managing the flow of materials and products from source to user."[1]

M

Machine Language. A language consisting of patterns of numbers and letters almost incomprehensible to a human being but understood by the computer. Instructions in machine language are the only instructions the computer can execute. See: *Computer,* Computer Language.

Management Control Systems. Systems for providing information or making decisions or initiating action according to rules set by management.

Management Information System. A communications process in which data are recorded and processed for operational purposes. The problems are isolated for higher level decision making and information is fed back to top management to reflect the progress or lack of progress made in achieving major objectives.

Mathematical Business Model. A mathematical representation that simulates the behavior of a business process, device, or concept.

Memory (Same as Storage). The physical part of the computer in which the program and data are stored temporarily while a program is being executed.

Memory Search, Associative. See: *Associative.*

Memory Access, Random. See: *Random Access.*

Memory Core. See: *Core.*

Memory Files. See: *Files, Memory.*

Memory, Laser. See: *Laser.*

Memory Module. The collection of all pieces of computer equipment used for memory or storage.

Memory, Plated Wire. See: *Plated Wire.*

Mnemonic. A device intended to assist human memory; thus a mnemonic term is usually an abbreviation that is easy to remember; e.g., mpy for multiply and acc for accumulator.

---

[1] Magee, John F., *Industrial Logistics,* McGraw-Hill, 1968.

"Model Aphasia." A disease common to mathematical models in which an abstracted sub-problem of the problem is solved; and then the solver convinces himself that he has solved the real problem.

Models, Mathematical. See: *Mathematical Business Models.*

Modern-Decision Theory. The theory that an optimal decision not only includes static objectives and constraints, but also requires subjective evaluation of the probabilities that hold for future events.

Multiplexor. A device which controls the transfer of data from several storage devices operating at relatively low transfer rates to one storage device operating at a high transfer rate in such a manner that the high-speed device is not obliged to wait for the low-speed devices.

O

Open-Loop. Pertaining to a control system in which there is no self-correcting action for misses of the desired operational condition, as there is in a closed-loop system.

Operations Research. The use of analytic methods adopted from mathematics for solving operational problems. The objective is to provide management with a more logical basis for making sound predictions and decisions. Among the common scientific techniques used in operations research are the following: linear programming, probability theory, information theory, game theory, monte carlo method, and queuing theory. Synonymous with O.R. and Operational Research.

Optical Reader. A device which transfers printed material to punched cards.

Output. Information received from the computer in the form of printed reports, punched cards, magnetic tape, disk or drum.

Peripheral Equipment. See: *Computer Peripheral Equipment.*

PERT Charts & Networks. A technique for planning a complex task consisting of many parts so as to accomplish it efficiently with respect to time or cost.

P

PL/1. A highly praised new compiler language which will, conceptually at least, contain as subsets COBOL, FORTRAN and ALGOL. Many instruction manuals have been written for it, but few PL/1 compilers currently exist.

Plated Wire Memory. A recently developed storage device that may provide substantial reductions in main memory costs.

Processor (or Central Processor). (1) The physical part of a computer that contains the main storage, arithmetic unit and special register groups. (2) All that portion of a computer exclusive of the input, output, peripheral, and in some instances, storage units.

Process Control. Descriptive of systems in which computers, most frequently analog computers, are used for the automatic regulation of operations or processes. Typical are operations in the production of chemicals wherein the operation control is applied continually and adjustments to regulate the operation are directed by the computer to keep the value of a controlled variable constant.

Program or Patch Boards (Hand Wired). Boards on which a program can be wired. Usually less flexible than a stored program but still in use for some special purposes.

Program Bugs. See: *Bugs.*

Program Debugging. See: *Debugging.*

Programmer. A person who, given a problem involving the computer, prepares *flow charts* and writes *programs* to solve the problem.

Programming. The act of writing *programs* for the computer in either *assembly language* or one of the *compiler languages.*

Project "Doctor". MIT, a program *conversational mode* which provides a light-hearted and limited "psychoanalysis" for the operation of a *remote terminal* of the MIT *time-sharing* system.

R

Radio Corporation of America. See: *Computer Manufacturers.*

Random Access. (1) The process of obtaining information from or placing information into storage where the time required for such access is independent of the location of the information most recently obtained or placed in storage. (2) A device in which random access, as defined above, can be achieved without effective penalty in time.

Real-Time System. A system which processes information or data in such a rapid manner that the results of the processing are available in time to influence the process being monitored or controlled.

Remote Console. A machine, much like a teletype in construction. It is one form of remote terminal.

Remote Terminal. A device physically distant from a computer at which input can be fed to the computer and output received from it.

Reprogramming. The act of writing a new program to solve a problem when an old program or part of an old program already exists.

Rerun Time. The time required to run a program again.

Robinson-Patman Legislation. A 1936 amendment to Section 2 of the Clayton Act of 1914. Its purpose is to make it unlawful "to discriminate in price between different purchasers of commodities of like grade and quality . . . where the effect of such discrimination may be substantially to lessen competition or tend to create a monopoly in any line of commerce, or to injure, destroy, or prevent competition with any person who either grants or knowingly receives the benefits of such discrimination. . . ."

S

Sabre Reservation System. A computerized system that American Airlines uses to make, cancel, and change flight reservations and waiting lists on an on-line real-time basis. Inquiries of the system are made from remote terminals that are located all over the country.

Savage Criterion. One of several criteria that the decision-maker can use as the basis for a strategy in games against Nature when no information is available about Nature. If the matrix of the game is such that the decision-maker selects a row and Nature a column, using the Savage criterion, the decision-maker first computes a matrix of regrets by subtracting the maximum element in each column from all elements in that column. The resulting matrix contains only negative elements; each element is a measure of the difference between the payoff actually obtained by choosing the row and the payoff that could have been obtained if the state of Nature had been known. The decision-maker selects the row which minimizes the maximum regret, i.e., then finds the minimum regret in each row (recall that regrets are negative), and chooses the row that maximizes the minimum regret.

Scientific Computers. See: *Computer, Scientific.*

Simulation. The representation of physical systems and phenomena by computers, models, or other equipment; e.g., an imitative type of data processing in which an automatic computer is used as a model of some entity; e.g., a chemical process. Information enters the computer to represent the factors entering the real process, the computer produces information that represents the results of the process, and the processing done by the computer represents the process itself.

Simultaneous Processing (Overlapping, Buffering). An ability of some computers to perform two operations at once, e.g., reading cards and writing tape.

Software. The totality of programs and routines used to extend the capabilities of computers, such as compilers, assemblers, narrators, routines, and subroutines. Contrasted with *hardware.*

Storage (Same as Memory). The physical part of the computer where the program and data are stored temporarily while the program is being executed.

Stored Programs. Programs which are stored in the computer before they are executed (contrasted with *program boards*).

System. An organized collection of parts united by regulated interaction, e.g., the "educational system," an accounting system.

Systems Analyst. A person skilled in the definition of and the development of computer techniques for the solving of a problem; usually, his description of the technique is given to a programmer, who will execute it.

System Auditing. Checking out a system to see that it performs according to the specifications established by management.

Systems, Corporate. See: *Corporate.*

Systems, Information. See: *Information.*

Systems, Integrated. See: *Integrated.*

Systems, Management Control. See: *Management.*

Systems, Real-Time. See: *Real-Time.*

Systems Specialists. See: *Systems Analysts.*

T

Tape Drive. The physical part of the peripheral equipment of a computer which reads magnetic tape.

Terminal. A point in a system or communication network at which data can either enter or leave or both.

Time Sharing. A system where a computer may be used for more than one purpose in the same time period, e.g., by executing an instruction from one program and then one from another program. The term is usually used to describe a system where many users enjoy more or less simultaneous access to a single computer by means of several remote terminals.

U

UNIVAC. See: *Computer Manufacturers.*

W

Wald (Maximin) Criterion. One of several criteria that the decision-maker can use as the basis for a strategy in games against Nature when no information is available about Nature. If the matrix of the game is such that the decision-maker selects a row and Nature a column, using the Wald criterion, the decision-maker first finds the element in each row which minimizes his gain and then chooses the row for which his minimum gain is maximized. This criterion would be chosen by a pessimistic decision maker who "always expects the worst."

Wilson Lot-Size Formula. Although the simple lot size formula of inventory control was first derived by Ford Harris of the Westinghouse Corp. in 1915, it is often called the Wilson formula because it was a part of an inventory control scheme sold to many organizations by R. H. Wilson who derived the formula later than, but independently of, Harris. The formula itself expresses the optimum order quantity, Q, in terms of the demand, D, in units per year (where D is assumed to be deterministic and uniform throughout the year); the cost of placing an order, A, in dollars; the unit cost per item, C; and the cost of carrying inventory, I, expressed in the unit's dollars per year per dollar of inventory. In terms of these parameters, the economic order quantity, Q, is given by:

$$Q = \sqrt{\frac{2DA}{IC}}$$

Bibliography

American Management Association, *Marketing Harnesses the Computer.* New York: AMA, 1967

Blanton, Alexander M. and Joseph Traut, *Computers and Small Manufacturers.* New York: Computer Research and Publications Associates, 1967

Boore, W. F. and G. Murphy, *Computer Sampler: Management Perspective on the Computer.* New York: McGraw-Hill, 1968

Boutell, W., *Computer-Oriented Business Systems.* Englewood Cliffs, N. J.: Prentice-Hall, 1968

Business Equipment Manufacturers Association, *Decisions from Data.* Washington: Thompson Book Company, 1967

Canning, Richard G. and Roger L. Sisson, *The Management of Data Processing.* New York: Wiley, 1967

Cross, Hershner, *Computers and Management: the 1967 Letherbee Lectures at Harvard Business School.* Boston: Harvard University, Graduate School of Business Administration, 1967

Cutler, Donald L., *Introduction to Computer Programming.* Englewood Cliffs, N. J.: Prentice-Hall, 1964

Higginson, M. Valliant, *Managing with EDP: A Look at the State of the Art.* New York: American Management Association, 1965

Lecht, Charles P., *The Management of Computer Programming Projects.* New York: American Management Association, 1967

Magee, John F. *Physical Distribution Systems.* New York: McGraw-Hill, 1967

Maley, Gerald and M. Heilweil, *Introduction to Digital Computers.* Englewood Cliffs, N. J.: Prentice-Hall, 1968

McLoughlin, Kevin, *Clarifying the Computer; A Practical Guide for Retailers and Manufacturers.* New York: Fairchild, 1967

McMillan, Claude, *Systems Analysis; A Computer Approach to Decision Models.* Homewood, Illinois; Richard D. Irwin, Inc., 1965

McRae, Thomas W., *Impact of Computers on Accounting.* New York: Wiley, 1964

Myers, Charles A., Ed., *The Impact of Computers on Management.* Cambridge, MIT Press, 1967

Prince, Thomas R., *Information Systems for Management Planning and Control.* Homewood, Ill.: Richard D. Irwin, Inc., 1966

Rico, Leonard, *The Advance against Paperwork Systems, Computers, and*

Personnel. Ann Arbor, Michigan: Graduate School of Business Administration, University of Michigan, 1967

Rosove, Perry E., *Developing Computer-Based Information Systems.* New York: Wiley, 1967

Sackman, Harold, *Computers, System Science and Evolving Society: The Challenge of Man-Machine Digital Systems.* New York: Wiley, 1967

Sadowski, Wieselaw, *The Theory of Decision Making: An Introduction to Operations Research.* New York: Pergamon, 1965

Solomon, Irving I. and L. O. Weingart, *Management Uses of the Computer.* Harper, 1966 (also in paperback, New American Library)

Tou, Julius T., Ed., *Computer and Information Sciences-II.* New York: Academic Press, 1967

Weinstein, Seymour M. and A. Keim, *Fundamentals of Digital Computers.* New York: Holt, Rinehart and Winston, 1965

Williams, William F., *Principles of Automated Information Retrieval.* Elmhurst, Illinois: Business Press, 1965

Withington, Frederic G., *The Use of Computers in Business Organizations.* Reading, Mass.: Addison-Wesley, 1966

G—Index

281